Who We Are Now

Who We Are Now

Sam Roberts

The Changing Face of America in the Twenty-first Century

TIMES BOOKS

Henry Holt and Company

New York

Times Books
Henry Holt and Company, LLC
Publishers since 1866
115 West 18th Street
New York, New York 10011

Library of Congress Cataloging-in-Publication Data

Roberts, Sam, date.
    Who we are now : the changing face of America in the 21st century /
Sam Roberts.—1st ed.
        p.   cm.
    Includes bibliographical references (p.   ) and index.
    ISBN 0-8050-7555-0 — ISBN 0-8050-7080-X (pbk.)
        1. United States—Civilization—21st century.   2. United States—
Civilization—1945–   3. National characteristics, American.
4. United States—Social conditions—1980–   5. Social change—
United States.   I. Title.

E169.12.R576 2004   2004048000
973.931—dc22

First Edition 2004

Illustrations designed by Matthew Ericson

Printed in the United States of America

(hardcover) 10   9   8   7   6   5   4   3   2   1
(paperback) 10   9   8   7   6   5   4   3   2   1

For Dixie Roberts Josephson,
With love and enduring respect
and gratitude for her strength,
inspiration, and unconditional support

CONTENTS

Who We Are Now

Who is the average American?

In 1900, he was a twenty-six-year-old man who lived in rented quarters in a rural community in the eastern United States. Only 1 in 20 Americans lived alone then. About the same small proportion of seventeen-year-olds had a high school diploma. More than a third of all adults worked on a farm and fewer than 1 in 5 women worked outside the home. Most Americans were married, and fewer than 1 in 100 were divorced. About 1 of every 7 Americans were foreign-born, a slightly higher proportion than the number of Americans who were nonwhite.

If 1900 seems like ancient history, consider 1950, when you or your parents or your grandparents were growing up. By then, the typical American was a thirty-year-old woman, still living east of the Mississippi, but now in a city and in her family's own home. Although the proportion of women who were divorced had doubled in a half-century (to about 1 in 50), the average woman was married and, as a result, wasn't working outside the home. The proportion of foreign-born Americans had fallen by half, and about 10 percent of the population was nonwhite.

Today, the average American is still a woman, aged thirty-five (if not a little older), living in a metropolitan area of the West or the South, more likely than not in a suburb. She owns her own home and probably lives with only one or two other people. More than a quarter of all Americans live alone. About 1 in 10 adults are divorced. More than 80 percent are high school graduates, and more than 3 in 5 women are in the workforce. About 1 in 4 Americans are black, Hispanic, or Asian.

By the time the twentieth century drew to a close, America was an altogether different place from when that century began. The changes that have reshaped society have been more than technological. The population changed, too. It had doubled in size by 1950 and then doubled again by 2000. Immigration altered the nation's complexion time and again. The mobility of native-born Americans and newcomers alike produced urban sprawl and seismic shifts in political power. Revolutions in civil rights and women's rights generated jarring upheavals in higher education, the workforce, and the family. Many of the trends that drove those twentieth-century changes accelerated in the 1990s, transforming America even more dynamically, redefining us as a nation—in some ways that were predicted and in many that were entirely unexpected—and posing profound challenges as we embark on a new century, one too young to be christened yet.

How we evolved, particularly in the second half of the twentieth century and during the transformations of the 1990s, helps explain who we are now and what makes the United States unique among nations.

✦   ✦   ✦

They were called "the good years," the historian Walter Lord recalled of the dawn of the twentieth century, not because everything going on in America at the time was in fact so good or that everyone benefited from its fruits, but because of the unshakable faith that what was wrong could be corrected and what was good would get even better. "These years were good," Lord wrote, "because, whatever the trouble, people were sure they could fix it."

Most of those people, Americans, could still trace their ancestry to England, Ireland, and Germany. Many were newly minted immigrants or their children, a growing number of them bringing new languages and unfamiliar customs from eastern and southern Europe. Some, largely confined to the South, were the descendants of slaves whose faith in what could be fixed and what could not had been tested mightily since the Civil War, which had ended only thirty-five years earlier. (More than a million veterans of that war were still alive.) The century had opened with Queen Victoria still on her throne, and, as the historian Henry Steele Commager wrote, "Already she had given her name to an era, and already men were beginning to pronounce that era the best, the most prosperous, and the most enlightened in history, forgetting or ignoring the poverty and misery, the cruel oppression and wars, that had stained its history."

For the most part, those optimistic people disregarded the debate (as most of the world did a hundred years later) over whether the new century began in 1900 or in 1901. At midnight on December 31, 1899, they ushered in what they and their descendants and successive waves of immigrants would transform into the American Century—a self-fulfilling prophecy first proclaimed by the journalist Henry Luce before the century was even half over. While other nations stood still or shrank or broke apart, America reinvented itself. It began the century uniquely as an experiment in racial and ethnic coexistence and would celebrate its success one hundred years later as the world's most multicultural society and a model for what other countries might eventually become.

"It is more than half a century since Carlyle said of the population of England that its workers were 'understood to be the

strongest, the cunningest, and the willingest our earth ever had,'"
a *New York Times* editorial recalled in 1900. "The praise was then
unchallenged and unchallengeable. But in the interval the population of the United States has not only vastly increased beyond
that of the British Islands, but its workmen have become clearly
the superiors of the British workmen in all the qualities Carlyle
mentions.

"Only three political systems—the British Empire, the Chinese Empire and the Russian Empire—have unquestionably
greater population than the United States," the *Times* intoned,
adding confidently, "For a young nation we are doing very well."

In the nineteenth century, the young nation's workmen had
perfected and mass-produced the telegraph, telephones, and
electric lights. Still, on the threshold of the twentieth, when the
Times envisioned "a still brighter dawn of civilization," who would
have imagined what innovations the coming decades would deliver: radio, television, the airplane. When the century began, Americans owned barely 8,000 private automobiles. When it ended, for
the first time personal vehicles registered in the United States outnumbered licensed drivers.

Between 1890 and 1900, the population of the forty-five
states had increased by a staggering 21 percent to 76 million. Los
Angeles soared in rank from the 135th largest city to the 36th
largest, and nearly 1 in 3 Americans now lived in a city. Whites
accounted for nearly 88 percent of the population (the "colored"
included blacks, Chinese, Japanese, and American Indians), but
the proportion of foreigners—9 in 10 of them from Europe—now
matched the highs of the 1850s and was rising with no ceiling in
sight. In Milwaukee, Detroit, Chicago, New York, Cleveland, and
San Francisco, more than three-quarters were either foreign-born
or the sons and daughters of immigrants. In North Dakota, more
than 1 in 4 people were foreign-born, the highest proportion of

any state. While the proportion of eligible voters who cast their ballots in the 1900 presidential election would fall to 74 percent from 79 percent in 1896 (women could vote in only four states and senators still weren't popularly elected), Americans still had plenty of issues to disagree about, not the least of which was whether unbridled immigration would mongrelize America or whether, regardless of social consequences, the influx of foreign labor was vital for industry. Concerns were being raised about the imbalance of wealth (U.S. Steel would be formed the following year, the first business capitalized at $1 billion) and about the challenges posed by a secular and scientific society to religion.

But these were, after all, the good years. "There is not a man here who does not feel 400 percent bigger in 1900 than he did in 1896," Senator Chauncey Depew proclaimed, "bigger intellectually, bigger hopefully, bigger patriotically, bigger in the breast from the fact that he is a citizen of a country that has become a world power for peace, for civilization, and for the expansion of its industries and the products of its labor."

Still, after the staggering gains that America registered in the 1890s, how much better could things get? New territories had just been spun into America's orbit by the Spanish-American War and five states would still be admitted to the Union, but the notion that the frontier was closed and that the nation was filling up faster than anyone had imagined placed a damper on the promise of manifest destiny. Thomas Edison, for one, refused to speculate about America's future. "I don't care to play prophet to the twentieth century," he said. "It's too large an undertaking."

＋　　＋　　＋

Edison was right.

Writing in 1950 about the first fifty years of the twentieth century, Henry Steele Commager declared: "One by one the buoyant hopes of the Victorians were doomed to disappointment. Within less than half a century prosperity gave way to ruin, universal peace to universal war, certainty to fear, security to insecurity, the ideal of progress to the doubt of survival. Never before in history had such bright hopes been so ruthlessly shattered."

Before the century was even half over, America had been sobered and steeled by two world wars and a depression and five decades of mind-bending scientific achievement that climaxed in the atomic bomb—a fearsome device that delivered promise and peril—and gave rise to a superpower rivalry that would define America's foreign and domestic policy for much of the next fifty years.

While Henry Luce had proclaimed the American Century a decade earlier, whose century was it, really, at least so far? Luce's own *Time* magazine declared Winston Churchill the Man of the Half-Century in 1950 and though native-born or naturalized Americans (Roosevelt, Wilson, the Wright Brothers, Einstein) were disproportionately represented on most Top Ten lists of men (not women) who had reshaped the world in the half-century, they were still largely relegated to a minority (outnumbered by the likes of Churchill, Gandhi, Hitler, Lenin, Stalin, and others) among those having had the greatest impact for good or evil.

Preaching from the pulpit of Riverside Church in Manhattan on the morning of January 8, 1950, the Reverend Dr. Robert J. McCracken gloomily contrasted the good years when the century began with civilization's precarious condition at its halfway point. "In 1900 the march of humanity was seen as a straightforward climb and all the omens appeared propitious," he said. "In the interval, man has annihilated space and split the atom, but nobody is predicting, as many were doing at the opening of the century, that he will soon banish poverty, abolish disease and usher in an era of peace and plenty. Instead, the complaint is that it requires a combination of audacity and faith to assume that civilization has any future. The high hopes and extravagant self-assurance of fifty years ago are gone, and in their place is a debilitating sense of frustration and futility."

Yet, as Commager also wrote, "notwithstanding war, ruin and misery, the first half of the twentieth century saw spectacular developments in medical science that saved millions of children, extended life, wiped out plagues and diseases, and alleviated pain. It saw a general spread of education and, on a somewhat obvious level, of enlightenment. It saw, for the Western world at least, an improvement in standards of living, a decline in child labor, a release from long hours of drudgery for adults and a general diffusion of new methods of entertainment and recreation. For the majority of mankind, and except in time of war, life was easier and pleasanter than it had ever been before."

And the majority could look forward to the prospect that life would become even easier and pleasanter in the future—if the planet managed somehow to survive and humanity was permitted to prosper in a world vastly improved by benevolent science. (This prospect was giddily heralded a few days before New Year's Eve 1949 when the *New York Times* proclaimed on its front page: "New Einstein Theory Gives a Master Key to Universe.") Commager warned that "the compelling consideration is that in the twentieth century population is increasing and basic resources are decreasing faster than ever before." But William F. Ogburn, a leading sociologist, predicted that by the end of the century the number of Americans would grow modestly and sustainably from about 151 million to between 175 million and 200 million, which meant that "the United States, from the population standpoint alone, seems assured of a rising living standard."

Without hinting at the upheavals that would reconstitute the typical American household, he cautioned that "while nutritional and other factors may have a great deal to do with unhappiness, the social institution most closely associated with happiness or unhappiness is the family."

◆   ◆   ◆

A typical American born in 1900 would not have lived to see 1950—life expectancy at birth was only about forty-seven years (and only thirty-three for blacks). But by midcentury, the average infant born in America could reasonably expect to still be alive during the first two or three decades of the new millennium. During his lifetime, he would witness a transformation in the United States that would prove as unnerving, if not quite as cataclysmic, as the changes that distinguished the first half of the twentieth century. By 1950, for the first time, more Americans owned their own homes than rented. Well more than half had telephones, but fully a third lacked complete indoor plumbing. Fewer than 1 in 10 Americans owned a television. Only 1 in 3 had even a high school diploma. The vast majority of families—nearly 4 in 5— were made up of married couples and, less than a decade after World War II had drawn more women to offices and factories, chances are that the only work a married woman did was as a full-time homemaker. America still counted more private household laundresses than librarians, more farmers than laborers, more blacksmiths than psychotherapists.

In 1950, the proportion of households with five or more people dropped below 25 percent and the share of two-person households climbed past that level. Between 1950 and 2000, the proportion of married-couple households would plunge from nearly 4 in 5 to barely 1 in 2. Married couples with children accounted for 55 percent of family households in 1950, a figure that the baby boom would boost to nearly 60 percent in 1960; in 2000, their share would fall to about 45 percent. In 1950, among women—including war widows—who headed a household without a spouse present, 34 percent had children at home. In 2000, nearly 59 percent would. In the decades after 1950, the share of people living alone would soar from fewer than 1 in 10 to more than 1 in 4.

In 1950, for the first time, a little more than half the population lived in a metropolitan area. By 2000, that would be true for 4 out of 5 Americans. The post–World War II spurt in affordable tract housing in former potato fields on Long Island on what the historian Kenneth Jackson dubbed the nation's "crabgrass frontier" in sparsely populated places sparked suburbanization. And that unbridled stampede for the American Dream dispersed people—white people, mostly—so that by 2000 the share of Americans living in the nation's central cities would shrink below the level in 1950. By 2000, the proportion of Americans living in the suburbs would more than double, to 50 percent.

Population and, with it, political power, still resided mostly in the eastern half of the United States in 1950. Pennsylvania, Illinois, and Ohio were still among the five largest states (after New York and California, which had just edged into second place). Among the ten largest cities, only Los Angeles and St. Louis were west of the Mississippi.

For half a century, the nation had been hailed as a melting pot, absorbing immigrants from every corner of Europe. But the degree of diversity pales compared to today. Only about 1 in 14 Americans had been born abroad, most of them from the same stock as the generations that had preceded them here. The big-city balanced political ticket typically consisted of an Irishman, an Italian, and a Pole or a Jew. Racial diversity was largely a matter of black and white, with whites just beginning their exodus from the central cities to the suburbs and the vast majority of blacks still segregated in the South.

Early in the twentieth century, only one state outside the South—Arizona—had a population that was more than 10 percent nonwhite. In 1950, the only states where more than 3 in 10 people were nonwhite were in the South. By 2000, the population of only ten states in the entire country would be less than 10 percent nonwhite and the population of five non-Southern states—Alaska, California, Hawaii, New Mexico, and New York—would count nonwhites as over 30 percent.

✦   ✦   ✦

America keeps changing. More than 281 million Americans were counted by the latest federal census on April 1, 2000—nearly four times the number in 1900 and nearly double the population in 1950. In the 1990s, the population grew by the biggest ten-year numerical leap ever. But we're already even bigger than that, even in the moments since you began reading this book. Every eight seconds, another American is born. Every 12 seconds, one dies. As each 25 seconds ticks by, there is a net gain of one immigrant from overseas. And so every 12 seconds, the nation's population clock records a net increase of one more American overall.

In contrast to most other developed countries, the United States has grown in total population in recent decades. And the reason for this, to a large degree, is immigration. Foreigners keep coming to this country, as they have for hundreds of years, because as refugees they can escape discrimination or death, or simply because, like during the good years when the twentieth century began, they seek the best opportunity to improve their own lives and those of their children.

As recently as 1970, the number of foreign-born people living in the United States—under 10 million, or 4.7 percent of the total population—was the lowest of any decade in the twentieth century. In the 1990s alone, the number soared by 57 percent to constitute more than 11 percent of the total population—below the historic highs in the first decade of the century but the highest proportion of foreign-born since the 1930s. In 2000, 56 million Americans—or 1 in 5—were foreign-born or the children of foreign-born parents.

This latest influx has also fundamentally altered America's racial and ethnic dynamic: for the first time, blacks are no longer the nation's biggest minority group. Jose is the no. 1 name for baby boys in Texas, no. 2 in Arizona, and no. 3 in California. Smith remains the most common surname in the United States, but the top 50 now includes Garcia, Martinez, Rodriguez, Hernandez, Lopez, Gonzalez, and Perez.

For the first time in the twentieth century, the census counted more people in each of the fifty states at the end of the 1990s than when the decade began. California's population swelled by more than 4 million people, Texas's by 3.9 million, and Florida's by 3 million. Spillover from those states, and the influx of foreigners, propelled the rate of growth among their neighbors. Between 1980 and 1990, Nevada's population exploded by 66 percent— the highest growth rate of any state, followed by Arizona and Colorado. For the first time in the twentieth century, Georgia's growth rate outpaced Florida's. Even states in the Midwest, which had been hemorrhaging population for decades, bounced back. Missouri's growth rate was the highest recorded since the last decade of the nineteenth century. Nebraska and Iowa grew faster than in any decade since the 1910s.

The nation's biggest cities grew twice as fast in the 1990s than in the 1980s. The population of eight of the ten largest cities expanded (Philadelphia shrank and Detroit tried valiantly but failed to avoid the dubious distinction of becoming the first city to slip below one million). New York City edged past 8 million for the first time and Chicago, reversing a fifty-year trend, gained 112,000. Americans are about as likely today as they were in 1950 to live in a big city, but the chances are greater that the city will be in the South or the West.

By 2000, 4 in 5 Americans lived in a metropolitan area. Still, most of the growth in the nation's metropolitan areas was outside central cities. Fully half of all Americans now live in the suburbs, a statistical milestone whose political, economic, and social implications elevated the so-called soccer mom from a harried homemaker into a cultural icon. Most cities, especially older ones in the Northeast and Midwest, are constrained by static political borders. But the suburbs sprawled, inexorably gobbling up fields and forests and, both literally and figuratively, redefining huge swaths of rural America. Atlanta grew by 22,000 people in the 1990s; its suburbs swelled by 2.1 million. The spotty small-town revival that erupted in the early 1990s was, by the end of the decade, vastly overshadowed by suburban and exurban spurts that expanded the official boundaries of metropolitan areas and further drained residents from rural communities. Kansas now has more frontier counties—defined as those with two to six people per square mile—than it did in 1890.

The average American also grew older in the 1990s—like residents of most other developed countries in Europe and Asia—although immigration helped keep the country from aging more rapidly, because immigrants are disproportionately young and have higher fertility rates. By 2000, the median age of Americans—meaning half were older and half were younger—was a record high of 35.3 years. More than 50,000 Americans are older than 100. While the 1990s was the first decade in which people over 65—the census calls them elderly—declined as a proportion of the population overall, that was just a blip, reflecting generally lower birthrates during the Great Depression. In 2011, the number of elderly will start to increase dramatically as the first of the baby boomers born after World War II turn 65.

Remember the nuclear family? The term was coined just two generations ago when the atomic age began, a social construct that invoked the laws of physics to explain how a mother, father, and children survived in relative harmony, like protons, neutrons, and electrons. The flesh-and-blood version on television was *Ozzie and Harriet* or, better yet, *Father Knows Best,* with two parents, a daughter, and a son (dog and station wagon optional). If, for most Americans, the nuclear family was the paradigm, it is one that fewer and fewer people actually experience. Today, think *Sex and the City* and *Will and Grace.*

In the 1990s, for the first time, so-called nuclear families constituted fewer than 1 in 4 of the nation's households. That's because more Americans have delayed getting married (the number of unmarried couples rose, too), postponed having children—or decided against parenthood altogether—and lived together longer after their children had grown. The fact that people were remaining single longer and also surviving longer combined to achieve another first: in the 1990s, the number of married-couple households with children was surpassed by the number of Americans living alone.

Overall, living standards rose during the decade, but at a price. The economic boom lifted many, but by no means all.

Home ownership rose to a twentieth-century record. Americans lived in larger houses (for the first time, the number of homes without indoor plumbing dropped below 1 million and also below 1 percent of total homes), but they also were saddled with bigger mortgages. More than 90 percent of households owned at least one car, van, or truck—the highest proportion ever—but they spent a longer time in those vehicles getting to and from work. "It's the American dream updated," said Robert E. Lang, an urban analyst at the Fannie Mae Foundation.

At the same time, about 1 in every 32 American adults was living in a prison or jail or was on probation or parole.

The proportion of families classified as poor in 2002—defined as earning less than $17,000 for four people—dipped below double digits to 9.6 percent, but 12 percent of the population, including 17 percent of American children, were still struggling below the government's official threshold of poverty. And, as in other categories, the states diverged from one extreme to the other. On average, people were poorest in West Virginia and richest in New Jersey, oldest in Florida and youngest in Utah, the most urban in New Jersey and the most rural in Maine.

On April 1, 2000, when Americans posed for the latest statistical profile of the United States, they didn't sit still long enough for the portrait to dry. The raw numbers recorded on that date, digested in the years since then and periodically updated, fill thousands of pages, but they represent a pixilated digital image that speaks with greater precision and clarity than is mathematically possible. The following chapters flesh out that portrait, providing greater perspective on why we count, how we live, how we're aging, where we've moved, where we dream, where we come from, how we live in black and white, whether we are smarter, and where we are today as measured against the rest of the world at the dawn of a new century.

2

Why We Count

Article I, Section 2, of the United States Constitution requires that Americans eyeball themselves in the mirror every ten years and assess their numerical growth so that their representatives and direct taxes can be "apportioned according to their respective numbers." But even the first census was fudged. Moreover, the Founding Fathers themselves foreshadowed the wrangling over guesstimates and the nation's preoccupation with race when, in their Great Compromise, they agreed to count slaves as three-fifths of free persons. In 1791, as sixteen United States marshals and their 650 assistants were completing the first official count that found 3,929,326 Americans (including 694,280 slaves and 59,557 "free Negroes"), Thomas Jefferson confided to George Washington on a cover sheet: "I enclose you also a copy of our census, written in black ink so far as we have actual returns, and supplied by conjecture in red ink, where we have no returns, but the conjectures are known to be very near the truth."

The first census posed only six questions: to distinguish free persons, their sex and color, and the number of free males age sixteen and over (to assess the nation's military and industrial potential).

By 1880, the census had gauged that more Americans were living beyond the nation's original boundaries than within them. By the census's centennial in 1890, the nation's population had grown sixteen-fold, to 63 million. The census questionnaire had grown even longer. So did the instructions. Enumerators were advised to "distinguish carefully between housekeepers, or women who receive a stated wage or salary for their services, and housewives, or women who keep house for their own families or for themselves without any gainful occupation." When listing the occupation of Indians, the instructions said, "special attention is to be directed to reporting 'Medicine-man,' as it is the only occupation among Indians resembling a profession in civilization."

In 1990, the government challenged Americans to complete their census forms with "a black lead pencil only." By 2000, the Census Bureau ushered in its third century of counting by acknowledging twentieth-century innovation: it invited the 120 million people to whom questionnaires had been mailed to fill them out with "a black or blue pen." The census is supposed to be all about precision, and for some sticklers that posed a problem. "I have a blue pen that writes with black ink; I suppose that's O.K.," mused William Safire, the *New York Times* wordsmith. "But I also have a black pen that writes with red ink: is that impermissible? The clear intent is 'use black or blue ink,'" he correctly concluded. "But if the Bureau of the Census, conscious of literal correctness, wrote those words, millions of people unfamiliar with the details of writing instruments would respond: 'I don't use ink; I use a ballpoint pen. Does this mean I have to fill this out with a fountain pen? There'll be big inkblots all over the form. What do they want from my life?'"

In 2000, the short form sent to most Americans contained seven questions—only one more than the original census in 1790—and officials estimated it would take only ten minutes to complete. The aptly named long form covered fifty-three questions on five pages—and more for each additional member of the household—and supposedly took thirty-eight minutes to fill out (which may be why there was a falloff in response rates between the short form and the long form—double the gap in 1990). Only one new subject was added to the questionnaire: the role of grandparents as caregivers. That question was mandated by Congress a few years earlier when the overhaul of welfare regulations generated a political maelstrom.

✦   ✦   ✦

What the census asks has profound political implications. So do the answers. Constitutionally, the census is conducted in order to reapportion the 435 seats in the House of Representatives and, as a result, each state's share of electoral votes (except in 1920 when rural states, fearing that their power would be eroded by the influx of foreigners to big cities, managed to block redistricting). The equation is complex, but the outcome is clear: one state's loss is another's gain. And with Congress so evenly divided politically, every seat counts. From 1900 through the 1940s, the Northeast accounted for 28 percent of the seats in the House. Since 1950, its proportion has declined; it's now 19 percent. The Midwest's share also shrank, from 35 percent in 1900 to 23 percent in 2000. The South's share fluctuated during the twentieth century, starting at 32 percent and ending at 35 percent. The West's share more than quadrupled, from 5 percent of House seats in 1900 to 23 percent today.

In 2000, the South and West each gained five seats. Arizona, Florida, Georgia, and Texas picked up two apiece. The California, Colorado, Nevada, and North Carolina congressional delegations each grew by one. New York, which claimed 45 seats in the 1930s and 1940s, had been losing seats ever since, and it lost two more after the 2000 census, reducing its delegation to twenty-nine—the first time since 1810 that the state was represented by fewer than thirty congressmen. Pennsylvania also lost two seats. Connecticut, Illinois, Indiana, Michigan, Mississippi, Ohio, Oklahoma, and Wisconsin each lost one. Most of the states gaining seats had been carried by George W. Bush in the 2000 presidential election; most of those that lost seats had been carried by Vice President Al Gore. Still, even under the revised electoral count, Bush would have needed Florida to win.

Today, each member of Congress represents about 647,000 constituents—up from about 193,000 in 1900 and 572,000 in 1990. One state, Montana, is too big for one representative but too small for two; the mathematical formula gives it one, though, so its sole congressman has 905,000 constituents.

Congressional seats aren't the only prize apportioned on the basis of population. So are federal funding and bragging rights.

Fearing that Detroit's population would fall below 1 million, city officials sponsored billboards, urging its citizens to be counted. Mayor Dennis Archer called it "a matter of pride." It wasn't enough. Detroit's official population count dropped to 951,270.

"We need more people if our state is to thrive and prosper," said Governor Tom Vilsack of Iowa, where the population in 44 of his state's 99 counties had peaked by 1900. The state has been wooing former Iowans and skilled immigrants to help bridge the gap between the number of working-age and retirement-age Iowans. Already, Iowans over the age of seventy-five outnumber those under five.

Results from more than 400 of the nation's 39,000 local governments were challenged, sometimes by the bureau itself. In Bossier Parish, Louisiana, the census counted 99,633 people— just short of the threshold that local officials had hoped to reach to qualify for additional federal financing. Bossier officials said they found 461 homes that the census hadn't counted. About 45 miles northwest of Pittsburgh, census-takers missed the entire population of the borough of Slovenska Nardna Podporna Jednota. Officially, the borough claims twelve adults and two children (an increase of one since 1990), but only four live there full-time. But no one was home when the census-taker visited. In Shepherdstown, West Virginia, the census recorded 800 fewer people in 2000 than 1990, until local officials discovered that residents of the town's three college dormitories hadn't been counted.

In fact, more than half the early challenges to the 2000 count involved dormitories, prisons, and other group quarters that were home to nearly 7.8 million Americans. "The supreme irony is the census did a really good job on the hard-to-count population this time around," said Warren A. Brown, a sociology professor at Cornell University, "and they fumbled the ball on the easy-to-count. What could be easier than counting somebody in prison?"

In counting Americans abroad, in some years the census included civilians employed privately, but the 2000 count recorded only federal military and civilian employees. That meant 11,000 Mormon missionaries from Utah weren't credited to that state. As a result, under the formula that awards congressional seats sequentially on the basis of population, Utah failed by 856 people to qualify for the 435th and final House seat. It went to North Carolina instead.

+   +   +

Effective marketing and dogged detective work on the part of the Census Bureau raised the response rate among ordinary citizens to 67 percent (compared to 65 percent in 1990, and 75 percent in 1980, and ranging from 76 percent in Iowa to 57 percent in Alaska)—a small but impressive reversal when so many other measures of public participation have been steadily declining. A $103 million advertising campaign reminded Americans that the federal government doles out about $185 billion on the basis of census population and economic figures. More than 440,000 temporary enumerators were hired to follow up the mailings.

What the federal government hailed as "the largest peacetime mobilization in the nation's history" was conducted at a cost of $6.5 billion, or about $56 per home or apartment in the United States (compared to $3.3 billion, or $32 per home, a decade earlier). The government spent $117 million on first-class mail alone.

Still, the census is only a snapshot—a snapshot of a moving target, no less, of hundreds of millions of people who are coming and going, some of them homeless and some of them away in vacation homes, and who speak a variety of languages (the questionnaire was printed in English, Spanish, Chinese, Tagalog, Vietnamese, and Korean—and nearly 18 percent of those five and older who responded said they spoke a language other than English at home). The count attempts to quantify the profound changes American society undergoes each decade. The latest count found that, for the first time, a majority of American households have access to a computer at home. The number of cellular telephone subscribers—a mere 5 million in 1990—rose dramatically to nearly 130 million by 2000. Motor vehicle registrations topped 200 million for the first time. Among adults, the number of college graduates surpassed 1 in 4, but the number living in college dormitories was exceeded by the number in prisons and jails. Crime declined, but 1 in 143 Americans were living behind bars.

The census provides benchmarks. Someone once compared it to a faulty scale: it may not tell you exactly what you weigh at any given moment, but it will give a pretty good idea of whether you've gained or lost weight since the last time. The count is subject to enormous variables, multiple interpretations, unintended consequences, and unexpected questions. Was there a measurable increase in gay and lesbian households compared to 1990 or, as the Census Bureau concluded, were the numbers not comparable? Did New York City's population really surge in the 1990s or, as some suggest, was at least half the growth the result of the city's success in verifying the bureau's address files and finding people who had been there all along?

By its own estimate, the census missed 3.3 million Americans in 2000. If the census is accurate enough to pinpoint how many people it missed, why not simply make a statistical adjustment and add them in? First, as a panel of census demographers concluded, the Constitution demands an otherwise undefined "actual enumeration." Second, adjusting for an undercount is fraught with political consequences, since most of the missing are presumed to be poor urban blacks and Hispanics and including them in the count would tend to favor Democrats. There's a third reason some experts shy away from a formulaic solution: a statistical adjustment might not make the census any more accurate. Successive improvements in methodology have shrunk the margin of error so that extrapolations from sampling of who wasn't counted but should have been and who was counted but should not have been are certain to produce a different result, but not necessarily a more accurate one.

Even so, the census relies on sampling and on a sophisticated and often mysterious process called imputation. Only about 1 in 6 Americans received the more detailed long form, but the census does, in fact, extrapolate from that sample. And when those forms are incomplete the Census Bureau imputes a plausible response, on the basis of answers from comparable residents of the same neighborhood, or even "corrects" an answer deemed to be implausible. In 1990, for example, the bureau didn't recognize same-sex marriages, so if someone reported sharing a household with a married partner of the same sex either the person's sex or relationship were edited to conform to the bureau's definitions or preconceptions at the time.

In 2000, imputation produced nearly 5.8 million bodies— more than 2 percent of the total population—that the census didn't actually count, but, nonetheless, believes existed on April 1, 2000.

"The census is actually probably precise to the millions," said Theodore M. Porter, who teaches history of science at the University of California at Los Angeles. "There are about six digits, maybe even seven, that are in some sense meaningless."

Kenneth Prewitt, who directed the 2000 census, described it as "the largest applied social science project in history."

"You either argue about numbers or you argue about anecdotes," Prewitt said. "And I think the public discourse is better when the argument is about numbers. But we should be sophisticated enough to understand that the number itself is an approximation. . . . The census is an estimate of the truth. It happens to be the best estimate that we have."

On April 1, 2000, the best estimate was 281,421,906. But there is a lot more to that number than meets the eye.

3

How We Live

At the turn of the twentieth century, a playwright coined the metaphor "melting pot" to describe the cauldron in which immigrants would shed all traces of the ethnic loyalties and traditions that defined them as foreigners and immediately emerge as honest to goodness Americans. The melting pot was largely a myth—America was always more of an emulsifier or even a mosaic—but the idealized vision would endure for more than a century. In 1949, at the dawn of the atomic age, a sociologist popularized another figure of speech to define how we live together. That term, too, was largely metaphorical, but would prove just as durable.

"Among the majority of the peoples on earth," George Murdock wrote, "nuclear families are combined, like atoms in a molecule, into larger aggregates." By nuclear family, he meant a married couple—a man and a woman—living with their own children (the dog, station wagon, and suburban dream house were still optional then, but within a few years would become all but obligatory). Murdock did not suggest, to paraphrase Tolstoy, that every family was combined haplessly in the same way. But he was unequivocal about the symbolism that the nuclear family inspired both as a sociological ideal and as an American moral in-dicator. It was, he wrote, "the type of family recognized to the ex-clusion of all others."

In our day, the nuclear family has atomized.

Fewer people are marrying altogether. Or, they're marrying later. As recently as 1970, 9 in 10 American women had been mar-ried at least once by their thirtieth birthday. Today, only 6 in 10 have married by then. Couples are divorcing more frequently. And they're living longer, often alone after being unmarried, widowed, or divorced. Over the course of just a few decades, those trends have profoundly altered the mix of households and families in the United States—changes that have been mirrored, to some extent, in other developed countries, particularly in Europe.

A mere 7 percent of all households in the United States con-sist of married couples with children, a working father, and a stay-at-home mother. Even among married-couple households, the statistics turn tradition on its head. Only 13 percent are fami-lies with children and in which only the husband worked, 31 per-cent are two-earner couples with children, 25 percent are two earners with no children. (The rest include other combinations, such as older couples whose children have left home.)

Calvin O. Butts Jr., the senior pastor of Harlem's Abyssinian Baptist Church, was stunned recently when couples who wanted him to preside at their weddings asked to amend the traditional marriage vows. Butts is a reasonable, modern man, but he couldn't believe the changes they requested. Drop the "till death do us part" prescription, they suggested, and substitute something a little more flexible, and realistic, like, "as long as our love shall last." Butts responded unequivocally, "Find another minister."

Most Americans still get married. Most stay married. Most have children. But in 2000, for the first time, fewer than 1 in 4 house-holds were composed of a married couple with children. In central cities, even the proportion of married couples without children plunged below 25 percent. For the first time, the proportion of single people living alone is higher than the share of nuclear families. The number of unmarried couples nearly doubled in the 1990s—a not insignificant minority of them same-sex partners, measured specifically for the first time. Those patterns can be— and have been—cited by some people as evidence of the nation's moral decay. But regardless of which way we're heading morally, the patterns reflect profound economic and cultural changes in American society, just as the nuclear family did in the 1950s and 1960s when, while it was never universal, it predominated as the way most Americans lived, or wanted to.

✦   ✦   ✦

When the twentieth century began, the American family was almost as different from the *Ozzie and Harriet* model as it would be when the century wound down. In 1900, almost half the entire population lived in a household with five or more people, a reflection, in part, of higher fertility rates and of the economic imperative and social convention of extended families. Two-person households didn't become the most common type until the 1940s. The sharpest decline in households with children took place in the 1970s baby bust, and by 2000 two-person households accounted for nearly 1 of every 3. In 1900, only about 1 in 20 households were made up of people living alone. By 2000, their proportion had surged to more than 1 in 4. Smaller size, in turn, accounted for a vast increase in the number of households. In 1900, when the population was 76 million, there were 16 million households. In 2000, with the population at 281 million, there were 105 million households. The average number of people per household had declined to 2.59, and per family to 3.14.

For a majority of the nation's children, the idealized nuclear family was a fact of life only for about half of the twentieth century, neither at the beginning nor at the end. A majority of children lived in a household presided over by a married couple only from the 1920s through the 1970s.

The most profound changes in family structure occurred during the last decades of the century. In 1950, married couples accounted for 78 percent of all American households. In 1990, they represented 55 percent. By 2000, the proportion had dropped to barely half, or 52 percent. The rate of decline has been slowing, however, as young immigrant families have kept the actual number up. Still, even among married couples, only 46 percent are living with their own children under the age of 18. Their declining share of households reflected the emergence of other living arrangements, including more single-person households, more single-parent households, and more households maintained by men. The decline has also had profound political implications, real and potential. It's hard enough to persuade property owners to raise taxes to pay for better schools for their own children. What about if they have no intention of marrying, are coupled and have no children, and never intend to?

If popular culture is a reflection of society, or of what society pretends to be, just look at what has succeeded *Ozzie and Harriet* and *Father Knows Best* in prime time—shows like *8 Simple Rules for Dating My Teenage Daughter, Friends,* or *Sex and the City.*

◆   ◆   ◆

Still, as Jason Fields, a Census Bureau demographer, says, "most people marry and marry only once." The majority of men and women over twenty-five are married. But, barely. Not until Americans reach age thirty are a majority of their age group married and living with their spouse.

For the most part, Americans marry later than they used to. In 1900, on average, men married for the first time at 26.1 years of age and women at 22. The averages hit a century low in the 1950s—during the baby boom—at around 21 for women and 23

"Traditional" Families Are Fading

Percentage of households in each category. Not shown are single people living alone and nonrelated people living together. "Children" are a family's own children under age 18 living at home.

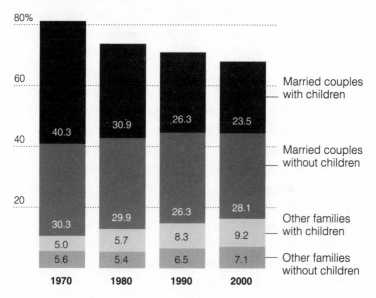

Source on all charts unless otherwise noted: Census Bureau

for men. Today, the average age at which men first marry is 26.9. Among women, it's 25.3.

A half-century ago, 77 percent of men and 56 percent of women age 15 to 24 had never been married. By 2000, the proportions had climbed to 88 percent for men and 82 percent for women.

Among 25- to 34-year-olds, the difference was much more striking. In 1950, 19 percent of the men and 11 percent of the women in that age group had never been married. In 2000, 39 percent of the men and 30 percent of the women had not married.

Among all Americans, the share who had never married rose from 24 percent in 1975 to 29 percent in 2002 (and from 32 percent to 43 percent among blacks, although that figure may be leveling off). And yet by the time Americans turn 60, fewer than 7 percent have never married—far fewer than a century or more earlier, when more than 1 in 5 women never married.

The marriage rate was highest in 1946, after men who had been separated from sweethearts for months or years returned home from World War II. It had sunk to its lowest point in the twentieth century in 1931, at the start of the Great Depression, but would rebound and not plunge to that level again until 1995. Among white women, the proportion who had ever been married has ranged from 57 percent in 1900 to 70 percent in 1960 toward the end of the baby boom. Among black men, not since 1970 were more of them married than not married. During the last several decades, the proportion of women who were widowed has remained about the same, but divorces are up. People 45 to 54 registered the highest percentage who had divorced than any other age group—15 percent among men and 18 percent among women (the slightly higher percentage among women reflects the fact that they tend to remarry less often than men do).

Today, among women in their early twenties, 67 percent have never married, but that proportion drops as women age, to 35 percent among women in their late twenties, just under 19 percent among women in their early thirties and only 14 percent among women in their late thirties. By their forties, though, only 49.2 percent of those who married once are still married to the same spouse; 37 percent have been divorced, of whom nearly half have remarried. Nonetheless, the proportion of single women in their early twenties has doubled in three decades, to 73 percent, and the share of never married women in their early thirties has tripled, to 22 percent.

Among men, nearly 79 percent in their early twenties have never married, a proportion that drops to 49 percent among men in their late twenties, 30 percent in their early thirties, 18 percent

Never Married

Percentage of people in each age group
each year who have never been married.

Women

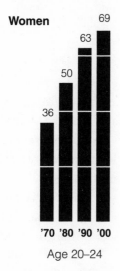

69
63
50
36

'70 '80 '90 '00
Age 20–24

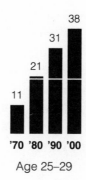

38
31
21
11

'70 '80 '90 '00
Age 25–29

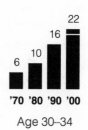

22
16
10
6

'70 '80 '90 '00
Age 30–34

Men

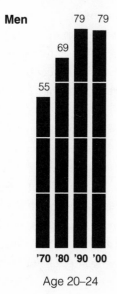

79 79
69
55

'70 '80 '90 '00
Age 20–24

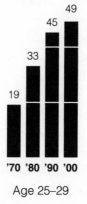

49
45
33
19

'70 '80 '90 '00
Age 25–29

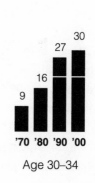

30
27
16
9

'70 '80 '90 '00
Age 30–34

in their late thirties, and about 12 percent by the time they are in
their forties. Among those in their forties who married once, 78
percent are still married to the same person; of people age 40 to
49, 36 percent have divorced at least once and 25 percent have
married twice.

◆   ◆   ◆

Married couples constitute the largest percentage of households
in the nation's burgeoning new suburbs, the antidote to higher-
cost cities and often the preferred place to raise a family. Married
households account for more than 69 percent of all households
in Gilbert, Arizona, and Naperville, Illinois, for instance, with the
share also over 60 percent in places like Plano, Texas; Simi Valley,
California; and Livonia, Michigan. Places with the largest proportion of formerly married people include Gary, Indiana, with
27.2 percent; followed by Clearwater, Florida; Birmingham, Alabama; St. Petersburg, Florida; Hollywood, Florida; Louisville,
Kentucky; and Cleveland, Ohio—all with over 26 percent. Generally, those are places with large concentrations of older Americans or of blacks, who have lower marriage rates overall.

The largest proportion of married couples with children in a
metropolitan area is Provo-Orem, Utah, where they account for
42.5 percent of all households. The lowest is in Punta Gorda,
Florida, with only 12.2 percent.

Since 1970, households headed by women have risen from
about 1 in 5 households to more than 1 in 3. One reason is purely
statistical: before 1980, in married-couple families the census
automatically declared the husband as the head of the household. (Since 1990, among blacks, women have been more likely
to be identified as the householder.) But the rise in households
headed by women is not merely a statistical artifact. It is a consequence, in large part, of more women marrying later or not at all
and of living longer usually alone.

Muted Wedding Bells

Number of marriages performed annually per
1,000 people in the United States.

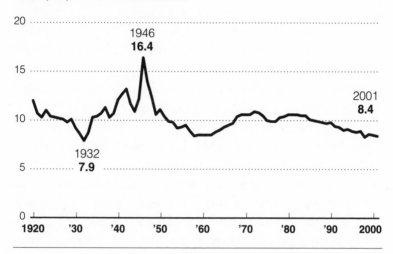

Among blacks over age fifteen, only 34 percent of men and 26 percent of women are now married and living with their spouse. The wide disparity could be a result of higher mortality rates among men and also the fact that black men are more likely to marry non-blacks than black women are. Those percentages among whites contrasted with 57 percent of men and 53 percent of women, 43 percent of men and 46 percent of women among Hispanics, and 53 percent of men and 56 percent of women among Asians.

Blacks were more likely never to have married (41.6 percent of men and 39.7 percent of women) or to have divorced (9.5 percent among men and 12.8 among women). In part, that could reflect the shortage of eligible black men for black women to marry.

Another trend confirmed by the latest census is that women are having fewer children and more women are having no children at all. Only a quarter century ago, among women in their early forties only 10 percent had never given birth. About 20 percent had delivered five or more children. By 1998, the proportion with no children had climbed to 19 percent, then dipped slightly to about 18 percent in 2002. The proportion with five or more children has plummeted to under 4 percent. Among women in that age group, blacks are most likely to be childless—more than 19 percent—and Hispanics the least likely—only 13 percent. About 1 in 5 married, divorced, and widowed women between the ages of 15 to 44 are childless. So are more than 3 in 4 women who have never married (the flip side of that statistic means that nearly 1 in 4 among those women do have children).

In the year ending June 2002, 1 in 3 babies were born out of wedlock—nearly 9 in 10 of those born to teenagers, half the babies born to twenty- to twenty-four-year olds. That breaks down to 1 in 4 of all the white babies, nearly 1 in 4 Asian babies, nearly 2 in 3 black babies, and more than 1 in 3 Hispanic babies. American-born women were more likely to give birth out of wedlock than foreign-born women in the United States. The birth rate among women living with an unmarried, opposite-sex partner is about the same as the rate among women living with their husbands, which suggests a further erosion of marriage as a social convention.

◆   ◆   ◆

Children under the age of eighteen account for about 26 percent of America's population. There are 72 million of them. While married couples account for 51.7 percent of all households, married couples living with children represent only 23.5 percent of all households (ranging from 35 percent in Utah to only 19.2 percent in Florida). More significantly, among all households in the United States including children under eighteen, fewer than half are headed by a married couple.

Murdock's nuclear family—"the type of family recognized to the exclusion of all others"—has actually been declining since 1960 as a proportion of married-couple households. In 1960, 3 in

5 of those households included at least one of their own children younger than 18. By 1990, the proportion had slipped below 1 in 2 and slid slightly again in 2000. Demographers attribute the decline to a myriad of factors: the decision of more and more young people to delay marriage; their decision, once they're married, to forgo having children; the rise in single-parent families; and the fact that an increasing number of parents are living longer after their grown children leave home.

From the children's perspective, surely, the nuclear family has atomized. In 1950, of the 20 million families with children under eighteen, only 1.5 million were one-parent families. In 1960, 9 percent of children lived with a single parent, but in 2000, 28 percent did. By 2000, of the 35 million families with children under eighteen, nearly 10 million were headed by a single parent. With whom do children live? In 1970, more than 83 percent of America's children lived with both biological parents. Only 10 percent lived with a single mother. Today, only about 60 percent live with both biological married parents. Nearly a quarter, 23 percent, live with their mother only. Another 5 percent live only with their father. And nearly as many, 4 percent, live with neither parent. About 7 percent live with one biological parent and a stepparent, nearly 2 percent live with their grandparents, and 7 percent live with couples—either their biological parents or one biological parent—who are not married.

✦ ✦ ✦

Since the 1970s an increasing number of American children have been living with one parent, with other relatives or nonrelatives rather than with both parents. Still, the proportion remains much higher among most nonwhites. While only 15 percent of Asian children live with one parent, 53 percent of black children do— 48 percent with a single mother—as do 30 percent of Hispanic children.

Shift Toward Single Parents

Percentage of families with children in each group.

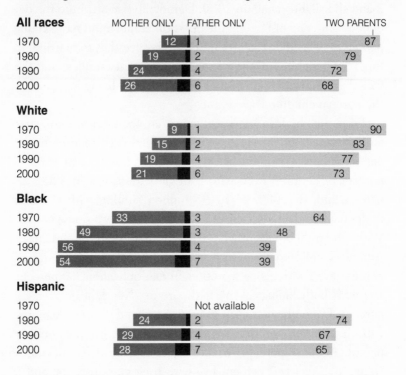

All races	MOTHER ONLY	FATHER ONLY	TWO PARENTS
1970	12	1	87
1980	19	2	79
1990	24	4	72
2000	26	6	68

White

	MOTHER ONLY	FATHER ONLY	TWO PARENTS
1970	9	1	90
1980	15	2	83
1990	19	4	77
2000	21	6	73

Black

	MOTHER ONLY	FATHER ONLY	TWO PARENTS
1970	33	3	64
1980	49	3	48
1990	56	4	39
2000	54	7	39

Hispanic

	MOTHER ONLY	FATHER ONLY	TWO PARENTS
1970	Not available		
1980	24	2	74
1990	29	4	67
2000	28	7	65

Meanwhile, among households headed by women, the proportion with no husband present and with their own children nearly doubled: from about 33 percent in 1950 to about 60 percent by 1980, which is just about where it remains today. Even given the moderating rates of divorce and out-of-wedlock births, the number of families headed by a woman grew five times faster in the 1990s than the number of married couples with children. The share of families headed by women with children under eighteen rose from 6.6 percent in 1990 to 7.2 percent by 2000. Even among whites, about 21 percent of families with children under eighteen at home are headed by a woman.

The census found that 3.7 percent of households were multi-generational. The most common was headed by a grandparent and included a child and grandchildren. About 8 percent of all children are living in a household that includes a grandparent. Responding to congressional concerns about the impact of changes in welfare regulation, for the first time the census also examined the role of grandparents as caregivers. Nearly 6 million, or 3.6 percent of Americans thirty and older live with their grandchildren and most of those (2.4 million) described themselves as having primary responsibility for raising their young grandchildren. Sharp differences emerged by race and ethnicity. While only 2 percent of non-Hispanic whites lived with their grandchildren, 6 percent of Asians and 8 percent of blacks and Hispanics did. More than half of the black grandparents identified themselves as primary caregivers. Among all grandparents sixty and older who lived with their grandchildren, nearly 3 in 10 were responsible for their care (including 25,000 grandparents who were 80 and over). Nearly two-thirds of the grandparents living with their grandchildren were women. About 1 in 5 grandparent caregivers were classified as poor.

◆　◆　◆

Another phenomenon has altered the composition of households, one that is a consequence of delayed marriage and of economic constraints—as well as of more indulgent parents. Some of the traditional benchmarks of adulthood—including achieving self-sufficiency with a full-time job and establishing an independent household—are taking longer to reach than they used to. Among young adults 18 to 24, 57 percent of men and 47 percent of women are still living with their parents. Even among older adults, between the ages of 25 and 34, 13 percent of men and 8 percent of women haven't left their parents' home yet—not a staggering percentage, but still about 50 percent higher than in 1970. This phenomenon is especially common in expensive cities like New York and Los Angeles and also among whites. One reason is that more and more college students are taking longer than four years to graduate even before they enroll for advanced degrees. As a result, parenthood and the obligations associated with it don't end after high school anymore, and while eighteen-year-olds are deemed mature enough to vote or enlist in the military social scientists say that many are struggling through what has been dubbed "transitional adulthood."

"There used to be a societal expectation that people in their early twenties would have finished their schooling, set up a household, gotten married and started their careers," Frank F. Furstenberg Jr., a sociology professor at the University of Pennsylvania told Tamar Lewin of the *New York Times*. "But now that's the exception rather than the norm. Ask most people in their twenties whether they're adults and you get a nervous laugh. They're not sure."

Take James Navarro, a thirty-year-old appellate court lawyer in Brooklyn who seems the model of a mature adult—except that he still lives with his parents in Queens, his bedroom is stocked with high school trophies, and his mother packs lunch for him several times a week. His two brothers and his sister—all in their twenties—are home, too. "When I was in college, I thought I'd be married by twenty-four and have a house and kids by thirty," Navarro said. "Now I think the idea of being an emotionally developed male by twenty-four is ridiculous. I want to get married and have kids someday. But I don't feel any pressure that it has to be soon."

Elisabeth Levy, a twenty-eight-year-old catering sales manager at a private club in Manhattan, agreed. "I think it's great, and really important, to take time to date and travel and hang out with your friends," she said. "This way, when you do finally settle down, you're really ready, and you don't wake up at thirty-three, married with two kids and a house, and trapped, like, 'How did this happen?' and 'What did I do with my life?'"

At the same time, the number of married teenagers jumped by

50 percent in the 1990s, although their proportion among all teenagers was still relatively low—4.5 percent compared to 3.4 percent in 1990, but that number was 9.5 percent in 1950. Among the married teenagers, though, 2 in 3 weren't living with their spouses—probably because one was away at college or in the military or still in their homeland, awaiting the opportunity to emigrate.

◆   ◆   ◆

The number of unmarried couples soared 72 percent in the 1990s, from 3.2 million to 5.5 million—still far fewer than the 55.4 million married couples. Some eventually marry.

Tying the Knot Later

Median age at first marriage.

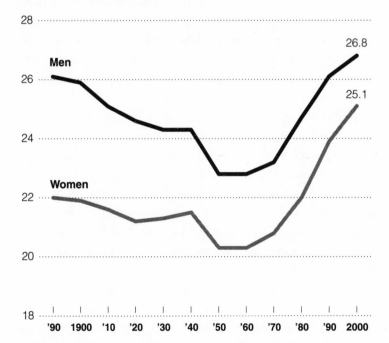

The census, which is all about self-identification, asked whether people living together with nonrelatives described themselves as boarders, housemates, foster children, or unmarried partners. In 2000, for the first time, the census accepted the possibility that unmarried partners could be of the same sex.

Among all unmarried-couple households, 4 in 10 included children. Unmarried partners were younger than married couples (37 years old for men and 35 for women, compared to husbands who averaged 49 years old and wives, 47), and were twice as likely to be black or Indian as white. About 12 percent of unmarried partners were mixed-race couples, compared to 6 percent of married couples. Unmarried couples were more likely to live in cities, particularly in the West and Midwest (Alaska, with 12 percent of all couples, claimed the most; Utah, the smallest share, with 4.4 percent). Among people aged 15 to 24, more women were living with men as unmarried partners than were wives in only four states: Maine, New Hampshire, Rhode Island, and Vermont. The highest proportion of wives to unmarried partners was in Utah. Paterson, New Jersey, claimed the highest proportion, 8.1 percent, of opposite-sex unmarried partners.

Same-sex couples accounted for about 594,000 or 1 in 9 of all the unmarried couples. About 301,000 were composed of male partners and 293,000 of female partners. California claimed the highest proportion of same-sex unmarried couples among all couples—1.4 percent—followed by Massachusetts, New York, and Vermont, with 1.3 percent each. Iowa, North Dakota, and South Dakota were lowest, at 0.5 percent. San Francisco, with 2.7 percent, was the city that reported the highest share of same-sex partner couples.

◆   ◆   ◆

Since 1950, the proportion of Americans who have divorced has increased exponentially. Then, among 25- to 34-year-olds, about

2 percent of the men and under 3 percent of the women were divorced. By 2000 more than 6 percent of men and nearly 9 percent of women in that group were divorced. Among people 35- to 59-years-old the frequency of divorce has been even more pronounced: around 3 percent for men and women in 1950, compared to 13 percent for men and 16 percent for women in 2000. Between 1960 and 1980 alone, the rate of failed marriages doubled, a consequence in part of no-fault and other liberalized state divorce laws. Since then, the rate has remained relatively constant: about half of marriages end in divorce.

The finding reverberated in alarm bells that have been ringing in the Bible Belt, where, in many places, the divorce rate is 50 percent higher than the national average, and even from the White House, as President George W. Bush proposed a "healthy marriage initiative" in 2003. In Oklahoma, Governor Frank Keating, a Republican, described divorce as the principal cause of poverty and vowed in 2000 to reduce the divorce rate by one-third in ten years. In Arkansas, Governor Mike Huckabee, also a Republican, went so far as to declare a "marital emergency" in 1999, promised to halve the divorce rate by 2010, and signed legislation that permits married couples to enter into a marital contract or covenant that would require a two-year waiting period before a divorce becomes final. "We are good in helping young people plan a wedding, but not in planning a marriage," said Rev. Anthony Jordan, executive director of the Baptist General Convention in Oklahoma.

Whatever the social costs of divorce, there is often an economic toll, too. "We know what the cause of poverty is in this country and, like it or not, it's divorce and non-wedlock childbearing," said Steve Nock, a sociology professor at the University of Virginia. "We know that for every three divorces, one family ends up below the poverty line. The average woman with dependent children who ends up in poverty stays poor for eight months.

The federal government pays for part of that, but states pay the balance. Divorce, by itself, is a major economic issue."

In 1990, 6 percent of all Americans were divorced or separated. By 2000, 10 percent were. Longer life spans and greater economic independence may be driving another trend: the increasing divorce rate among elderly Americans. Maybe anthropology is, too. Margaret Mead maintained that marriage worked when couples raised children and died by their fifties—not necessarily when they continued living together for decades beyond child-rearing.

+   +   +

The conflicted working mother was immortalized as an advertising icon in an AT&T Wireless telephone commercial in 1997. When she tells her children that she had to get ready for an important conversation with a client while they play on the beach, a daughter asks, "Mom, when can I be a client?"

In the 1990s, for the first time, families in which both spouses work became a majority, even among married couples with children. Among children living with two parents, 62.4 percent are the children of two working parents.

Mothers who had given birth within the previous year were less likely to be working than mothers of older children. Among all mothers with infants, blacks and whites were more likely to be working than Asians or Hispanics. About 1 in 3 of all mothers with an infant work full-time. The greater the new mother's educational attainment, the more likely she was to be working, and working full-time. Nearly half the new mothers with a college degree worked full-time.

Among mothers of children older than one, nearly 3 in 4 work. About half work full-time, including a disproportionate share of blacks, women without a husband, and women with a graduate or professional degree.

The proportion of working mothers with children aged six to seventeen increased in the late 1990s, to 79 percent, and the proportion who worked during pregnancy was up, too. But the proportion of working mothers with infants dropped for the first time in twenty-five years, from 59 percent of working women in 1998 to 55 percent in 2002. That 55 percent broke down as follows: 34 percent worked full-time, 17 percent worked part-time, and 4 percent were looking for jobs. The decrease was driven by a decline among women with working husbands. Martin O'Connell, who studied the reversal for the Census Bureau, attributed it to two causes: "One is that as more women delay their childbearing, which many now do until their thirties or forties, they have a chance to build up a nest egg that allows them to take more time off," he said. "And the other is that, looking down the road in a good economy, there's the anticipation that it will be easy to find a job whenever you want to go back to work." Given the subsequent recession, it was too soon to declare a trend.

Overall, the sharpest decline in working mothers was among married moms, from 60 percent in 1998 to 54 percent in 2000 (compared to 40 percent in the early 1960s). The decline was limited to white women with some college education. Among women with older children, aged six to seventeen, the proportion remained higher.

✦   ✦   ✦

In 1994, the federal government replaced "welfare as we know it" with a system intended to rectify decades of good intentions that helped contain poverty, but provided little incentive—disincentives, in many cases—to graduating from welfare to permanent work or to getting married. These new welfare regulations, combined with a booming economy, propelled more single mothers into the workforce. In 1993, 44 percent of them were working. By 1999, 65 percent were. Since 1986, the share of married

Mothers and Jobs

Percentage of women with children under 6 years old in March 2002.
"Unemployed" women were those seeking jobs.

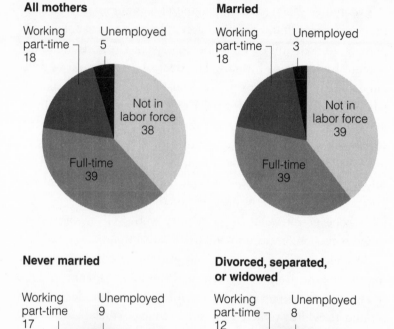

All mothers

Working part-time 18 | Unemployed 5 | Not in labor force 38 | Full-time 39

Married

Working part-time 18 | Unemployed 3 | Not in labor force 39 | Full-time 39

Never married

Working part-time 17 | Unemployed 9 | Not in labor force 37 | Full-time 37

Divorced, separated, or widowed

Working part-time 12 | Unemployed 8 | Not in labor force 31 | Full-time 49

mothers with jobs grew steadily and plateaued at 68 percent by the end of the 1990s. The proportion of single mothers with jobs hovered around 58 percent until 1993, when it began climbing sharply, to 71.5 percent by the end of the decade. For the first time in more than a decade, single mothers were more likely than married mothers to be employed. A separate analysis of whether welfare recipients worked produced similar results. In 1995, about 40 percent of welfare recipients reported working at least part-time. In 1999, the proportion had soared to 58 percent.

Five years after the system was revised, several studies found a significant increase in the number of poor children living in households headed by two adults—the arrangement with the greatest potential for economic prosperity. The proportion of black children living with two married parents increased from 34.8 percent in 1995 to 38.9 percent in 2000, according to an analysis by the Center on Budget and Policy Priorities. During the same period, the proportion of black children living with a single mother declined, from 47.1 percent to 43.1 percent. A separate study by the Urban Institute concluded that welfare reforms also prodded more mothers to live with partners, whether they married them or not.

In Milwaukee, Stephanie Brown, a welfare-to-work mother, married Truneil Brown, the father of her youngest child, in 2000. "We did it pretty much for the family's sake," she explained to Blaine Harden of the *New York Times*. "He was good with the kids. Marriage is a better example for the kids. They feel more secure experiencing the wedding. They feel like an average American family." For children, most research concurs, growing up in a household headed by two biological parents who largely get along with each other offers the most supportive environment. But welfare-to-work programs, while a prod, are not a solution in and of themselves and don't necessarily guarantee stability. Even after marrying, Stephanie Brown's life was far from perfect. Her husband lost his job; she holds two jobs, working with mentally disabled adults and as a home health aide, and was told in 2001 that she was making too much money to continue collecting $200 in food stamps each month. "These marriages and cohabitating households are all about survival," said Helen Gee, a supervisor for Community Advocates, Wisconsin's largest advocacy agency for low-income families. "They are crisis-driven. Women need help with high rent, utilities, child care, and transport. Their struggle is so great they think that two heads are better than one. Many women are leaving their kids at home all day with these guys they hardly know. We are seeing a lot of stressed-out clients."

That stress, in part, produced an unintended consequence: more and more children, blacks in big cities, in particular, living with neither parent and living instead with relatives, friends, or in foster care. By 2002, research by the University of California and the Rand Corporation found that among black children in central cities the proportion living with neither parent had more than doubled in the late 1990s, from 7.5 percent to 16.1 percent.

✦   ✦   ✦

In 1990, the proportion of people living alone constituted one-quarter of all households. By 2000, for the first time, the proportion of Americans living alone (26 percent of all households) surpassed the proportion of married-couple households with children under 18 (23.5 percent of all households).

In 1900, the West had the highest proportion of people living alone, reflecting the single men and immigrants lured by what was left of the frontier. By 1980, the Northeast ranked first, a consequence both of the disproportionate share of widowed elderly and also of young people living alone in big cities. By 2000, one-person households accounted for at least 20 percent of all households in every state except Utah. North Dakota and Rhode Island ranked highest, with 29 percent living alone. Utah was lowest, with 18 percent. Typically, the highest proportion of people living alone are in places with high concentrations of young adults—like college towns and big cities—and the elderly, many of whom may be widowed. In Alexandria, Virginia, 43 percent of the households are composed of people living alone; in Cambridge, Massachusetts, 41 percent are. Pittsburgh (with 34.9 percent), St. Louis (32 percent), and Fort Lauderdale (29.1 percent) had high percentages of people living alone, a reflection mostly of disproportionately large elderly populations. Americans age sixty-five and older account for the largest proportion of people maintaining one-person households.

Not all these people are alone, though, nor are they necessarily longing for companionship, despite the stigma attached to being

Living Alone

Percentage of all people living alone by age group. In 1970, 7 percent of all people lived alone; in 2000, 10 percent did.

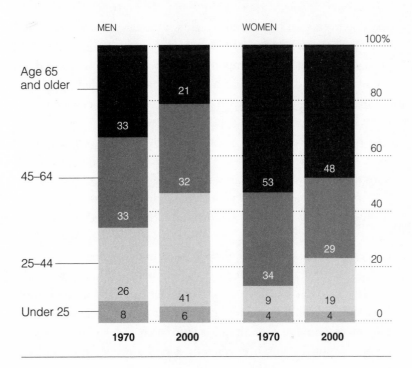

"never married." Ethan Watters, a writer from San Francisco, re-called: "As if the connotation of 'never married' weren't negative enough, the vilification of our group has been swift and shrill. These statistics prove a 'titanic loss of family values,' according to the *Washington Times*. An article in *Time* magazine asked whether 'picky' women were 'denying themselves and society the benefits of marriage' and in the process kicking off 'an outbreak of *Sex and the City* promiscuity.'" Writing in *The New York Times Magazine,* Wat-ters explained his initiation into the group of never married, while he searched for a female soul mate, was much more benign. He wrote: "The constant in my life—by default, not by plan—became a loose group of friends. After a few years, that group's membership and routines began to solidify. We met weekly for dinner at a neigh-borhood restaurant. We traveled together, moved one another's fur-niture, painted one another's apartments, cheered one another on at sporting events and open-mike nights. One day I discovered that the transition period I thought I was living wasn't a transition period at all. Something real and important had grown there. I belonged to an urban tribe." But while such urban tribalism conflicts with the instinct to pair off and marry, Watters argued that the experience is more likely to produce a "happily ever after" ending. "Those of us who have entered our mid-30s find ourselves feeling vaguely as if we're living in the latter episodes of *Seinfeld* or *Friends,* as if the plot lines of our lives have begun to wear thin," he wrote. "Could it be that we who have been biding our time in happy tribes are now ac-tually grown up enough to understand what we need in a mate? What a fantastic twist—we 'never marrieds' may end up revitalizing the very institution we've supposedly been undermining."

Since 1960, the number of single-person households in-creased in each of the four possible categories: for men and women householders and for householders over 65 and under 65. The biggest ten-year increases occurred in the 1970s for each group, except for men over 65, whose ranks swelled most in the

1990s as they continued to close the longevity gap with women. Who lives alone? As recently as 1960, the largest group was women under 65. By 1970, women over 65 predominated. Since 1980, men under 65 have been the biggest group. In 2000, they accounted for 35 percent of all one-person households, compared to nearly 30 percent for women under 65, 27 percent for women over 65, and 9 percent for men over 65.

Still, of all four groups differentiated by gender and age, women over 65 are most likely to live alone. In 2000, fully 77 percent of them did, compared to 29 percent of women under 65, about 20 percent of men over 65 but less than 17 percent of men under 65.

✦   ✦   ✦

Divorce rates may have moderated, but more marriages end in divorce these days than by death. The proportion of births to unmarried white women is as high as it was for black women in 1965. The number of unmarried couples is rising and marriage is, literally, being redefined. Proportionately, as the number of people living alone rises, the typical American household has been reconstituted to one without children. Even among families, the paradigmatic couple with children and with only one spouse working has declined from more than half a generation ago to about one-fifth.

Television is often a reflection of society rather than a bellwether and these days, as Julie Salamon wrote in the *New York Times,* the most enduring family on television, the Simpsons, is constituted by cartoon characters. And when a group of advertisers came together a few years ago to encourage family-friendly programming, the first creation was "Gilmore Girls." The program was about a 32-year-old single mother and her 16-year-old daughter and it provoked nary a peep compared to the political outcry that had greeted Murphy Brown's single motherhood a decade before.

4

How We're Aging

No county in the nation has a higher proportion of people over age 85 than McIntosh County in North Dakota. Florida, Pennsylvania, and West Virginia are home to a higher proportion of people 65 and older, but North Dakota has the highest proportion of people older than 85. Maybe the weaker ones were driven away by the rigors of agriculture and the 120-degree temperature swings between January and July. Maybe the fittest are among the descendants of a self-selected group of Germans who emigrated first to Russia and then fled to America. They were hardened by the Depression and the Dust Bowl and fortified by vigorous work and clean air to survive well into their eighties and beyond. The median age in McIntosh County is 51, and more than 1 in 3 residents are over 65. More than twice as many households include people over 65 than children younger than 18. There's another reason for the high proportion of elderly, of course: so many younger people have moved away from McIntosh County. But it's not as if they've been replaced by people in their eighties. Something about North Dakota, and about these people, has kept them alive longer than most other Americans. It is not uncommon for gas station attendants to wash windshields, for supermarket clerks to carry groceries to customers' cars. Buses ferry people from the senior center to medical appointments with specialists in Bismarck. The Ashley Medical Center does triple duty as a hospital, a nursing home, and an assisted living residence.

"They live longer in the Great Plains States," Richard M. Suzman, associate director of the Behavioral and Social Research Program at the National Institute on Aging in Washington, D.C., told the *New York Times*'s Peter Kilborn. "Community and neighborhood are important. So is the level of positive integration, neighborliness, looking out for others. Close-knit communities can be oppressive at one level. But they're also associated with higher life expectancy and better health."

◆   ◆   ◆

By one estimate, nearly two-thirds of all the people in the world who have survived past their fiftieth birthday are still alive.

America may be growing older, but the rest of the industrially developed world is growing older faster. Immigration has masked and slowed the aging of America, but we are on the verge of the greatest surge ever. In 2011, the first baby boomer will turn 65 (and those who can take early retirement at 62 will begin leaving the workforce in 2008). The last baby boomer will turn 65 in 2029. Already, the median age of Americans is the highest ever—a shift that has profound implications for an enormous range of variables, from the demand for health care to the design of automobile dashboards to the ratio of retired Americans to the number of working people, which will dictate the viability of Social Security. More generations are alive—if not necessarily living together—than at any other time. The proportion of Americans over age 65 now stands at about 13 percent of the population, and by 2030, they are expected to constitute 20 percent. Much

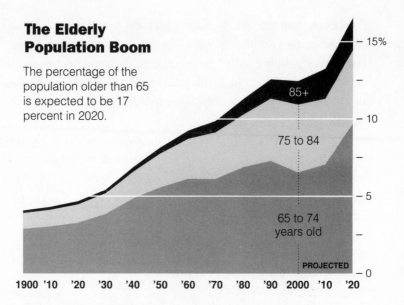

The Elderly Population Boom

The percentage of the population older than 65 is expected to be 17 percent in 2020.

85+

75 to 84

65 to 74 years old

PROJECTED

15%

10

5

0

1900 '10 '20 '30 '40 '50 '60 '70 '80 '90 2000 '10 '20

sooner than that, as early as 2010, more Americans will be older than 65 than younger than 15.

What seems certain, though, is that the convergence of two trends—more older Americans retiring and more young adults still living with their parents or moving back home—will create a potentially enormous financial burden on all the working people squeezed in the middle.

✦   ✦   ✦

The traditional graphic depiction of how a nation ages is called a population pyramid, but it isn't shaped like a pyramid anymore.

It used to be. In 1900, children under five represented the largest five-year age group, about 12 percent of the total population, and each older group was smaller enough so that the tiny proportion over the age of 85 formed the pinnacle to an almost perfect pyramid. But by 1940, after declining birthrates in the

1920s and then during the Depression, the 15- to 19-year-old group (born between 1920 and 1924) was the biggest. The post–World War II baby boom propelled the under five group to the biggest again in 1950, about 11 percent of the population, and it has shaped the population pyramid ever since. Now the pyramid is more like a rectangle or a pillar, resembling less a pyramid than a person, pinched slightly at the waist (people in their twenties) with burly arms (representing baby boomers in their mid-thirties to mid-fifties). The figure lists slightly to the right, symbolizing the greater number of women compared to men among the older age groups. (How many baby boomers are still alive? Between 1946 and 1964, the nation recorded 76 million births; an estimated 4 million of them had died by 2000, which left 72 million American-born baby boomers aged 36 to 54.)

In 1900, Americans under the age of 15 were the largest group—so big that 1 in 3 people was under 15—and people 65 and older were the smallest. Today, the elderly are still the smallest group but the biggest groups are now 25 to 44 and 45 to 64. Youngsters under 15 now account for 1 in 5 Americans.

Infants and toddlers, up to the age of two, account for about 16 percent of all people under age 18. Children of elementary and high school age, 5- to 17-year-olds, account for 73 percent. The school-age population has been increasing since the mid-1980s and by the end of the 1990s it matched the record baby boom peak of the early 1970s.

The West has the largest proportion of young people, 27 percent, and the highest growth rate for that age group. Children under 18 constitute 26 percent of the population in the Midwest and South and 24 percent in the Northeast.

While the number of young people grew by 14 percent nationwide during the 1990s, in five states the growth rate surpassed 25 percent. Nevada led with 72 percent, followed by Arizona at 39 percent, Colorado at 28 percent, Florida at 27 percent, and

The Aging of America

Projected share of population for each age group through 2100.

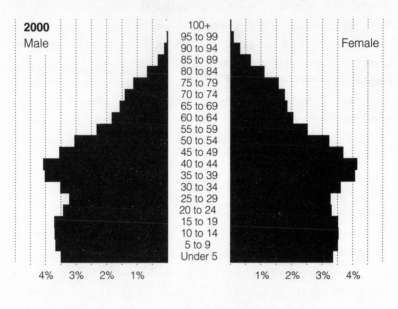

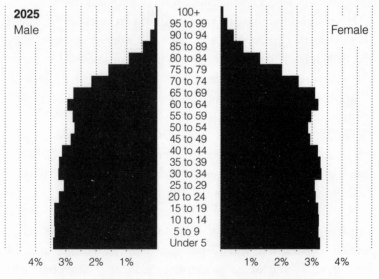

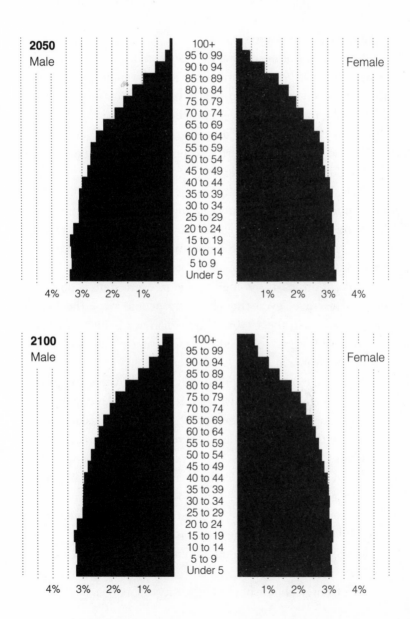

Georgia at 26 percent. Five other states actually suffered a net loss of young people. West Virginia lost 9 percent, or nearly 1 out of 10 people under 18. North Dakota, Wyoming, Maine, and Louisiana also registered losses.

Another way of measuring the age or youthfulness of a society is by its median age. The median age is the point at which half the population is older and half is younger. In 1900, it was age 22.9, and it rose to 29 in 1940, peaked at 30.2 in 1950, and then, driven by the baby boom, dipped to 29.5 in 1960 and 28.1 in 1970. The median age has risen every decade since and reached 35.3 in 2000, the oldest ever.

A closer look at median age by race and ethnicity hints at just how America's complexion is changing. Non-Hispanic whites have the highest median age, 38.6 years. People who reported two or more races had the lowest median age, 22.7 years, followed by Hispanics at 24.6, blacks at 30.2, and Asians at 32.7.

In the Northeast, the median age in every state is above the national average, even though young people were the fastest-growing group in the 1990s. The median age is highest in West Virginia, 38.9 years, followed by Florida at 38.7, Maine at 38.6, and Pennsylvania at 38.

By far, the youngest population is in Utah where the median age is 27.1—the only state where it is below 32. Among the other youngest populations are Texas at 32.3 years and Alaska at 32.4.

Among the larger counties, four recorded median ages below 26: Utah County, Utah, at 23.3; Brazos County, Texas, at 23.6; Onslow County, North Carolina, at 25; and Clarke County, Georgia, at 25.4.

Among the nation's ten largest cities, the highest median age is in Philadelphia, 34.2. The lowest is in Dallas, 30.5.

Among cities with 100,000 or more people, Provo, Utah, had the lowest median age, 22.9, followed by 25.4 in Athens-Clarke County, Georgia, home of the University of Georgia.

In Fontana, California, 37.8 percent of the residents are under 18. Fontana, a Los Angeles suburb, has been among the nation's fastest-growing cities and the two phenomena are closely related. Growth is not always good, but it is considered one sure sign that jobs and housing are available. Affordable housing, lower living costs, and extension of the freeway system attracted younger couples to Fontana, and the fact that many of those families are Hispanic also meant they were likely to have more children, further reducing the median age.

◆   ◆   ◆

While the nation's total population tripled in the twentieth century, the number of people 65 and over multiplied 10 times. In 1900, the 3.1 million Americans over 65 represented 4.1 percent of the total population. By 2000, that group had swollen to more than 35 million, or 12.4 percent of the total. (The 1990s was the only decade in the century in which the 65-and-over group grew more slowly than the total population.) An American born in 1900 was expected to live 47.3 years. Life expectancy rose to 68.2 by 1950 and 76.9 in 2000. Among people born in 1900, only about half were expected to survive until age 60. Today, nearly 90 percent are. In 2000, a person turning 65 was likely to survive another 17.9 years.

More than 1 in 4 elderly people are between ages 65 and 69, with about another 1 in 4 aged 70 to 74. Put another way, the 18.4 million Americans who are 65 to 74 years old account for 53 percent of the nation's elderly (and 6.5 percent of the total population). The 12.4 million people aged 74 to 85 represent 35 percent of the elderly (and 4.4 percent of the total population). The 4.2 million who are over 85 have grown to nearly 12 percent of the elderly (and 1.4 percent of the total).

For almost the first half of the twentieth century, the gap in life expectancy between men and women was marginal, only about two or three years. But the gap grew to seven years in the 1970s and 1980s. The 1990s signaled another trend among the elderly. Widows still outnumber widowers by about 4 to 1. But though women outlive men and the number of men per women decreases in each age group, the longevity gap between them finally appears to be narrowing. Earlier in the century, medical advances vastly improved maternal mortality rates, but death rates among men did not level off until the 1960s. Among people born in 2000, women are expected to live 79.5 years and men 74.1.

Among all people 65 and over, there were 67 men for every 100 women in 1990 and 70 men in 2000. Among those 65 to 74, the ratio was highest: 78 men for every 100 women in 1990, and 82 men in 2000.

There is also a racial gap among the elderly, although it is beginning to narrow, too. While non-Hispanic whites constitute 69 percent of the total population, they account for 84 percent of the elderly. The life expectancy at birth for white women is about five years longer than for black women. Among men, it's about seven years longer for whites than blacks. But that disparity evaporates among Americans who have already reached their golden years: it is about 1.7 years for those who are age 65 and zero for those age 85. Among people who reach 90, black men and women are likely to live a bit longer than whites.

Since 1940, the population 85 and older increased every decade even faster than the younger elderly—the groups from 65 to 74 and 75 to 84. In 1900, the census counted only 122,000 Americans 85 and older, or 4 percent of the elderly. By 2000, there were 4.2 million, or 12 percent of the elderly (but still only 1.5 percent of the total population).

In 1950, fewer than one-third of the elderly were over age 74; today, nearly one-half are. Only 1 in 20 were over 85, compared to 1 in 8 today.

Between 1990 and 2000, the number of Americans 85 to 89

years old, 90 to 94, and 95 and older each grew by more than one-third, or 35.4 percent, 44.6 percent, and 34.7 percent, respectively.

The 2000 census counted a record 50,454 centenarians, or 1 for every 5,578 Americans. That represented an increase of about 35 percent from the 37,306 recorded only ten years earlier. California and New York have the most in sheer numbers, but South Dakota and Iowa have the highest proportion of people over 100.

◆   ◆   ◆

Migration and fertility rates altered the relative age of America's regions in the twentieth century. Until 1960, the South was the youngest region, with the highest share of people under 15 and the smallest share 65 and over, largely as a result of higher birthrates among blacks. By the end of the century, the West had emerged as the youngest region, mostly because of higher fertility within the disproportionate share of Hispanics. Since 1950, the highest proportion of people 65 and over has been in the Northeast.

Those patterns were generally reflected within the states, although every state had a smaller percentage of people under 15 in 2000 than in 1900 and a higher percentage over age 65.

In 1900, people under age 15 accounted for 42.8 percent of the population in South Carolina, 42 percent in Mississippi, and 41.8 percent in Texas. By 2000, Utah was the youngest state, although its share of the people under age 15 had dropped sharply, to 26.6 percent, followed by Alaska with 25.2 percent and Texas with 23.5 percent.

The Northeast and Midwest accounted for 8 of the 10 oldest states in 1900 (those with the highest proportion of elderly), all 10 of the oldest in 1950, and 7 of the 10 by 2000. Vermont, Maine, and New Hampshire ranked highest at the beginning of the twentieth century, with about 8 percent each. By 2000, Florida was first, with 17.6 percent, followed by Pennsylvania with 15.6 percent and West Virginia with 15.3 percent. California and Florida shifted in opposite directions from the beginning to the end of the century. In 1900, Florida ranked 42nd oldest, and catapulted to first place in 2000. California was the sixth oldest in 1900 and became the sixth youngest.

Of the 35 million elderly Americans in 2000, one-quarter lived in California, Florida, or New York. Another quarter reside in Illinois, Michigan, New Jersey, Ohio, Pennsylvania, or Texas. No state has more elderly people than California, with 3.6 million, followed by Florida, with 2.8 million, and New York, with 2.4 million. Alaska has the lowest proportion (5.7 percent) and the lowest number (36,000) of people over 65. Utah registered 8.5 percent, followed by Georgia with 9.6 percent, Colorado with 9.7 percent and Texas with 9.9 percent.

Growing Old in America

Percentage of the population that was 65 years or older in 2000.

Total U.S. 12.4%

5.6%   10.0   12.5   15.0   17.6%

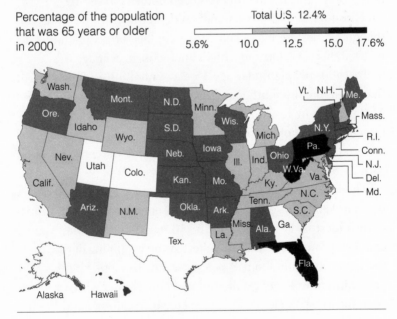

In the late 1990s, Florida recorded the biggest net gain in people over 65—149,000—although slightly more people 85 and over left the state than moved in, suggesting that some retirees were returning home to be closer to their families as they got older. (Alaska, Colorado, Connecticut, Maryland, Minnesota, and Washington, while winding up with fewer people 65 to 74, recorded a gain of people 85 and over.) Nearly 1 in 3 of the older migrants to Florida came from New York or New Jersey. About 1 in 4 of the elderly migrants to Arizona came from California or Washington. Nevada drew most from California and Arizona, and also drew heavily from Florida and Illinois. Three in 4 elderly people who migrated from New York moved to Florida, North Carolina, Virginia, South Carolina, or closer to home to New Jersey, Pennsylvania, and Connecticut.

Looking county by county, a swath of the Midwest, from the Mexican border north through the Great Plains to Canada, and also a band in the Northeast are home to a disproportionate number of elderly—reflecting two ongoing migration patterns: an exodus of young people to other parts of the country and the decision of their parents and grandparents to stay put.

More than 82 percent of the counties in the Midwest are home to a higher proportion of elderly than the national average of 12.4 percent. Still, Charlotte County, Florida, claims the highest share—35 percent. Among the biggest counties, Charlotte also has the highest median age, 54.3, followed by two other Florida counties, Citrus at 52.6 and Sarasota at 50.5.

The lowest proportion of elderly is in Chattahoochee County, Georgia, home to a big military base, where those 65 and older constitute only 2 percent of the population.

Six of the 10 cities with the greatest proportion of elderly are retirement communities in Florida. Clearwater ranks first, with 21.5 percent, followed by Cape Coral with 19.6 percent. The top ten also include Honolulu, Hawaii; Warren and Livonia, Michigan;

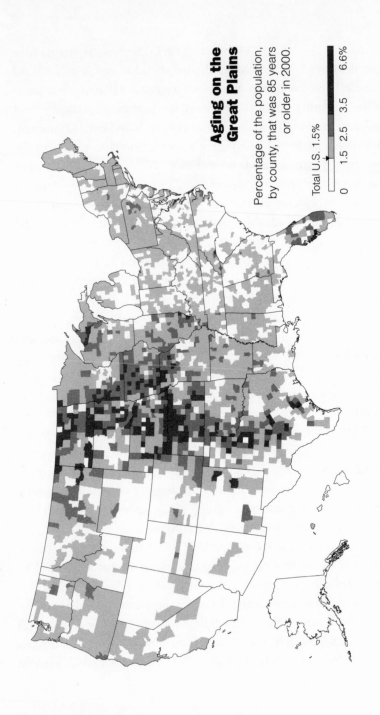

Aging on the Great Plains

Percentage of the population, by county, that was 85 years or older in 2000.

Total U.S. 1.5%

0   1.5   2.5   3.5   6.6%

and Scottsdale, Arizona. (Clearwater also has the highest median age of any large city, 41.8; it's also over 40 in Cape Coral, Scottsdale, and Livonia.) Among the ten largest cities in the United States, Philadelphia has the highest proportion of elderly, 14.1 percent—the only one of the ten to exceed the national average—followed by New York, with 11.7 percent. Phoenix and Houston have the lowest proportion of elderly, 8.1 percent and 8.4 percent, respectively.

Places with disproportionately small elderly populations tend to have large numbers of immigrants, young families, college students, and military installations. Among the lowest were Gilbert, Arizona (3.8 percent); Fontana, California (4.7 percent); and Plano, Texas (4.9 percent).

The pattern of growth among the elderly population pretty much mirrored regional population growth in general. In the 1990s, the number of elderly grew fastest in the West, by 20 percent, and in the South, by 16 percent, and trailed considerably in the Midwest, where it grew by only 7 percent and the Northeast, by 5 percent.

The number of elderly residents rose in every state, but nowhere as much as in Nevada, where it soared by 72 percent, followed by Alaska, with a 60 percent increase, Arizona, with 39 percent, and New Mexico, with 30 percent.

An estimated 1 in 20 or so baby boomers have already retired, the vanguard of an army of Americans over 60 that will about double from 35 million today to well over 65 million by 2030. By then, projecting on the basis of current trends, the elderly will account for 20 percent of the population. Where they settle will go a long way toward defining the demand for jobs—in restaurants, home health care, housekeeping, construction, and related fields—and which places grow fastest in the first decades of the twenty-first century. Already, there is some evidence that suburban empty-nesters are returning to downtowns where transportation is convenient and cultural activities abound. Self-contained retirement communities are being carved out of rural and exurban farmland, not only in predictable places like the Southwest, but—bypassing traditional retirement magnets like California, Florida, and Arizona—in Georgia, North Carolina, Virginia, and even places in the Northeast, like the Poconos in Pennsylvania and Jackson Township, New Jersey.

So many retirees who originally settled in Florida have migrated north to Georgia, North Carolina, and Virginia that they have already earned their own nickname—halfbacks. They have moved halfway back, or so, in the direction of their original home states. Other states not typically known as retirement havens have begun luring baby boomers from other parts of the country. Each June, a group of marketers from Mississippi pitches a tent in New York's Central Park, fries up samples of catfish and begins mining for gray gold by touting its twenty "certified" retiree-friendly towns. Alabama tapped state pension funds to build a trail of Robert Trent Jones golf courses. "Retirees are a clean industry," said Dr. Mark Fagan, a sociologist at Jacksonville State University in Alabama. Over the longer term, though, it's a gamble. Those localities are betting that, on balance, retirees will help revive local economies rather than impose a burden on health care and other social services.

◆   ◆   ◆

One sector of the economy that the elderly unquestionably drive is medical care. At lunchtime outside the Boca Urology office in Boca Raton, Florida, patients mill about, even calling the receptionist on their cell phones, asking to be admitted. "We never used to lock the door at lunch, but they came in an hour early," Ellie Fertel, the office manager told Gina Kolata of the *New York Times*. "It's like they're waiting for a concert. Sometimes we forget to lock the door and they come in and sit in the dark." Visiting the urologist or other specialists has become a social activity around many retirement communities. Patients bring their spouses and plan shopping and lunches around doctors' appointments. Money is no object, because Medicare, the federal health insurance program for the elderly, pays. Obviously, this is a lifesaver for people who otherwise could not afford it. Also, for people who happen to be sick. Many aren't. South Florida has a large pool of well-to-do older people aware of what they are entitled to and plenty of doctors to accommodate them. By some measures, patients there make more office visits, see more specialists, and take more tests than anywhere else, which is why the cost of Medicare per person is twice as much in South Florida as it is, for example, in Minneapolis.

At Boca Urology, one patient, eighty-three-year-old Leon Bloomberg, was asked how many doctors he visited regularly. Between himself and his wife, Esther, he said, ten or twelve, including a neurologist, a cardiologist, a rheumatologist, and the urologist for his prostate. "You get recommendations at the clubhouse, at the swimming pool," Bloomberg explained. "You go to a restaurant here and nine times out of ten, before the meal is over, you hear people talking about a doctor or a medicine or a surgery."

Still, many places with disproportionately older populations are struggling with the high cost of medical care—few more so than rural counties in upstate New York, a state that mandates expensive Medicaid programs and requires localities to pay a quarter of the cost, the most of any state. When Mark Thomas became county executive of Chautauqua in 1998, the bill for health care for its poorest residents was $13 million. In five years, the cost more than doubled, to $29 million, which amounts to more than half the county's revenue from property taxes. "We are dealing with seniors burning through their financial sources and having to go on Medicaid," Thomas told Lydia Polgreen of the *Times*. Among them is eighty-nine-year-old Helen Grover, who gets Meals on Wheels and also housekeeping, which allows her to stay in her own home. Katie Smith, the director of the county's Office for the Aging, explained, "We get state money to help people with housekeeping. At budget time the county legislature gets tempted to cut the $95,000 it costs us to keep the program. But if having someone help a ninety-year-old with her chores means that ninety-year-old can stay in her house and keep paying property taxes rather than us spending $60,000 a year in taxpayers' money on long-term residential care, it is money well spent." In Chautauqua, 16 percent of the residents are sixty-five or older, compared to the national average of 12.4 percent. In Hamilton County in the Adirondacks, 20 percent of the residents—some left behind by children and grandchildren who have left for other opportunities—are elderly. Most of the more than $3 billion that New York spends on Medicaid for the elderly outside New York City pays for nursing home care.

But one sign that Americans are not only living longer but are in better shape to care for themselves is the nursing home population. Cost, availability, quality of care are among the other variables, of course. The proportion of people in nursing homes who are elderly increased in the 1990s, but barely, from 90 percent to 91 percent. In 2000, more than 1.5 million people age 65 and over lived in a nursing home. At the same time, the proportion of elderly people living in nursing homes decreased from 5.1 percent to 4.5 percent. The decline was most pronounced among people 85 and over. In 1990, 24.5 percent of Americans 85 and over, or nearly 1 in 4, were confined to a nursing home. In 2000, 18.2 percent were.

That same year, though, Americans continued a decade-long trend of making more visits to their doctors each year. We visited doctors 823 million times in 2000, as the average age of patients climbed to 43.

Better access to medical care is one reason people are living longer. Longer than their parents and, in many cases, longer than they themselves expected to live. Robert Bezanson retired to Green Valley, Arizona, in 1990, after being raised in Massachusetts, moving to Montana, and living wherever his pipe-laying work took him. He planned to live on Social Security and spend down his nest egg of government bonds, which would keep him going for ten years, until he turned seventy-five. But in 2003, he celebrated his seventy-eighth birthday, lucky enough to have his health, but looking warily at neighbors who survive on fixed pensions and whose investment portfolios were brutalized by the recession and the stock market. "The biggest problem I have is that I'm living too long," he said.

+   +   +

For individuals, the consequences of longer life are challenging enough. For society, the implications are enormous.

According to the Census Bureau's middle-range projections, the nation's median age will peak in 2035 at 38.7, and then dip just slightly, to 38.1 by midcentury. But no one is certain. On the basis of the bureau's middle-level estimate of mortality, by 2040 America will have about 14 million people over 85. But if death rates continue to fall at recent rates, the number could be more than 50 million.

If people are not only living longer but are also healthier (and if work, generally, is less strenuous), they may want to retire later, which could mean more competition for younger people entering the workforce and for workers in their thirties and forties hoping to get promoted. (Seventy was first proposed as the eligibility age for Social Security benefits in the 1930s, but the government set it at 65, in part to free up jobs for younger workers.) As recently as forty years ago, more than 3 in 4 American men in their early sixties were still in the labor force. By 2000, even with the virtual elimination of mandatory retirement and of tax penalties on older workers receiving Social Security, the proportion had dropped to fewer than half.

But the expected avalanche of retirements beginning in less than a decade promises to have a profound impact on the dependency ratio, which the government defines as the number of children and elderly compared to the number of people considered to be of working age (which, at the moment, means people 18 to 64 years old). According to the Census Bureau's middle-range projections, there are expected to be about 60 dependent people for every 100 working age people by 2010. As the baby boomers retire, the ratio is projected to soar to 68 in 2020, 79 by 2030, and 80 at midcentury. For perspective's sake, that's lower than it was in the 1960s, when baby boomers swelled the ranks of dependent younger Americans.

As more and more baby boomers approach retirement age— and as all those retirees begin applying for Social Security and Medicare, placing an unprecedented drain on the retirement and health care systems—regulations, incentives, and even societal mores that govern those trends may transform both those systems. Early in 2004, Alan Greenspan, the Federal Reserve chairman warned that the real fiscal calamity is not the deficit but the ballooning cost of entitlement programs like Social Security and Medicare when baby boomers begin to retire. Greenspan urged Congress to forsake future tax increases as a means of shrinking the federal deficit and to reduce spending—including entitlement programs—instead.

In the twenty-first century, Americans will live longer, healthier, and more productive lives—lives that at every stage, from childhood on, will be reshaped by the fact that, on average, they promise to last more than twice as long as life spans did a century ago. When Gail Sheehy wrote her book *Passages* in 1976, she defined thirty as the beginning of midlife. Today, she says, thirty "is the new twenty-two." That means adulthood is being delayed, more multigenerational families are emerging (in 1940 only about

13 percent of people over 60 had a living parent, today 44 percent do), more women will survive into their seventies and even eighties with their spouse and as many as 1 in 20 baby boomers will live to be 100. "You know what Florida looks like?" said Laurence Kotlikoff, a Boston University professor, "The whole country's going to look a lot older than that." By 2030, he estimates, the number of retirees will have doubled, but the number of working people will have risen by only 18 percent—producing a gap of $51 trillion between payroll taxes and costs of medical care and Social Security. Who's going to make up the difference?

In 2003, Audry Blaylock, the oldest of four sisters, celebrated her hundredth birthday in an Iowa nursing home where, she told Susan Dominus of *The New York Times Magazine*, that her greatest fear about growing old had been loneliness. "When my husband died, I was terrified of being alone, and all my children wanted me to come stay with them, but I said, no, let me face it right away, don't put it off," she recalled. "The longer you put something off, the harder it is to face it."

Where We've Moved

For the third decade in a row, a tiny town in Missouri defined how, why, and where America grew.

That America grew at all defied what has been going on in the rest of the economically developed world. Given those trends, the dimensions of the population growth in the United States were nothing short of astounding. Overall, the nation registered 32.7 million more people in 2000 than in 1990—the largest ten-year numerical increase ever. For the first time in the twentieth century, every state recorded more people than it had counted a decade before. While most of the biggest cities reversed population losses, the 1990s signaled the triumph of the suburbs, now home to more than half of all Americans. What drove that growth, universally, was the same dynamic that has historically defined American expansionism: the migration of a self-selected group of people with the gumption to quit familiar surroundings and seek out more promising opportunities—or, simply, a less onerous lifestyle—elsewhere for themselves and their families. In the 1990s, that migration accelerated sprawl into formerly rural counties on the fringes of metropolitan areas. The borders of ballooning suburbs bumped one another, bruising political and geographic sensibilities, but co-alescing into seemingly indistinguishable megalopolises in coastal corridors that claimed tens of millions of Americans.

If Edgar Springs, Missouri, seems an implausible place to per-sonify those trends, it's a demographer's paradise. A 25-pound brass plaque sunk into a concrete post 2.8 miles east of Edgar Springs marks the spot where government experts pinpointed the nation's center of population in 2000.

The official center of population is a device only a statistician could contrive. It marks the pivot at which a perfectly level map of the United States would balance if each resident of the coun-try weighed exactly the same. (We obviously don't, but that's an-other story.) The demographers' mythical fulcrum is a mobile manifestation of mathematical constants that have defined the nation's internal migration since the first census two centuries ago. It's the fleeting landfall of a nation in flux, a nation in which emerging regional agendas—or, at least, metropolitan ones—cut across county and state lines and have rendered anachronistic the original political boundaries of the continental United States, last codified nearly one hundred years ago.

Edgar Springs was originally known as Edgar Prairie, but, as legend has it, its current name was derived from the popularity of a still that Reuben Edgar, who settled there in the mid-nineteenth century, operated near a local spring. People would say coyly that they were going to visit Edgar's spring and the name caught on. Today, the city has one restaurant (Hot Lips, named for the CB handle of the owner, who formerly drove a truck), no traffic lights or stop signs, and more dead people in the local cemetery than liv-ing residents (about 190 in the latest census, down from 215 a decade earlier). Edgar Springs pretty much exemplified the rural Midwest: compared to the United States overall, the population was older (the median age was over 41) less diverse (97 percent of the residents were white and only two people said they were foreign-born), and less mobile (between 1995 and 2000, fewer than 1 in 10 residents moved there from as far away as another county; no one came from another state or from abroad). And so on April 23, 2001, experts from the Census Bureau, the National Geodetic Survey, the National Oceanic and Atmospheric Administration's National Ocean Service, the Missouri Department of Natural Resources, and officials from Phelps County and proud residents of Edgar Springs braved a rainstorm to ceremoniously plant the marker atop a concrete post flanked by two buckets of flowers. It was too soon to tell whether the designation would leave any enduring mark, besides the brass marker, on Edgar Springs, but its designation by the Census Bureau signaled the inexorable shift of America's population and its state of mind westward and, as much relentlessly if less dramatically, southward.

Moving Out of State

The 10 largest migration flows between 1995 and 2000.

MOVED FROM	TO	NUMBER OF PEOPLE
New York	Florida	308,230
New York	New Jersey	206,979
California	Nevada	199,125
California	Arizona	186,151
California	Texas	182,789
Florida	Georgia	157,423
California	Washington	155,577
California	Oregon	131,836
New Jersey	Florida	118,905
Texas	California	115,929

On the basis of the first federal census in 1790, census enumerators later plotted the nation's population center at Chestertown, Maryland, 23 miles east of Baltimore. Over the course of every decade, on average, the center inched about 40 miles west and 3 miles south until it was plotted in Bartholomew County, Indiana, in 1900; finally crossed the Mississippi River from a soybean field in Mascoutah, Illinois, in 1970; to De Soto, Missouri, in 1980; and then edged to Steelville, Missouri, in 1990. Edgar Springs is nearly 33 miles west and 12 miles south of Steelville—a shift in the population center of nearly 1,000 miles west since 1790 and 324 miles west and 101 miles south since the twentieth century began (79 miles of that shift south occurring since 1950). The Census Bureau also measures regional changes another way. It plots the median center of population, an imaginary intersection of one line that divides the population evenly in the east and west and another line that splits it into equal portions north and south. That nexus straddled the border of Ohio and Indiana during the 1900s and ended the twentieth century southwest of Indianapolis in Daviess County.

Whichever way it was calculated, the inexorable southwestward shift in the population midpoint vividly exemplified America's manifest destiny and its density.

✦   ✦   ✦

Americans move a lot and, along with births and deaths and the influx of foreigners, internal migration is a key component of population growth. In fact, in the fifteen months before the 2000 census, nearly 1 in 5 of the nation's 105 million households changed residences. That's twice as many as the proportion who've stayed put for fully thirty years or more. Among home owners, stayers outnumbered recent movers. The reverse was true for renters, by a wide margin. Between 2002 and 2003, though, movers constituted only about 1 in 7 Americans.

Nevada is the most transient state, and no place in the country was more rootless than Stateline, Nevada, a casino and ski community in the Sierra Nevada on the south shore of Lake Tahoe. Of Stateline's 1,146 residents in 2000, only 4.5 percent were born in Nevada. No other place in the nation had a smaller proportion of its population living in the state where they were born. The median home price in 2002 was about $400,000, displacing affordable housing and driving out residents who worked in Stateline's resorts industry.

In the late 1990s, 5 million people moved from the Northeast, the Midwest, and the West to the South, and 3.2 million left the South for another region. Most of the gain was in states near the Atlantic coast, from Delaware to Florida. Overall, in terms of domestic migration, the South gained nearly 1.8 million people, and the West a mere 12,000 (2.7 million moved in but almost as many moved out). The Northeast had a net loss of 1.3 million residents, and more than 540,000 moved out of the Midwest than moved in. At the state level, 22 million people moved from one state to another in the second half of the 1990s. Nevada and Arizona had the highest rates of net immigration from other states. Between 1995 and 2000, those two states gained many residents from California, which recorded a net loss of 755,000 people to other states, second only to New York's net loss of 874,000. A closer look at internal migration reveals how newcomers from overseas were instrumental in the net population gains that states registered in 2000. In New York, 726,000 moved in from other states, but 1.6 million moved out. In California, 1.4 million people moved in, but 2.2 million moved out. In Texas, 1.4 million people moved in, but another 1.2 million moved out. If it hadn't been for immigrants from abroad, Connecticut, Hawaii, Illinois, Iowa, Louisiana, Massachusetts, New Jersey, Ohio, Pennsylvania, among others, would have lost population.

Domestic and foreign-born migrants gravitated to some of the same places. Georgia, Florida, North Carolina, Arizona, and

Newcomers

Percentage of people born
in the state in which they
were living in 2000.

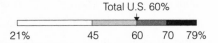

Total U.S. 60%

21%   45   60   70   79%

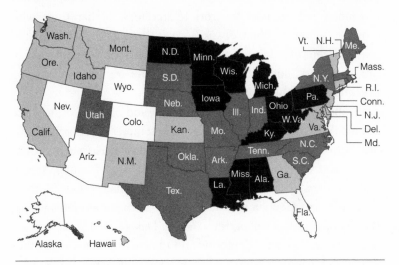

Texas attracted the most people from other states (with Florida
and Texas slipping in rank since 1990). California, Texas, New
York, Florida, and Illinois drew the most from abroad. But the
foreign-born population, like the native-born, is dispersing. The
demographer William H. Frey of the University of Michigan has
found that 65 percent of immigrants who arrived in the 1990s
live in the gateway states of California, Texas, New York, Florida,
Illinois, and New Jersey, compared to 71 percent of the foreign-
born residents who arrived before 1990.

+   +   +

Why do people move? The conventional wisdom is that most
moves within a county are to find better housing or a safer neighborhood, while most moves from one county to another (or one

state to another) are work-related. But the latest figures challenge a basic economic tenet, that mobility is a mechanism to redistribute people and wealth because workers move to where jobs are plentiful. Census surveys suggest that unemployed people aren't any more likely to move for work-related reasons than those with jobs are. Moreover, the Census Bureau concluded, "Work-related reasons were not as important for movement of the poor as economic theory suggests, with housing-related reasons taking precedence for this group."

Young adults between the ages of 25 and 39 tend to be more mobile. Where they go is also a good barometer of where the jobs are. Between 1995 and 2000, they constituted more than one-third of movers. Calculated another way, about 3 in 4 young, single, college-educated adults reported moving in that period. Nevada, Colorado, and Georgia had the highest net migration rates within that group; North Dakota, Iowa, South Dakota, and West Virginia had the lowest. While California and Illinois lost migrants to other states, they gained among the young, single, and college-educated group. New York lost fewer among that group than it did among the general population. Several other states, including Utah, Kentucky, South Carolina, and Missouri, gained people overall, but lost population in the younger, single, college-educated group. Metropolitan areas that were the biggest magnets for that group included Las Vegas, Nevada; Charlotte, North Carolina; and Atlanta, Georgia. Among the twenty largest metropolitan areas, only Philadelphia, Detroit, and Cleveland suffered a net loss among that group. A number of other metropolitan areas—including New York, Chicago, Los Angeles, and Washington—experienced a net loss of migrants overall but were popular destinations for the young, single, college-educated group.

Mobility also differs by race and ethnicity, although it's largely a factor of other variables, like income, education, and whether people own or rent their homes. In the five years preceding the 2000 census, non-Hispanic whites were the least mobile. Among them, only 43 percent moved to a new residence, compared to 49 percent of blacks, 54 percent of Asians, and 56 percent of Hispanics. While non-Hispanic whites moved less frequently, when they did switch residences they were typically more motivated—for work-related reasons or for retirement—than members of other ethnic or racial groups to move to a different state altogether.

Regional differences also emerged as a result of internal migration, and, as a result, racial and ethnic groups that had already settled in the United States were further redistributed.

Between 1995 and 2000, more blacks moved to the South than left it, while every other region registered more blacks leaving than arriving. Moreover, the net influx of 300,000 blacks altered the southern black profile. As a proportion, blacks who left the South were more likely to be college-educated men between 25 and 44 years old than the blacks who arrived. The disproportionate number of older blacks among those who moved to the South from other regions suggest, to some extent, a return migration by some who had gone elsewhere when they were younger.

More Hispanics left the West than arrived from other states, while the South and the Midwest recorded a net influx. Asians, meanwhile, were redistributed from the Northeast and the Midwest to the South.

Internal migration hardly depleted the Northeast, but it lost members of all four major racial and ethnic groups and at the highest rates of any region: 22 non-Hispanic whites (for every 1,000 living in the region), 42 blacks (for every 1,000 blacks living there), 34 Hispanics, and 23 Asians. Numerically, that meant a net loss to the region by domestic migration of 832,000 non-Hispanic whites, 233,000 blacks, 151,000 Hispanics, and 39,000 Asians. (Most of the losses were in the Middle Atlantic states; New England recorded a net gain of Hispanics and Asians from domestic migration alone.)

The Midwest also lost non-Hispanic whites, blacks, and Asians to domestic migration. The West gained non-Hispanic whites, but lost blacks and Hispanics to domestic migration. (As in the Northeast, within the region the results were divided; the Mountain states gained from all four racial and ethnic groups while the Pacific states lost from all four.)

Among states, Florida recorded the largest net gain of non-Hispanic whites from other states (450,000; 190,000 of those from New York alone), followed by Arizona (including 109,000 from California) and North Carolina. Florida also gained more Hispanics (92,000) than any state, followed by Nevada, Arizona, and Georgia. Georgia gained more blacks than any state (130,000, nearly half of them from Florida and New York), followed by North Carolina, Florida, Maryland, and Texas. Nevada (18,000), Texas (15,000), and Georgia (14,000) gained the most Asians.

The most lopsided migration pattern was between Hawaii and Nevada. Nevada gained 563 native Hawaiians for every 1,000 native Hawaiians living in Hawaii. The shift of 1,600 people probably reflected the decline of Hawaii's economy—a result, in part, of the Asian recession—and Nevada's demand for workers with tourism, hospitality, and marketing experience.

Immigration from overseas profoundly affected population distribution, too, and offset some of the results of domestic migration. The Northeast registered an influx of nearly half a million non-Hispanic whites and Hispanics, more than 300,000 Asians and 200,000 blacks from abroad. More than a million Hispanics settled in the South from overseas, a million more moved to the West, and more than 300,000 moved to the Midwest.

California recorded the largest number of non-Hispanic white movers from abroad (269,000), followed by New York (200,000).

California also gained the most Hispanic movers from overseas, 660,000, followed by Texas (447,000), Florida (348,000), New York (223,000), Illinois (146,000), and New Jersey (117,000). New York (112,000) and Florida (85,000) had the largest number of blacks from abroad. Among Asians from abroad, the largest number moved to California (377,000) and New York (157,000).

Of the 120 million people aged five and older who moved between 1995 and 2000—nearly 46 percent of all such Americans—more than half changed residences within the same county. Another 1 in 5 moved elsewhere in the same state, and slightly fewer moved from one state to another. City residents were the most mobile. Fully half changed residences.

Nonetheless, foreign immigrants aside, almost two-thirds of Americans still live in the state where they were born. The proportion ranged from 21 percent in Nevada to more than 65 percent in New York. Even in California, historically a destination state, more than 50 percent of the residents were born in the state. That's a consequence of two factors: fewer people moved there for work during the 1990s when the economy boomed in other states, and high birth rates among Hispanic and Asian newcomers to California increased the proportion of residents born in the state.

At the other end of the spectrum from Stateline, Nevada, is Warren, Michigan. Nationwide, most people stay in their homes for six years on average. But in Warren, which abuts Detroit, nearly 20 percent of the homes haven't changed hands in more than three decades—more than twice the national proportion. Joseph Bieda, a retired engineer for General Motors, is a case in point. He and his wife bought their three-bedroom brick ranch house for less than $17,000 in 1961. Since then, they renovated their kitchen and two bathrooms three times; their house is now worth about ten times what they paid for it. But they have no intention of moving. "It suits us just terrific," Bieda told Motoko Rich of the *New York Times*. "I don't see any reason to move to Florida."

In Warren and stay-put places like it across the country, one common denominator is that the population is disproportionately older. In Warren, where more than 17 percent of the residents are sixty-five and older, Deputy Mayor Michael Greiner said: "These are hardworking, middle-class people who settled in their homes, take very good care of them and then burn the mortgage when it's paid off." Among towns (like Warren) with more than 100,000 people, 4 of the 10 with the least mobile residents are in Pennsylvania, which has the highest percentage of longstanding residents of any state—17 percent—followed by West Virginia, Connecticut, and Massachusetts.

All this back and forth, the proliferation of cellular phones and the transformation from an era not long ago when air travel was the province of jet-setters raises a fundamental question: Are Americans more mobile than before? By one measure, the frequency with which we cross county lines to find a new home, we're less mobile. An analysis by Kimberlee Shauman of the University of California, Davis, found two reasons for the apparent decline in long-distance mobility. One reason is the rise in dual-career married couples, which means that neither partner is as willing to sacrifice a managerial or professional job just because a spouse is offered a better opportunity elsewhere. Another reason is that, on average, heads of households have grown older since a few decades ago, and older people are less likely to move.

✦   ✦   ✦

In the twentieth century, the population of the Northeast and the Midwest more than doubled. But the South, the most populous region since 1940 (in part because the Census Bureau's definition includes Texas), nearly quadrupled in population, from 25 million in 1900 to 100 million in 2000. The West saw its population grow more than fifteen-fold, from 4 million to 63 million. By 1980, more than half the nation's population lived in either the

South or the West. Still, the West alone (with nearly half the nation's land area) had the smallest proportion of the nation's population until 1990, when it overtook the Northeast (which has the
smallest land area), and the West is now poised to dislodge the
Midwest from second place.

In the 1990s, while the population of the Northeast grew
by nearly 6 percent and the Midwest by almost 8 percent, the
South expanded by more than 17 percent and the West by nearly 20
percent. And for the first time in the twentieth century, the South
gained black residents from every other region. In fact, the South
registered the most people moving in and moving out.

The West is also home to the most and least populous states:
California (in first place since 1970 after dislodging New York),
with 33.9 million, and Wyoming, with 494,000. Texas, with 20.9
million, officially edged New York for second most populous in
2000. Florida was the only state that grew from less than a million when the twentieth century began to more than 10 million in
2000. Since 1900, six states—Illinois, Michigan, New York, Ohio,
Pennsylvania, and Texas—have remained in the ranks of the ten
most populous. Indiana, Iowa, Missouri, and Massachusetts fell
off the list, California, Florida, and New Jersey joined the top
ten, North Carolina made a brief appearance in 1950, and Georgia, which was no. 10 in 1910, bounced back in 2000. Florida's
population grew astoundingly, by 2,924 percent, during the twentieth century, but it was outpaced by two other states—Nevada,
whose population soared by 4,620 percent, and Arizona, which
grew by 4,074 percent. (Among the ten states that gained between 5 and 10 million residents over the century, Arizona was
the only noncoastal state.) Together, only four states—California,
Texas, Florida, and New York—accounted for 38 percent of the
nation's population growth in the twentieth century. (In 1900,
California and Kansas had about the same population, 1.5 million, but by the end of the century Kansas's hadn't even doubled

and California's increased by more than 32 million.) More states lost population—especially in the exodus from the Dust Bowl—in the 1930s than during any other decade. Since 1950, states in the West accounted for 8 of the 10 fastest growing. During the same period, most of the states that grew slowest were in the Midwest and Northeast (the population of West Virginia actually declined by 10 percent).

The 1990s was the only decade of the century in which every single state gained population. Numerically, California grew the most, by 4.1 million, Texas by 3.9 million, and Florida by 3 million. Proportionately, none of those was the fastest growing. Nevada grew by 66 percent, Arizona by 40 percent, Colorado by 31 percent, Utah by 30 percent, and Idaho by 29 percent. In the Northeast, New Hampshire grew the fastest, by 11 percent, as a result of spillover from Massachusetts. In the Midwest, Minnesota was the fastest-growing state, by 12 percent. In the South, Georgia was the fastest growing, with 26 percent, outpacing Florida's growth rate for the first time in the century (with many of the newcomers to Georgia coming from Florida). Even Nebraska and Iowa grew faster than any time since the 1910s. Missouri registered growth rates unseen since the last decade of the nineteenth century. In the last half of the 1990s, the largest flow of people between one state and another was from New York to Florida. While 70,000 left Florida for New York, another 300,000 moved from New York to Florida.

In the late 1990s, for the first time, more Americans left California than moved in. Again, as in other states, the influx of immigrants more than made up for the loss. The reversal in a trend that the government has recorded consistently since 1940 but that probably began before California became a state reflects both a dissatisfaction with high housing prices and sprawl and the availability of cheaper alternatives nearby. Although California attracted 1.4 million people from other states, it lost 2.2 million of

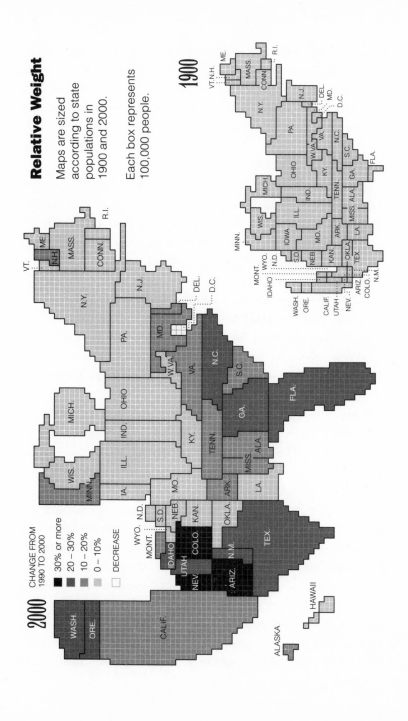

Relative Weight

Maps are sized according to state populations in 1900 and 2000.

Each box represents 100,000 people.

1900

2000

CHANGE FROM
1990 TO 2000

30% or more
20 – 30%
10 – 20%
0 – 10%
DECREASE

its own residents. Nearly 200,000 of them settled in adjacent Nevada. Another reason for the exodus is California's role as a gateway for immigrants. "The only way you can balance that is by exporting people out of state," said Dowell Myers, a demographer at the University of Southern California.

❖   ❖   ❖

A half-century ago, about 36 percent of Americans lived in rural areas, but in 1950, for the first time, a majority of rural Americans no longer lived on farms. Today, the rural population has risen to about 1 in 5—slightly higher, numerically, than it was fifty years ago (although definitions have changed), but only about 1 in 100 Americans lives on a farm.

Development of prisons, casinos, resorts, and retirement communities drove the revival of some enclaves in rural America. The Great Plains was the great exception and even in more robust regions it wasn't certain whether population gains—or, at least, the reversal of losses—would endure much into the twenty-first century.

Calvin Beale, a senior demographer with the Department of Agriculture's Economic Research Service, pronounced the rebound as real. The evidence: in the 1990s, the number of nonmetropolitan counties with declining populations was halved, compared to the previous decade.

The Great Plains has been exporting people for seventy years, so much so that 70 percent of its counties register fewer residents today than in 1950. The hemorrhaging wasn't stanched in the 1990s and accelerated since then, despite the efforts of people in places like Superior, Nebraska, to attempt a last stand against the exodus. Some people, too old or too unskilled, lack the resources to leave. But others, typically lured by family ties and links to the land, forgo the lure of bright lights and remain or, after leaving for college, military service, and even after raising families elsewhere, return to their depopulated hometowns. In Cheyenne, Oklahoma, population 718 and falling, Stuart Sander, a thirty-four-year-old bank vice president, and his wife, Kimberly, struggled to give their children the same small-town opportunities that they had. "Out here, people are more content with what they have," he told Peter Kilborn of the *New York Times*. "I have a good job. I'm home every night to see my kids. I'm very happy with that." But those values become sorely tested when it becomes difficult to depend on reliable ambulance service or when schools are closing or consolidating. "I'm very worried about this place, this bank, what this town will be," Sander said.

"Our greatest asset is the psychological loyalty of people who left here," said Don Crilly, a retired surgeon in Superior. He was one of those people. He and his wife, Sylvia, returned a decade ago from the San Francisco Bay area.

But the obstacles for revival are daunting. Of the nation's twelve poorest counties, seven are in Nebraska, including the nation's three poorest. "As an urban person who lived within blocks of the East Oakland ghettos, I have been just shocked by some of the poverty I have seen here," Sylvia Crilly told the *Times*'s Timothy Egan. "Some of these people are just drowning."

All but two of the ninety-nine counties in the United States with the highest percentage of elderly people are in the Plains states. "People live a lot longer here," she added, "or, as the old joke goes, it just seems that way." According to one survey, more teenagers in the rural Plains admit to using illegal drugs than in cities or suburbs. Only 11 percent of the people in small-town Nebraska say they are satisfied with where they live.

"This is a huge shift from earlier polls," said John C. Allen, director of the Center for Applied Rural Innovation at the University of Nebraska. "In some of those rural counties, we've lost 40 percent of the eighteen- to forty-nine-year-olds. This is where your entrepreneurs come from. Those are your optimists, your future."

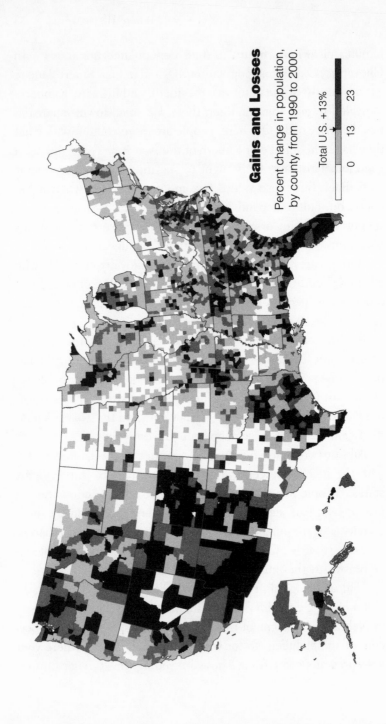

Gains and Losses

Percent change in population,
by county, from 1990 to 2000.

Total U.S. +13%

0   13   23

Among the nation's 3,141 counties, losses were most pronounced in a depopulated swath that reached across America's
midsection from Mexico to Canada. In the 1970s, more people
moved into rural areas than left them, for the first time since the
census began counting. That flow subsided in the 1980s, but by
the late 1990s rural areas—officially, nonmetropolitan ones—
were registering a net gain again. Most of the gain was a consequence of urban sprawl in counties adjacent to metropolitan
areas. The rural heartland hollowed out at a slower pace in the
1990s, with fewer counties losing 10 percent of their residents
than during the decade before, but the Great Plains show only a
shadow of their peak population in the 1930s, before small farmers drawn there by federal homesteading were driven away by
punishing droughts and subsidy programs began to favor agribusi-
ness conglomerates. Bison thrive again on the Great Plains, but
not people. Kansas now claims more frontier counties—which the
census defines as from two to six people per square mile—than it
did in 1890. Graham County, Kansas, lost 17 percent of its population in the 1990s and, like many other small towns in the wheat,
ranching, and oil belt from Texas to the Dakotas, dead people outnumber the living as young people leave for greener pastures. Tiny
Morland, Kansas, stripped even of the Union Pacific Railroad
tracks that ran by the town, shrunk from 234 to 164. In 2001,
Morland High School graduated its last class and closed its doors.
Rolling prairies and pastures surrounding Morland are dotted with
boarded-up farmhouses, and in town, too, the housing market has
collapsed. "How do you sell houses to people that aren't here?"
asked Fred Pratt, a real estate agent.

◆　　◆　　◆

Whatever the virtues of life in rural America and the agrarian
ethos that Thomas Jefferson touted, most Americans have lived
in one metropolitan area or another since 1950. By 2000, four

times as many people lived in a metropolitan area—consisting of a central city and its suburbs—than in a nonmetropolitan area. During the 1990s, the metropolitan population grew more—by 33.3 million people—than in any other decade. The Northeast has always had the highest proportion of people living in metropolitan areas. By 2000, more than 3 in 4 people in the Northeast, West, and South lived in metropolitan areas. In the Midwest, edged out by the South to become the least metropolitan region, nearly 3 in 4 lived in metropolitan areas.

As recently as 1970, no residents of Alaska, Vermont, and Wyoming lived in a metropolitan area. By 2000, in eight states (California, Connecticut, Florida, Maryland, Massachusetts, New Jersey, New York, and Rhode Island) at least 9 in 10 residents lived in a metropolitan area.

Within metropolises, growth was uneven. Between 1910 and 1960, residents of the central cities outnumbered their suburban neighbors. But beginning in 1910, when 21 percent of Americans lived in central cities and only 7 percent lived in the suburbs, the suburbs began growing faster. By 1960, the central cities (with 32 percent) and the suburbs (with 31 percent) each was home to about 1 in 3 Americans. By 2000, the suburbs themselves accounted for half the nation's population. By one estimate, suburban sprawl is gobbling up two acres of farmland every minute on the fringes of metropolitan areas where roads, malls, and supersized homes on 10-acre plots are uprooting orchards and crops. "We are consuming more land per person than at any time, in the most wasteful way," said Ralph Grossi, president of the American Farmland Trust.

Those metropolitan areas are monsters. In 1950, only fourteen metropolitan areas had a million or more people. Four decades later, 50 percent of Americans were living in metropolitan areas of a million people or more. And by 2000, the fifty metropolitan areas with a million or more people accounted for 57 percent of the nation's population. Whatever the virtues of small cities, much less rural America, a smaller proportion of Americans are living in metropolitan areas with fewer than 250,000 people and in areas ranging from 250,000 to 999,999 people than they were fifty years ago. At the same time, nearly 1 in 3 Americans now live in a metropolitan area with at least 5 million neighbors.

Metropolitan sprawl, meanwhile, has redefined the notion of downtowns. In some suburbs that have graduated into big cities in their own right, downtown is in a nearby bigger city—a trend that has already infiltrated the argot of demography. To suburbs, ex-urbs, fringe cities, and strip cities, now add the "boomburbs." The Fannie Mae Foundation identified fifty-three boomburbs, which they defined as suburban cities with populations of more than 100,000 that have grown by double digits every decade since they achieved status as cities. The four biggest were founded in 1950 and all are in the West (where they have been able to annex unincorporated neighbors): Mesa, Arizona, in metropolitan Phoenix, which mushroomed from 16,790 to 396,375 in 2000; Santa Ana in metropolitan Los Angeles, which grew from 45,533 to 337,977; Arlington, Texas, in metropolitan Dallas, which multiplied more than forty-fold, from 7,692 to 332,969; and Anaheim, also in metropolitan Los Angeles, which exploded from 14,556 to 328,014.

They began as a loose collection of strip malls and subdivisions, of bedroom communities and small towns. "They have now coalesced into suburban super cities that have all the functions of a traditional city but are built for a drive-through society," said Robert Lang, a coauthor of the Fannie Mae analysis.

Metropolitan sprawl also drove development in the nation's fastest-growing counties—five of which doubled their population in the 1990s. The most dramatic growth was in Douglas County, Colorado, south of Denver, which swelled by 191 percent, and in

Forsyth County, Georgia, north of Atlanta, which grew by 123 percent.

Again, immigration is what drove population gains in major metropolitan areas. Metropolitan areas with fewer than 5 million people recorded a net gain in people from elsewhere in the United States. The biggest metropolitan areas, those with 5 million or more people, suffered a net loss of 2.1 million people to domestic migration, but the influx of foreigners—more than 3.3 million—more than compensated.

But the premise that the suburbs are the place to escape the city and raise children is being challenged by the changing economics of the suburbs. Places like Lopatcong Township, New Jersey, have limited new multifamily housing to two bedrooms each—ostensibly, to place some reasonable limits on runaway development but, in fact, to stem the influx of couples with young children. In Lopatcong Township, elementary school enrollment has nearly doubled since 1995, severely straining property taxes. Many communities prefer to attract retirees or commercial property owners and the most desirable development, says James W. Hughes, dean of the Edward J. Bloustein School of Planning and Public Policy at Rutgers University, is "one that doesn't have smokestacks and doesn't generate children." From suburban Boston to Naperville, Illinois, near Chicago, communities are imposing "vasectomy zoning" that limits new house buyers to people fifty-five and older, which the federal Fair Housing Act permits in developments specifically reserved for senior citizens. But communities that restrict skateboarding because it damages sidewalks or impose 5-acre minimums on residential lots may be sacrificing something else. "You cannot deal with smart growth in an environment where, in the back of people's minds, they're saying, 'If we have another unit, will this cost us tens of thousands of dollars in school costs?'" Edmund O'Brien, the mayor of

Metuchen, New Jersey, told Laura Mansnerus of the *New York Times,* "You can't have a town without kids."

In the suburbs, the growth of non-family households—composed of, among others, younger single people (gay and straight) and elderly widows—has transformed the familiar post–World War II vision of the suburbs. In the hundred largest metropolitan areas, these non-family households now slightly outnumber married families with children. While some southern and western cities with a suburban feel are attracting more young families, young singles and immigrants are following the jobs to the suburbs.

Meanwhile, the proportion of Americans living in the nation's ten largest cities has declined, from a peak of 15.5 percent in 1930 to 8.5 percent by 2000. That pattern exemplified two factors: the influx of immigrants to those cities earlier in the twentieth century and the growth of the suburbs as the century progressed. Surging growth in the Sun Belt also drove membership in the top ten. In 1900, 8 of the 10 biggest cities were in the Northeast or Midwest (the West was represented only by San Francisco and the South by Baltimore). New York, Chicago, and Philadelphia, the only cities with at least a million people each in 1900, remained among the top ten throughout the century. By the end of the century, though, Pittsburgh, St. Louis, Boston, Baltimore, Cleveland, San Francisco, and Washington had fallen off the list and Los Angeles, Houston, Dallas, San Antonio, Phoenix, San Diego, and Detroit had nudged their way into the top ten.

While Detroit and Philadelphia lost population, the nation's largest cities generally grew nearly twice as fast in the 1990s as in the 1980s. Three-quarters of them gained population. Most of the cities that recorded gains shared a number of characteristics, including booming economies that also made them attractive to immigrants. Cities in the West and South—among them, Las Vegas, Nevada, and Charlotte, North Carolina—grew the fastest.

Gains in Population

Change in population between 1990 and 2000.

Fastest Growing Metropolitan Areas	POPULATION IN 2000	PERCENT CHANGE SINCE 1990
Las Vegas, Nev.	1,563,282	+83%
Naples, Fla.	251,377	+65
Yuma, Ariz.	160,026	+50
McAllen-Edinburg-Mission, Tex.	569,463	+49
Austin-San Marcos, Tex.	1,249,763	+48
Fayetteville-Springdale-Rogers, Ark.	311,121	+48
Boise City, Idaho	432,345	+46
Phoenix-Mesa, Ariz.	3,251,876	+45
Laredo, Tex.	193,117	+45
Provo-Orem, Utah	368,536	+40

Ten Largest Cities

New York, N.Y.	8,008,278	+9%
Los Angeles, Calif.	3,694,820	+6
Chicago, Ill.	2,896,016	+4
Houston, Tex.	1,953,631	+20
Philadelphia, Pa.	1,517,550	-4
Phoenix, Ariz.	1,321,045	+34
San Diego, Calif.	1,223,400	+10
Dallas, Tex.	1,188,580	+18
San Antonio, Tex.	1,144,646	+22
Detroit, Mich.	951,270	-8

So did college towns (including Madison, Wisconsin, and Columbus, Ohio) and also cities where residents tend to drive (like Phoenix, which was the fastest growing among the biggest cities, at 40 percent) rather than use mass transit. Augusta, Georgia, quadrupled in size to nearly 200,000 people in the 1990s. Henderson, Nevada, nearly tripled, to 175,000.

Five big cities that lost population in the 1980s—Atlanta, Chicago, Denver, Memphis, and Yonkers—reversed those declines in the 1990s, and most of those did so after concerted campaigns to stem the decline. Denver rebounded from an energy recession by revitalizing downtown with libraries, parks, and a baseball stadium so the city was poised to recover more quickly when the economy came back.

Even Midwestern cities like Detroit, Cleveland, and Milwaukee that suffered population losses shrunk more slowly than before— perhaps because more of the people remaining lacked the resources to leave. Detroit lost 7.5 percent of its residents overall, including 53 percent of its white population. Except for Columbus, the fifteen largest cities in Ohio, which was buffeted by declines in the steel, auto, and chemical industries, lost people. Cleveland, which lost about 1 in every 4 residents in the 1970s, shrunk by only about 5 percent in the 1990s and new stadiums and the Rock and Roll Hall of Fame signal a revival of downtown. "People don't feel that Cleveland's a national joke anymore," said Eric Hodderson, president of Neighborhood Progress, Inc., a development organization. Thomas Bier, director of Cleveland State University's housing policy research program, said, however: "Cleveland still has a very serious problem of a very large population of poorly educated, low-income people. They survive, but I'm not sure the world is getting better for them."

Still, Hartford, St. Louis, Gary, Baltimore, Flint, Buffalo, Norfolk, and Syracuse registered double-digit population losses in the 1990s.

For more than two hundred years, one city predominated for any number of political, economic, and cultural reasons but also in direct proportion to its population. It still does. New York was the nation's biggest city according to the first census in 1790, and though it was displaced as the nation's capital first by Philadelphia and then by Washington, the city remains preeminent and so does the greater New York metropolitan area. A study by the United States Conference of Mayors concluded that if the New York metropolitan area were a separate country in 2000, its $437 billion economy would have ranked 14th in the world, behind South Korea but ahead of Australia and Taiwan. (Los Angeles would have ranked 16th and Chicago 18th, ahead of Argentina and Russia.) With more than 21 million people, metropolitan New York now accounts for 7.5 percent of the nation's total population, or about 1 of every 13 Americans. Los Angeles ranks second, followed by Chicago, Washington, San Francisco, Philadelphia, Boston, Detroit, Dallas, and Houston. In 1950, when the Census Bureau first defined metropolitan areas, none of the ten most populous was in the South. Today, three (Washington, Dallas, and Houston) are.

In every decade, New York's population has been at least twice the number of people in the second-largest city in the nation, and in 2000 it surpassed 8 million for the first time. The 1990s was the first decade since the 1930s that New York led the nation's cities in the number of people it gained, and its 6 percent growth spurt outpaced the rate in its suburbs and in New York State overall. "This is about the changing prospects of New York and big cities," said Robert Yaro, executive director of the Regional Plan Association, a venerable planning advocacy group. Not only are many cities "really safer, cleaner, and more livable," he said, but "baby boomers can live wherever they want. The kids are out of the house. They're tired of mowing the lawn. So we have this big countertrend of folks staying in the city or moving back in. That was an aberration until this decade."

+   +   +

"What are we doing here alone?" asked Debbie Giacomo, a thirty-one-year-old elementary schoolteacher perched on a bar stool alongside three friends at Nola's in Palo Alto, California. "We're young. We're cute. We're available. So what are we doing here alone?" Single people all over America have asked that question at one time or another, but it rings especially true among women in Silicon Valley. It's one of the few places in the Western Hemisphere where men outnumber women. In Palo Alto, Jim Aronson, a thirty-year-old sales rep for a semiconductor company told Evelyn Nieves of the *New York Times,* "The girls know they have the pick of the litter."

In the United States today, there are 86 unmarried men over the age of fifteen for every 100 unmarried women. Alaska has the highest ratio, 114 men to 100 women, among the states, probably attributable to the predominantly male workforce in forestry, mining, and construction there. Most places with lopsided ratios of unmarried men to women include prisons, military installations, or all-male colleges. Among places with 100,000 or more people, Paradise, Nevada, has the highest ratio, 118, followed by Fort Lauderdale, Florida; Tempe, Arizona; and Sunnyvale, California.

When the twentieth century began, sex ratios diverged widely by region. In 1900, the ratio was 100:100 in the Northeast, meaning parity in the number of men and women, but 128.1:100 in the West, where the frontier still lured more single men than couples and families and drew immigrants to mining and railroad building. Women outnumbered men in only eleven states. The gap peaked in 1910 then narrowed for most of the century.

In 2000, the ratio of men to women was 93.5 in the Northeast

and 99.6 in the West to every 100 women. Women outnumbered
men in forty-three states and the gap among them was the lowest
ever, ranging from 92.5 in Rhode Island to 107 in Alaska. (In addition to Alaska, the states with more men than women are Colorado, Hawaii, Idaho, Nevada, Utah, and Wyoming.)

In America's cities, the sex ratio dipped to 90.7 for every 100
women in 1970 but rose to 94.6 in 2000, a forty-year peak. Seven
of the ten places with more than 100,000 people where men outnumber women are in the West and five are in California. The
highest sex ratio of men to women was in Salinas, California,
113.7, followed by Fort Lauderdale, Florida, 110. The lowest was
in Gary, Indiana, 84.6, followed by Birmingham, Alabama, 85.7.
Among the nation's ten largest cities, men outnumber women
only in Phoenix, San Diego, and Dallas. The lowest sex ratios are
in Philadelphia and Detroit. The differentials are among the greatest in small counties or their equivalents, where typical population
patterns can be skewed by the presence of institutions, like a
prison, military installation, or single-sex college. Crowley County,
Colorado, had the highest sex ratio of any county, 205.4:100. It's
home to a privately operated prison in Olney Springs for male inmates from Colorado and Wyoming. Clifton Forge, Virginia, home
to a women's community college, had the lowest, 78.9:100.

Because the Hispanic population is younger, the sex ratio is
higher: more than 104 men per 100 women, overall. Among non-
Hispanic whites, it's nearly 96.

The ratio is lowest among blacks. Black women outnumbered
black men during every decade of the twentieth century. The sex
ratio figure of black men to black women plunged to a low of 89.6
in 1980.

The absence of men makes the Bronx the most female county
in New York State. If group quarters aren't counted—jails,
mostly—it is the seventh most female county in the United
States, with more than five women for every four men. One rea-

son is widows in large apartment complexes. Another is patterns of immigration, with Bangladeshis, among whom males predominate, tending to settle in Queens and Dominicans and West Indians, whose ranks are more balanced by gender, moving to the Bronx. Still another reason is jail and prison. About three times as many of the inmates in city jails list the Bronx as their residence than list Queens—leaving many poor black women in housing projects to fend for themselves. "Many of these places are just full of women," said Elijah Anderson, a University of Pennsylvania sociologist, because men fear relationships in which they may fail as providers. "They do go off to the military. They do go off to prison. They do go off to be free to consort with other women." Among blacks living in the Bronx, 50 percent more households are headed by women than by married couples. The Bronx is also one of only five counties in the entire country where more than 30 percent of the households are headed by single mothers. (Among the other four, one is Holmes County, Mississippi, and the rest are in Indian reservations in South Dakota.) Which is why Brunilda Bonilla hangs a condom on her Christmas tree in her small apartment in the Hunts Point section of the Bronx. As she explained to the *New York Times*'s Alan Feuer, her eldest daughter, who is twenty-four, already has a three-year-old; her eighteen-year-old often sleeps at home with her boyfriend. "You need it, you take it," Mrs. Bonilla says.

✦   ✦   ✦

America is getting more and more crowded, but there's still plenty of room, at least compared to the rest of the world. And compared to ten years ago, there's even more land in which to grow. In 1990, one reason for the increase in density was that the nation's landmass had shrunk. Collectively, the expanse of land and water was the largest ever. But officially, the land mass of 3,536,342 square miles was the smallest since before the purchase of Alaska. The shrinkage was attributed, in part, to the fact that the census had begun measuring bodies of water, including reservoirs, more precisely and subtracting their mass from land area. Another reason was more ominous: coastal erosion. Bayous coursing through parishes that are partly below sea level fulfilled Randy Newman's warning—"They're tryin' to wash us away"—from his mournful ballad "Louisiana." In 1970, Louisiana's land area measured 49,000 square miles. By 1990, the state had contracted to 44,500. In 2000, the census counted 43,561 square miles.

In 2000, the nation's land area had grown again, this time to 3,537,438 square miles. But the overall population density also had increased—to 79.6 people per square mile, compared to 70.3 in 1990; 64 in 1980; 37.2 in 1940; 17.8 in 1890; and only 4.5 recorded in the first census in 1790, when the nation's boundaries were much narrower.

That average masks wide disparities, though. Regionally, the Northeast, now with about one-fifth of the nation's people living in about one-twentieth of the nation's land area, remains the most dense. Despite enormous growth elsewhere, none of the three other regions has reached the density recorded in the Northeast more than one hundred years ago. From the beginning to the end of the twentieth century, the average number of people per square mile swelled in the Northeast from 130 to 330, in the Midwest from 35 to 86, in the South from 28 to 115, and in the West from 3 to 36.

Density by state varies widely, too, since it is based not only on population but on landmass. In 1900, only three states (New Jersey, Rhode Island, and Massachusetts) had more than 200 people per square mile. By 2000, twelve did (including Connecticut, Maryland, New York, Delaware, Florida, Ohio, Pennsylvania, Illinois, and California). When the century began fourteen states had fewer than 10 people per square mile. Today, only five do (South Dakota, North Dakota, Montana, Wyoming, and Alaska).

In 1960, the new state of Alaska displaced Nevada as the least densely populated state. With about one person per square mile, it retains the title. And most of the fastest-growing states still have plenty of room. Only about 45 people live in every per square mile of Arizona and only 6 per square mile in Montana. In 1970, New Jersey overtook Rhode Island as the most densely populated state. With more than 1,134 people per square mile, New Jersey remains the most congested.

No city comes even close to New York in people per square mile—26,402—and even that figure is dwarfed by the density of 67,000 in Manhattan, where 1.5 million people are crammed into 23 square miles. (At the other extreme among counties, if you prefer the wide open spaces the density is one-tenth of a person, or one person in every 10 square miles, in Loving County, Texas, where only 67 people were counted living in 673 square miles.) Among the biggest cities, San Francisco was second with 16,634 people per square mile, followed by, among others, Chicago (12,750), Boston (12,165), Philadelphia (11,233), Miami (8,098), and Los Angeles (7,876). Older cities, especially in the Northeast, tend to be more dense, in part because their political boundaries are more rigid. They are less able to grow geographically by annexing adjacent jurisdictions.

The exodus to the suburbs that depleted central cities also dramatically reduced their density. Between 1950 and 2000, density of the nation's central cities declined from 7,517 people per square mile to 2,716 in 2000. Suburban density increased dramatically from 1950 to 1970 and more slowly since then.

As one-fifth of Americans move every year, the shifts that defined the 1990s appear likely to endure—producing more suburban sprawl, bigger cities, the inevitable shift of the nation's center of population west and south, and growth driven by immigration even in unlikely places.

6

Where We Dream

If owning one's own home typifies the American Dream, more and more Americans had their dream come true in the 1990s. For the first time, 2 in 3 householders owned, rather than rented, their own house, apartment, mobile home, or other dwelling.

In 1900, fewer than half the households in the United States lived in their own homes. About 8.2 million households occupied rented houses and apartments and about 7.2 million owned their own homes. The home ownership rate declined until 1920, and fell further during the Depression, but after World War II, the home ownership rate rebounded and more, to 55 percent in 1950—the first time in the twentieth century that most people owned their own homes—and to 61.9 percent by 1960. It inched up in 1970 and 1980, dipped slightly in 1990 to 64.2 percent, and ended the century at 66.2 percent, the highest rate ever recorded. The biggest numerical and percentage increase occurred in the 1970s, but in the 1990s, the number of occupied rented units rose 8.3 percent to 35.7 million, while the economic boom and lower mortgage rates sent the number of owner-occupied units soaring by 18.3 percent to 69.8 million.

Only four states—Idaho, Nevada, North Dakota, and South Dakota—had lower rates of home ownership in 2000 than they did in 1900.

Of the nearly 116 million housing units in the United States in 2000—up from 102 million in 1990 and 37.3 million in 1940, when the first census of housing was conducted—3.8 million were for sale or for rent.

Another 3.6 million were temporarily vacant, largely reserved for seasonal, vacation, or recreational use. The three states with the highest percentage of those homes are all in New England: Maine, where they total 15.6 percent of all the housing; Vermont, with 14.6 percent; and New Hampshire, with 10.3 percent. In Florida, 6.6 percent of the housing was identified as vacation homes or apartments, but that constituted the highest number of any state—483,000—followed by California with 237,000, New York with 235,000, and Michigan with 234,000.

Home ownership rates ranged from 61.5 percent in the West to 70.2 percent in the Midwest, and from 53 percent in New York (which only passed the 50 percent mark for the first time in 1990) to 75.2 percent in West Virginia. Among counties, Alcona County, Michigan, claimed the highest rate of home ownership, 75.9 percent, closely followed by Elbert County, Colorado, with 89.6 percent. Among metropolitan areas, 5 of the 10 with the highest rates of home ownership were in Florida, led by Punta Gorda, with 83.7 percent. The top ten also included Jackson and Saginaw-Bay City-Midland in Michigan, Barnstable-Yarmouth in Massachusetts, Houma in Louisiana, and Sharon, Pennsylvania.

Not surprisingly, rates of home ownership are higher in the suburbs than in central cities. Both have risen steadily, although since 1970 home ownership rates in nonmetropolitan areas surpassed those in the suburbs. Between 1960 and 2000, the rates have climbed from 70 to 73 percent in the suburbs and from 47 to 51 percent in central cities, the first time more people in cities owned than rented their houses and apartments.

Renters outnumbered owners in only five metropolitan areas: Jersey City, New Jersey (though across the Hudson River from New York, a metropolitan statistical area in its own right); New York City; Los Angeles-Long Beach and San Francisco in California; and Bryan-College Station, Texas, the home of Texas A&M University. They outnumbered home owners in only 36 of the nation's 3,141 counties, including 3 in New York City (the Bronx ranks lowest, with 19.6 percent home ownership). Among the others with a high percentage of renters are Manhattan with only 20.1 percent home ownership, and Chattahoochee County, Georgia, with 27 percent. On the island of Molokai in Hawaii, all 115 occupied units in Kalawao County—containing a former leper colony—were rented rather than owned. Among the nation's ten largest cities, renters outnumber owners in the top four (New York, with 69.8 percent renters; Los Angeles, with 61.4 percent; Chicago, with 56.2 percent; and Houston, with 54.2 percent) followed by San Diego (with 50.5 percent) and Dallas (with 56.8 percent).

The rate of home ownership peaks among people age 65 to 74, with 81.3 percent, and is lowest among householders under age 25, although low interest rates in the late 1990s drove the proportion to over 20 percent. The highest percentage of home ownership, 84.8 percent, was recorded among married couples without children under age 18, which includes empty-nesters. By 2000, 63 percent of householders under 65 owned their own homes and 78.1 of those householders sixty-five and older did. For both age groups, those were the highest home ownership rates ever, although the differential between the groups was also the highest since 1960.

Ownership rates also differed by race and ethnicity. The highest was among non-Hispanic whites: 72 percent. Among black and Hispanic householders, the rate was 46 percent, which means that more of them rent rather than own their homes. Among Hispanics, though, home ownership rates varied widely, from 58 percent for Cubans to 48 percent for Mexicans and 35 percent for Puerto Ricans (each up, respectively, from 51 percent, 47 percent, and 26 percent in 1990).

Rates also differed by whether the householder was living alone or with others, a reflection of several factors, including income. Since 1950, householders living with other people have been more likely to own their own homes. By 2000, for the first time, people living alone who owned their own homes outnumbered people living alone who rented.

Growth in the housing inventory largely mirrored growth in the population. Nationwide, it grew by 13.3 percent. In Nevada, nearly 300,000 homes and apartments were built in the 1990s, an increase of 59.5 percent. No state gained more homes than Florida, where 1.2 million units were built in the 1990s, an increase of 19.7 percent. In California, the percentage increase was much smaller, 9.2 percent, but that still amounted to one million homes and apartments.

◆   ◆   ◆

"Americans put home ownership on a pedestal," said Howard Decker, chief curator of the National Building Museum in Washington, D.C. The twentieth century provided the technological and economic means to elevate that pedestal several notches. "When you understand how central the single-family home is to the American Dream and American mythology," Decker added, "you can understand why a bigger version of the home is better."

About 60 percent of the nation's housing units are single-family homes. They predominate in the Midwest, accounting for more than 3 in 4 homes in Iowa, Kansas, Nebraska, and Michigan. Single-family homes accounted for less than half the housing units in only one state—New York, where, like Hawaii, nearly

1 in 3 homes were in buildings with five or more apartments. The largest proportion of older housing is in Massachusetts, where more than a third of all the units were built before 1940. Nevada led the nation in new housing; more than 25 percent of its homes were built since 1995.

Between 1970 and 2000 alone, the size of new homes expanded by more than 50 percent, from an average of 1,500 square feet to 2,200 square feet. More than half have two or more floors, compared to fewer than one-fifth in 1970. Fully one-third have four or more bedrooms, compared to one-fourth thirty years earlier, even though families are smaller. The proportion with at least two and a half bathrooms more than tripled and went from 15 percent to 54 percent. Just since 1990, the average house expanded from 5.2 rooms to 5.8 rooms. More than 1 in 4 had seven or more rooms.

Still, overcrowding persists and increased in the 1990s. The census defines homes and apartments as crowded if they are occupied by more than one person per room and severely crowded if they are occupied by more than 1.5 persons per room. Among owners, 3.1 percent of all occupied homes and apartments were crowded and 1.2 percent were severely crowded. Among renters, the proportions were considerably higher: 11 percent crowded and 5.8 percent severely crowded. Overcrowding also varied significantly by race and ethnicity. Among householders nationwide, 1.9 percent of non-Hispanic white households and 8.5 percent of black households had more than one person per room, but 29.3 percent of Hispanic households did and 17 percent were severely overcrowded. Housing in which a foreign-born person headed the household were also disproportionately crowded. Households in California and Hawaii were the most crowded, and these were the only states where overcrowded units accounted for more than 10 percent of all housing. In California, 15.2 percent of the units were rated as crowded, with 9.1 percent severely overcrowded. Nine of the ten cities with the highest proportion of overcrowded housing were in California (with Santa Ana, at 50.3 percent, the highest of any city with more than 100,000 people).

Outhouses, those telephone-booth-shaped shacks with a crescent moon carved in the door, have been the butt of American humor for as long as anyone can remember. Finally, they are fast being relegated to an artifact of the past. In 1940, only half the homes in the United States had hot and cold running water, a flush toilet, and a bathtub or shower. By 1960, 17 percent lacked plumbing. By 1990, 3 million people in 1.1 million houses, or 1.2 percent of the total, still lacked indoor plumbing. In 2000, for the first time, the number of homes without indoor plumbing dropped below 1 million (to 671,000) and below 1 percent of the total (to 0.64 percent), in part the result of concerted efforts by the federal government and by state and county health programs. "Although the numbers look infinitesimal, at the county level you see a dramatic change," said Robert E. Lang, director of Virginia Tech's Metropolitan Institute. In 1990, 854 of the 2,362 homes in Hamilton County in New York's Adirondacks lacked indoor plumbing. By 2000, only 20 still did. In Bath County, in the Allegheny Mountains of Virginia, the number of houses with little or no indoor plumbing shrank from 349 to 31. In West Warm Springs, a subdivision not far from Warm Springs, the terrain was too rocky for septic tanks and the county resisted laying water lines until the late 1980s, when it took the tentative step of installing small hydrants in residents' front yards. Without sewers or septic tanks, though, homeowners couldn't hook up the lines to indoor faucets or drains. By late 1996, Peggy Stewart, whose family had hauled a galvanized tub into the kitchen for the ritual Saturday night bath for generations, was belatedly enjoying the benefits of domestic technology. "I told all my neighbors, 'If you call I won't answer because I'm going to be in the bathtub all day,'" she told Peter Kilborn of the *New York Times*.

As recently as 1960, more than 1 in 5 households did not even have access to a telephone, either inside or outside the house. By 2000, only 1 in 50 said they did not have a phone in their home.

◆   ◆   ◆

Between 1990 and 2000, the median value of a single-family American home rose 18 percent, to $119,600. Adjusting for inflation, the median value was $44,600 in 1950 and has increased every decade since then (by a high of 43 percent in the 1970s and a low of 8.2 percent in the 1980s).

But since 1980, values have diverged dramatically—dividing the nation into real estate rich home owners in California and in the Boston-New York-Washington corridor and people elsewhere in the country where prices for property have barely budged in two decades. Apart from the implications for where people live and whether they move, the divergence has created enormous disparities in wealth. Houses and apartments that doubled or tripled in value not only created nest eggs for retirement but provided the equity against which home owners borrowed billions of dollars to cushion the impact of economic ups and downs. In the most expensive cities, on average, homes cost six times more than in the least expensive—compared to three times as much two decades earlier. In Boston, the median home price has risen 167 percent since 1980; in Decatur, Illinois, it rose 9 percent.

In 2000, the most expensive homes were in the West ($171,000) and the least expensive in the South ($96,300). But in the Northeast, the median value dropped by 12 percent in the 1990s to $139,400, driven by a 27 percent drop in Connecticut, mostly in the state's cities, following a boom in the late 1980s.

Hawaii recorded the highest median value in 2000, $272,700, as it did in 1990. California ranked second, at $211,500, followed by Massachusetts at $185,700, New Jersey at $170,800, Washington at $168,300, Connecticut at $166,900, Colorado at $166,600, and Oregon at $152,100 (where the median value rose the most, to 78 percent). Oklahoma was lowest, at $70,700.

In a corridor of counties from Washington, D.C., north to the Boston suburbs and along the California coast, the median value of a single-family home exceeded $150,000. In Manhattan, it topped $1 million; in Nantucket, Massachusetts, $577,500; and in Marin County, California, $514,600. Among places of 100,000 or more people, Sunnyvale, California, ranked highest in median home value, at $495,200, followed by Cambridge, Massachusetts, at $398,500. Seven of the ten highest-priced places were around San Francisco Bay and two were in New England. Cambridge, Massachusetts, boasts the highest percentage of million-dollar single-family homes, nearly 12 percent of all owner-occupied single-family dwellings, followed by California's San Francisco, Pasadena, and Los Angeles (with 15,501 homes valued over $1 million); Fort Lauderdale, Florida; Berkeley, California; Stamford, Connecticut; Honolulu, Hawaii; Atlanta, Georgia; and Fremont, California.

In contrast, in nearly one-half of the counties, mostly in the Great Plains from Texas to North Dakota, median home values were less than $75,000. In King County, Texas, the median value was $13,800. Among localities with 100,000 or more people, the lowest median value of a single-family home was recorded in Flint, Michigan, $49,700.

Among householders who identified themselves as Asian, the median home value was $199,300, a factor, in part, of the disproportionate number of Asians who live in Hawaii and California, states with the highest median home values. Blacks lived in homes with the lowest median value, $80,600. Homes owned by Hispanics were valued higher, at $105,600.

◆　　◆　　◆

Mobile homes have been the fastest-growing form of housing and they have come a long way since the mid-1990s, when James Carville, the political strategist, tried to dismiss Paula Corbin Jones's sexual harassment charges against President Bill Clinton by saying: "Drag a hundred dollar bill through a trailer park and there's no telling what you'll find." Mobile homes have gone more upscale.

Since 1980, the number of single-family homes in America increased by 30 percent, to 70 million. During the same period the number of mobile homes doubled to 9 million, or nearly 1 in 10 of all residences. For every five detached single-family homes that were built, one mobile home was manufactured. Today, while 60 percent of housing units are detached, single-family residences, there are more mobile homes than apartment houses with fifty or more units. Most of these are not your father's mobile home. And don't dare call them "trailers," which is what they were called in 1950, when the census counted 315,000. They are "manufactured housing," and though many occupants would prefer to live in one of those single-family houses on a tree-lined street in suburbia, this is what they can afford.

In South Carolina and New Mexico, 1 in 5 families live in a mobile home. In Idaho and Georgia, nearly 1 in 8 do. In Brantley County, Georgia, the third-highest concentration of mobile homes in the country (after adjacent Long County and Eureka County, Nevada, where nearly 70 percent of the units are mobile homes), 58 percent of the housing units are mobile homes. In many places in the South and Southwest, in particular, they define the outer ring of urban sprawl—a largely unsowed frontier of individual lots and of subdivisions that give the appearance of geometric order, until a storm comes along.

"Typically it was thought of as a blue-collar factory worker buying manufactured homes," Chris D. Bosky, director of administration and information services for the Manufactured Housing Institute, a national trade association, told Kevin Sack of the *New*

York Times. "Now it's professional couples with families. People can't afford $150,000 homes anymore, and consumers would rather spend their money on other things."

At Hunter Ridge, a ten-year-old "manufactured home community" south of Atlanta, residents are limited to one pet per lot, cars and trucks can't be repaired within the community, and lawns must be trimmed to less than three inches high. "I would never live in a trailer park," said John W. Guiton, a forty-five-year-old trucker who lived in a house until losing it in a divorce and now prefers his $22,000 double-wide home on a lot that he rents for $215 a month. "This is a mobile home community," he said.

A new mobile home costs an average of nearly $50,000 (the median value of mobile homes, according to their owners, was $31,200). The lot, which more and more owners are choosing to buy, is extra. (According to industry estimates, about 2 in 3 mobile home owners lived in trailer parks or mobile home communities a decade ago; today, about 2 in 3 have planted their mobile homes on their own private lots.) A down payment of only several thousand dollars will buy a double-wide mobile home with fireplace, two bedrooms, two bathrooms, and a game room, and though it's the best that a lot of lower income families can afford, it's not necessarily a great investment. Mortgage rates are higher than on conventional homes and mobile homes tend to lose value rather than appreciate. Even with all the niceties, with all the flexibility and mobility—when people drive off to a new site they give a whole new dimension to the phrase, there goes the neighborhood—the homes still carry a stigma. "This is not a house," said David Brown, a welder who lived with his wife in a 24- by 60-foot mobile home in rural Georgia. "It's a cheap way of putting a roof over your head."

Nationwide, 8.6 million people, or about 7.5 percent of the population, live in mobile homes or trailers (although the census may have underestimated because it doesn't specifically ask about "manufactured homes," the most expensive category). Mobile homes accounted for 11.6 percent of all housing in the South and 7.1 percent in the West. South Carolina claims the highest proportion, 18.5 percent, followed by North Carolina with 18.1 percent, New Mexico with 18 percent, and West Virginia with 17.3 percent.

In 2000, Florida led the nation in the number of mobile homes and trailers. The census counted 842,701 of them there, nearly 1 in 10 of the total in the United States. In several counties, including Gilchrest, Glades, and Dixie, more than half the population lives in mobile homes. But while Florida's inventory of mobile homes grew by more than 86,000 in the 1990s, the proportion of Floridians living in them, compared to conventional housing, dipped from 12.5 percent to 11.6 percent.

◆   ◆   ◆

Other Americans live in homes not of their own choosing: prison populations quadrupled in the 1980s and 1990s. Draconian sentencing laws in the 1990s, coupled with an economic boom that enabled states to build more prisons, drove the inmate population to record levels at the beginning of the twenty-first century.

By the end of 2002, a record 2,166,260 Americans, including 97,491 women, were counted in local jails, state and federal prisons, and juvenile detention centers (1.4 million in state and federal prisons, including 163,528 in federal prisons; 665,475 in local and county jails; and 110,284 in juvenile centers). Of those, more than 93,000 prisoners were being housed in privately operated correctional facilities. That meant 1 in every 110 men and 1 in every 1,656 women were sentenced prisoners in state or federal institutions. At the end of 2002, there were 701 prisoners per 100,000 U.S. residents (compared to 601 in 1995), the first time the rate had surpassed 700. One in every 143 U.S. residents was being housed in a state or federal prison or local jail.

An analysis by the U.S. Bureau of Justice Statistics confirmed earlier large racial disparities in the prison population, and found that 10.4 percent of black men in their late twenties were imprisoned, compared to 2.4 percent of Hispanic men in that age group and 1.2 percent of non-Hispanic white men.

California had the most inmates, 162,317, followed closely by Texas with 162,003. Louisiana had the highest incarceration rate—794 inmates per 100,000 residents—compared to Maine and Minnesota, which tied for the lowest rate, 141 inmates per 100,000 people.

Economically depressed communities coveted jails and prisons because of the jobs they generate, but by the end of the decade large inmate populations were straining already overburdened state budgets and some states were revisiting the mandatory sentencing provisions in the drug, violent crime, and gun laws that had sent the number of inmates soaring in the 1980s and 1990s.

✦   ✦   ✦

Most people live in some form of what the Census Bureau defines as conventional housing. Some don't. Who they are, how many of them there are, and even what to call them have challenged the ingenuity of government demographers since homelessness emerged as a national issue in the 1980s.

In 1990, the Census Bureau conducted a special survey of emergency shelters and of some previously identified street corners and other outdoor sites where homeless people typically congregate. The Census Bureau found more than 168,309 people in emergency shelters, 10,329 in shelters for runaways, and 11,768 in shelters for abused women. Another 49,734 were counted "visible in street locations." Because the 1990 homeless count was subject to misinterpretation—it was delivered replete with caveats—the 2000 census was more circumspect in its effort to calculate the number of people without conventional housing. The latest count of people in emergency and transitional shelters included runaways and neglected children and adults in hotels, motels, and other living quarters where people identified as home-less were staying overnight.

In 2000, the census included this disclaimer: "The tabulated population in emergency and transitional shelters is not repre-sentative of, and should not be construed to be, the total popula-tion without conventional housing, nor is it representative of the entire population that could be defined as living in emergency and transitional shelters." Nonetheless, the census recorded 170,706 people in emergency and transitional shelters (com-pared to the official count of 178,638 in 1990). New York State topped the list, with 31,856, followed by California, with 27,701. About 3 in 4 of the people in shelters were adults, and a little more than 6 in 10 of those adults were men. Non-Hispanic whites constituted about 1 in 3 of those surveyed, blacks repre-sented about 4 in 10, and Hispanics about 2 in 10.

✦   ✦   ✦

Home ownership rates keep going up, setting new records—nearly 70 percent in 2003. But the latest rise in the home owner-ship rate has been driven, in part, by another trend: more and more Americans are at the age when they are more likely to own their own home. The ownership rate rose to nearly 43 percent among people under age 35, but the rate was twice as high among people over age 55 (that, in turn, contributed to another trend: the disproportionately higher home ownership rates among non-Hispanic whites). Moreover, as interest rates were plunging, only half of families who owned their own home in 1995 and only 1 in 20 families who rented could afford a median-priced, single-family house in their own communities. In 2003, a study by the National Low Income Housing Coalition, an advocacy group, found that with housing costs outpacing wages, a low-income worker cannot reasonably afford a modest one- or two-bedroom apartment to rent, much less to buy.

7

Our Changing Complexion

In Queens, the borough of New York City that may be the most diverse county in the country, Northern Boulevard in Flushing looks like a street in Seoul. Most of the businesses are adorned with signs in Korean that give no hint of what goes on inside, which makes English-speakers feel like foreigners in their own neighborhood. One large sign, on a supermarket, included only these words in English: "Now" and "24 Hours." "You tell me what that sign is for; I can't figure it out," Ken Westerfield, who lives in nearby Whitestone, said outside the store. "A lot of white people who've grown up here resent Koreans setting up businesses that sell only to other Koreans, buy from other Koreans, and do business only with other Koreans. They ruin the economy for regular Americans." A 1909 New York State law, dating from an era when many signs were in Italian or German or Yiddish, requires some English on billboards. But it's generally considered unenforceable. Some city council members are mulling over new legislation.

Just across Flushing Meadow Park, an apartment building in the Corona section embodies what Joseph Salvo, the director of the City Planning Department's population division, calls "probably the greatest social experiment in history." The 110 apartments of the brown-brick Calloway Chateau building are home to Uzbeks, Afghans, Indians, Pakistanis, Bangladeshis, Koreans, Filipinos, Ukrainians, Russians, Argentines, Colombians, Dominicans, Puerto Ricans, Peruvians, African-Americans, and Guyanese. The common denominator is food. On the Muslim holy day Eid al-Adha, Pakistanis distribute goat liver and testicles to the Indians. On the holiday of Diwali, Hindus present boiled milk sweets to the Muslims. And everyone gives samples of their ethnic favorites to the Puerto Rican building superintendent, who at the end of the day relaxes by studying the tropical fish in his aquarium. "It's like our building," he told Suketu Mehta of the *New York Times,* referring to the coexisting starfish, crayfish, shrink, anemone, and other varieties in the tank. "They don't eat each other."

◆   ◆   ◆

Managing the nation's unprecedented diversity may be the greatest challenge facing America as it begins the twenty-first century.

The trends toward greater diversity are unmistakable: In the United States, nonwhites account for only 16 percent of the population over age 65, but fully 39 percent of those younger than 25. In 1970, only 7 percent of the nation's population under age 25 was foreign-born or first generation. By 2000, that proportion had swelled to 21 percent. Immigration has had such a profound impact on America's families that 1 in 5 children today has at least one foreign-born parent (although among the 11.5 million children with at least one foreign-born parent, 8 in 10 were born in the United States).

No single group changed the face of America more in the 1990s than immigrants. And during no other decade in the nation's history have foreigners so profoundly altered the country's complexion in so many ways. Its digestion, too. Frito-Lay began promoting a spicier line of snacks under the slogan *"A Todo*

America's Face

Percentage of the population. Hispanics, who make up
12.5 percent of the population, may be of any race.

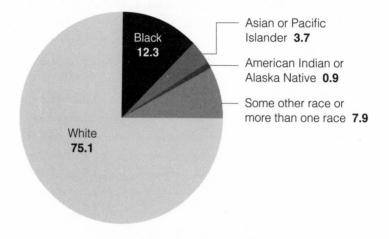

Black **12.3**

Asian or Pacific Islander **3.7**

American Indian or Alaska Native **0.9**

Some other race or more than one race **7.9**

White **75.1**

Sabor," or "full-flavored." Pork heroes called *carnitas* appeared on
the Subway sandwich chain menu. English is still the nation's
primary language, and will remain so, but those who studied
French in high school must be having some second thoughts as
they flip by Spanish language television stations, peruse the
"international" section of supermarkets (the pictures help), mis-
takenly reach for the *en Espanol* line of Hallmark cards, or listen
to George W. Bush become the first president to deliver a White
House speech in Spanish. Billboards for the Spanish-language
television network Univision proclaim it to be "as American as
flan." When New York launched its new 311 telephone information line in 2003, the city government boasted that the service
would be available in more than 170 languages. In Richmond,
California, forty-six-year-old Michael Cox, a University of California, Berkeley, graduate who runs his own travel agency in San
Jose, played Santa Claus at the Hilltop Mall in Tagalog, Punjabi,

Hindi, Arabic, French, Spanish, Portuguese, and Mandarin as well as English. And, in perhaps the greatest validation of grow-ing political clout, alternate-side parking rules are suspended in New York City not only on legal holidays, Christian and Jewish holidays, and the Chinese New Year, but on six Muslim holy days as well. Hindus are lobbying the city council to suspend the street-cleaning rules for at least one day of Diwali, the five-day celebration honoring the goddess of wealth.

Between 1990 and 2000 alone, America's foreign-born popula-tion increased by 57 percent to more than 31 million, a record high, making America now the least "American" it has ever been by the conventional definition—or the most American, if Latin America counts as American, too. Immigrants and their children account for more than 1 in 5 residents of the United States (a modern high, though lower than the 1 in 3 during the first two decades of the twentieth century). Because foreign-born women now account for one-fifth of all births in the United States—up from just 5 per-cent three decades ago—the proportion of foreign-born and first-generation Americans is projected to grow even higher.

"The twenty-first century will be the century in which we re-define ourselves as the first country in world history which is lit-erally made up of every part of the world," said Kenneth Prewitt, the former census director.

✦   ✦   ✦

The first human migrants to the New World came across Beringia, the land bridge that stretched across what is now the Bering Strait between Siberia and Alaska, about 18,000 years ago. Since then, they've never stopped coming.

The fusion of immigrants into an idealized American was al-ways integral to American mythology, as Philip Martin and Eliza-beth Midgley deconstructed the concept for the Population Reference Bureau. Most of the metaphors suggested metallurgy.

Ralph Waldo Emerson spoke of a "smelting pot." Henry James preferred a "cauldron." And the hero of Israel Zangwill's 1908 play, *The Melting Pot,* which immortalized the term, exhorted immigrants: "Germans and Frenchmen, Irishmen and Englishmen, Jews and Russians—into the Crucible with you all! God is making the American!" Zangwill, a Jewish playwright living in London and married to a non-Jew, recast the melting pot as an American icon. His play was produced in New York City at the height of a massive surge of immigration; in 1909 a record 1.7 million legal immigrants would enter the nation.

That one-year record still stands. If the United States was the world's first truly multicultural society, the first universal nation, only the degree of diversity today is new, not its existence or its consequences. After all, in the mid-seventeenth century, when New York was still called New Amsterdam, its 500 residents spoke eighteen languages.

Drawing on historical records and earlier research, Campbell Gibson, a Census Bureau demographer, estimated that when Columbus arrived in the Americas in 1492, about 96 percent of the people living in what is now the United States were Indian and the rest were of Polynesian origin. (Another estimate suggests that there were about 3.5 million Indians then, who belonged to at least seventeen language groups.) Well before the English landed in Jamestown in 1607, the Spanish had established a foothold in what is now New Mexico to become America's first minority. By the middle of the eighteenth century, Benjamin Franklin figured "there are suppos'd to be now upwards of One Million English Souls in North-America (tho; 'tis thought scarce 80,000 have been brought over Sea). This Million doubling, suppose but once in 25 Years, will in another Century be more than the People of England, and the greatest Number of Englishmen will be on this Side of the Water."

By 1790, when the first federal census was conducted, the

population of what is now the United States is estimated to have been about 64 percent white—or less white than it is today—16 percent Indian, 11 percent black, and 4 percent Polynesian. In the original 13 states, Indians, decimated by disease and colonization, were reduced to only about 1.2 percent of the population by 1790. By other accounting, black slaves, beginning with the first recorded arrival of an African in 1619 in Jamestown, Virginia, by 1790 constituted 19 percent of the population. Judging by their surnames, well over half the whites were of English origin (about another 10 percent were from Germany and the Netherlands), and for nearly a century the vast majority of whites in America could trace their roots to northwestern Europe.

That would change dramatically over the century that followed, as a result both of immigration and of territorial expansion (the war with Mexico in 1846–48 added about 80,000 Latinos or Hispanics [the census uses the terms interchangeably] in the Southwest and, as a result of the war with Spain in 1898, the United States acquired Puerto Rico). As recently as 1900, though, 9 in 10 residents of the United States were non-Hispanic whites, mostly of western European ancestry. By the end of the twentieth century, however, more Americans could trace their roots to the more than 48 million people who had emigrated to the United States since 1790 than to the English, Dutch, Spanish, Indian, and Polynesian people who lived within the nation's boundaries before then. (Fully 1 in 4 Americans believe they are descended from the Pilgrims, according to the General Society of Mayflower Descendants, which says that, in fact, eight U.S. presidents were: John Adams, John Quincy Adams, Zachary Taylor, Ulysses S. Grant, James A. Garfield, Franklin D. Roosevelt, and both Presidents Bush.)

The enduring debate over what defines an American—were the original European settlers, as they maintained, the first Americans or merely immigrants themselves?—entered a new dimension in 1850 when the census began distinguishing between residents who were born in the United States and those born abroad. What the census confirmed was already apparent to urban Protestants and nativists who greeted the arrival of each shipload of Roman Catholics from Ireland and newcomers from northern Europe with growing alarm. That debate resonates today. As Kenneth Prewitt, the former census director, recalled: "The effort by nativists to close down immigration was opposed by economic interests: factory owners needed workers, as did the railroads pushing across the country. The frontier was there to be settled, and shipping interests benefited from the huge cross-Atlantic traffic. Economic interests prevailed. Immigration continued, though naturalization was not made easy."

Before 1875, immigration was virtually unrestricted, except for convicts and prostitutes, but ethnic rivalries—like the violent turf wars between native Protestants and transplanted Irishmen depicted in the film *Gangs of New York*—began finding their way into congressional restrictions on would-be Americans. Each new group tried to slam the Golden Door behind it. Cheap Chinese labor helped build America's railroads, but Chinese women were largely excluded—not out of compassion for their working and living conditions, but to prevent couples from procreating and producing American-born Chinese who would be automatically eligible for citizenship. Concerns over potential competition for jobs inspired the Chinese Exclusion Act of 1882, which led to six successive decades of decline in the nation's Chinese population— until World War II, when the Chinese were redeemed as America's allies against Japan.

The so-called New Immigration at the end of the nineteenth century distinguished between the western and northern Europeans who had predominated during America's first century and the masses from eastern and southern Europe who were deluging the nation's cities and challenging their political and social elites.

In 1921, Congress enacted the National Origins Quota Act, which was intended to freeze America's racial and ethnic profile at its 1910 contours (but which was amended three years later to impose the even more restrictive 1890 proportions as the ideal instead). Quotas by national origin were largely repealed by 1965. In 1986, illegal immigrants who had lived in the United States continuously since 1982 were granted eligibility for citizenship. In 2004, the Bush administration proposed a guest worker program that would grant legal status to illegal immigrants in the form of three-year, renewable work permits.

The latest surge in immigration echoed the boom at the beginning of the twentieth century, and not only in its dimensions. Both times the nation's economy was shifting, then from agriculture to industrial mass production and now from service industries to information. Like the sudden influx of eastern Europeans and Russian Jews in the 1890s and early 1900s, the latest wave of foreigners is more foreign, or at least less familiar, than the immigrants who arrived during the preceding decades. The preponderance of brown faces, coupled with the influx of Asians, has revived America's historic ambivalence about immigration: Does unrestricted population growth from abroad place an unsustainable burden on the environment and social services and cost native-born workers jobs? Or do barriers at the borders constrict economic growth, deprive the nation of self-selected strivers who infuse whole neighborhoods and cities with renewed vitality, and challenge the very foundation of America's unique multiculturalism? Notwithstanding the disparaging remarks in 1999 by John Rocker, the Atlanta Braves pitcher, about New York's immigrants— "You can walk an entire block in Times Square and not hear anybody speaking English"—outright bigotry is no longer acceptable politically or culturally.

Diversity—call it racial and ethnic pride or raw political and economic rivalry—has always been grist for competition and conflict.

Increasing Diversity

Percent change in the population of each group during the preceding decade.

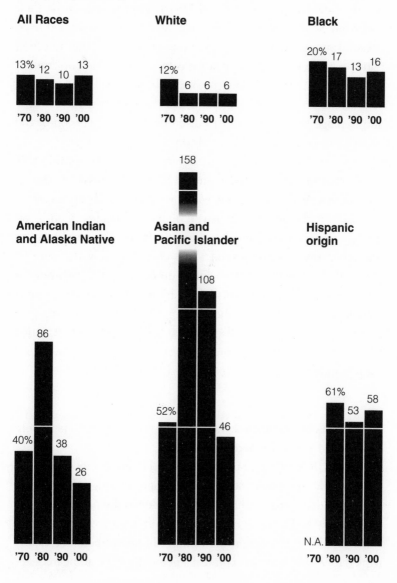

All Races

13% 12 10 13

'70 '80 '90 '00

White

12% 6 6 6

'70 '80 '90 '00

Black

20% 17 13 16

'70 '80 '90 '00

American Indian and Alaska Native

86
40% 38 26

'70 '80 '90 '00

Asian and Pacific Islander

158
108
52% 46

'70 '80 '90 '00

Hispanic origin

61% 53 58
N.A.

'70 '80 '90 '00

Americans often forget that before the nation was founded and even in its early years, non-Hispanic whites from Europe were outnumbered in many places by American Indians who had been here for thousands of years, settlers of Hispanic origin who made their way from Spain and South America, and blacks kidnapped from Africa. Immigrants typically arrive poorer and less educated than native-born Americans and place greater demands on government social services. However, they are generally a self-selected group of strivers—often downtrodden, but with the gumption to leave history and heritage behind in order to discover their own version of the American Dream. Most eventually do so.

Arriving during an economic boom in the 1990s, immigrants filled jobs and reinvigorated abandoned neighborhoods and vacant downtowns. At the same time, each new group has been resented, or worse, by the group that arrived before. Advocates of curbs on immigration warn that opening the nation's doors to a million or so foreigners a year depresses the wages of American workers or displaces them altogether. But while Europe struggles with how to assimilate its own immigrants from Africa and Asia, and as it joins with Japan in confronting the challenge of how a dwindling proportion of young people will support an aging population, America has grown and been rejuvenated by newcomers from overseas. Immigration has always enriched this nation culturally.

◆   ◆   ◆

Two factors distinguished the latest wave of immigrants: where they came from and where they settled.

In the 1960s, when about 320,000 legal immigrants were arriving annually, 40 percent were from Europe, although the number of West Indians arriving had already exceeded the number of Italians. In 1970, Japanese newcomers overtook arriving Scandinavians. By the 1990s, when the number of newcomers had nearly tripled to 900,000 a year, a mere 13 percent were Europeans.

More Americans can still trace their roots to Germany than to any other country, but the nearly 43 million who reported German ancestry in 2000 represented only 15 percent of the population. In traditionally German neighborhoods like Ridgewood in Queens, a German enclave since the 1880s, fewer than 3,000 residents identified their ancestry as German in 2000 compared to more than 10,000 only twenty years earlier. German-Americans (Donald Trump and George Steinbrenner, among them) may still march up Fifth Avenue in the annual Steuben Day Parade, but only two neighborhood churches in Ridgewood continue to hold services in German, and other vestiges of Germanic heritage— from the Oktoberfest in Forest Park in Queens to the dozens of German shops on Myrtle Avenue—have vanished or are disappearing. "There's been so many Germans here for so long that Germans feel very comfortable here," said Kathleen Hulser, public historian at the New-York Historical Society, "but the polar opposite is that after two wars and the Holocaust, the term German is so toxic that nobody wants to identify themselves as that." Even in the Midwest, because of the surge in newcomers from elsewhere and the passage of time since the last influx of Germans, the proportion of people identifying their ancestry as German has dropped. In Wisconsin during the 1990s it fell from 54 percent to 43 percent. The proportion of Americans who reported Irish ancestry plunged to 10.9 percent and English, to 8.7 percent. In contrast, the number of Americans of Italian origin actually increased slightly during the decade, to 15.7 million, although their share of the population dipped to 5.6 percent.

While 1 in 4 Americans still identify their heritage as German or Irish, a legacy of nineteenth- and early-twentieth-century political and social upheaval in Europe, the vast majority of new immigrants come from two other continents. In 2000, for the first time, the majority of Americans born abroad—fully 52 percent— were from Latin America. And more than 26 percent arrived from

Asia. What's more, they came from all over Latin America and Asia. Among all the foreign-born people in the United States today, about 36 percent were born in Mexico and Central America, nearly 10 percent in the Caribbean, 6 percent in South America, 26 percent in Asia, and 14 percent in Europe. Mexicans alone account for more than 25 percent of all foreign-born residents of the United States—the largest proportion from any single country since 1890, when immigrants from Germany constituted about 30 percent of the foreign-born.

In California, for the first time since the late 1850s, shortly after the territory was seized from Mexico, a majority of the babies being born in the state are Hispanic. Non-Hispanic whites now constitute a minority of the population in California and New Mexico—*again*—and are close to becoming a minority in Texas, too. In the late 1990s, Hispanics, propelled by both immigration and higher birth rates, achieved numerical parity in the United States with blacks or African-Americans (the census uses the terms interchangeably). That portends enormous political implications when more Hispanic immigrants become eligible for citizenship and register to vote. Nowhere was that shift more dramatic than in Florida, where Spanish explorers and settlers had originally been the largest minority when they founded St. Augustine 500 years ago. In the 1990s alone, a million more Hispanics moved to Florida, overtaking blacks in population and dispersing from earlier pockets in the southern part of the state.

America's Asian population, meanwhile, topped 10 million. More than 1 in 3 Asian-Americans live in California, but newer Asian immigrants are far less concentrated geographically than they used to be and also far more diverse by country of origin. Indians from Asia advanced to the third-largest group of Asian immigrants, behind Chinese and Filipinos.

There have also been smaller, but significant additions to the American mosaic. A total of thirty-three ancestry groups reported populations of over one million each, among them Arabs. The 2000 census found 1.2 million people of Arab ancestry in the United States, probably a conservative and imprecise estimate, although it represented a sizable increase from the 610,000 recorded in 1980, when the census first measured ancestry, and 860,000 in 1990. The Arab population rose by 41 percent in the 1980s and 38 percent in the 1990s. In 2000, they accounted for less than half a percent of the population. More than 1 in 3 identified themselves as Lebanese, followed by Syrian and Egyptian (12 percent each), and Palestinian (6.1 percent). About half the Arab population lived in five states: California, Florida, Michigan, New Jersey, and New York. California gained the most, 48,000, in the 1990s, but even in smaller states, like Tennessee, the Arab population more than doubled, from 6,000 in 1990 to 13,000 in 2000. Arabs had the highest share of the population in Michigan, 1.2 percent. Among places with 100,000 or more people, Arab-Americans accounted for nearly 4 percent of the population in Sterling Heights in southeastern Michigan (and close to 30 percent in nearby Dearborn, which has about 98,000 residents and where Pharoah's Café offers Christmas, New Year's, and Ramadan greetings in English and Arabic), and nearly 3 percent in Jersey City. In New York City, about 70,000 residents identified themselves as Arab-American. While 4 in 5 Arabs identified themselves as white only, more than 1 in 4 reported one Arab and one non-Arab ancestry. Between 1995 and 2000, the number of mosques in the United States rose 25 percent, to about 1,200.

✦   ✦   ✦

While the degree of diversity remains uneven geographically, never before have so many people from so many other countries settled in so many places.

The foreign-born population grew by 90 percent in the South (where the baseline was smallest), 65 percent in the Midwest, 50 percent in the West, and nearly 40 percent in the Northeast. In North Carolina, Georgia, and Nevada, it multiplied by more than 200 percent, and it expanded by between 100 percent and 199 percent in sixteen other states and only in one—Maine—was the rate lower than 10 percent. Six cities with populations of 100,000 or more, all in California and Florida, achieved the distinction of becoming majority foreign-born. Only one county did—Miami-Dade, where the 1.1 million immigrants constituted 51 percent of the population. But in nearly 200 other counties, the proportion of foreign-born residents surpassed 1 in 9, the national average. And in sixty more counties—places like Clark County in Idaho and Seward, Finney, and Ford Counties in Kansas, places far from gateway cities like New York, Los Angeles, Chicago, and Houston—foreigners accounted for 2 in 10 residents.

The sheer volume of arrivals from overseas drove up the foreign-born population to 60 percent in Miami and 40 percent in Los Angeles. (Los Angeles was on the verge in 2001 of electing its first Hispanic mayor—the first, that is, since 1872; California's changing complexion was accompanied by a telling reminder that economic and social assimilation typically precedes political assimilation: among all the state's voters in November 2000, 73 percent were white.) In California, the written portion of the test for driver's licenses is conducted in twenty-eight languages, including English, Spanish, Chinese, Korean, Tagalog, Armenian, Russian, and Vietnamese.

In 1990, California, New York, Florida, Texas, and Illinois accounted for 75 percent of all the nation's immigrants. By 2000, those states' share had dropped to 66 percent. As recently as 1990, immigrants accounted for 10 percent or more of the population in only five states. By 2000, the foreign-born population topped 10 percent in 15 states. More than 4 in 10 private household workers and farmworkers are immigrants. But foreigners also followed native-born movers from other states to Tennessee and Utah—where the foreign-born population doubled in the 1990s—to fill the construction, service, and retail jobs generated by the influx of migrants. If one stands at the corner of Elden Street and Alabama Drive in suburban Herndon, Virginia, one can see scores of Central American day laborers queue up for construction jobs in the booming high-tech corridor near Dulles International Airport. During the 1990s alone, the Hispanic share of Herndon's population more than doubled, from under 10 percent to 26 percent.

California, Texas, and New York still claim the largest populations of any states—and the largest number of immigrants. But the greatest percentage growth in immigration was in Nevada, Georgia, and North Carolina. In Nevada, the number of foreigners drawn by hotel and casino construction and other jobs more than tripled, from 105,000 in 1990 to 316,000 in 2000. In North Carolina, the number almost quadrupled, from 115,000 to 381,000. For the first time in a century, more California residents were born in a foreign country than in another state. Arkansas registered the biggest percentage increase in Hispanic immigrants of any state—more than 170 percent, to 54,000. Even in cities like Nashville, where immigrants accounted for a tiny 1.8 percent of the population in 1990, the proportion more than doubled (to 4.7 percent) by the end of the decade. In Atlanta and in Gwinnett County, Georgia, the Hispanic population soared more than 215 percent in the 1990s to more than 27,000, and the number of Asians was up 180 percent to 29,000. In Fort Bend, Texas, the number of Asians rose by more than 127 percent to 33,000. At St. Charles Borromeo Catholic Church in Morgantown, North Carolina, mass is delivered in English, Spanish, and Hmong. Minidoka, Idaho, lost its church, school, hotels, and stores as population dwindled, but its cheap housing attracted Hispanic farm and potato-processing workers. Of the city's 129 residents in 2000, 100 identified themselves as Hispanic.

Foreign-born residents now constitute a majority in six cities with populations bigger than 100,000, including Hialeah, where they account for more than 7 in 10 people; Miami, where they make up 6 in 10; and for more than half the population of Glendale, Santa Ana, Daly City, and El Monte in California.

Historically, immigrants gravitated to the cities and then, after a generation or two, graduated to the suburbs. But in the 1990s, nearly as many immigrants settled in the suburbs as in the central cities. In 12 of the 20 largest metropolitan areas—Los Angeles, Washington, Atlanta, Miami among them—the number of foreigners who settled in the suburbs surpassed those who stayed in the cities. Immigrants accounted for about 40 percent of the population increase in metropolitan areas. In fact, in the sixty-nine metropolises where at least 1 in 10 residents are foreign-born, more foreigners moved into the suburbs than the central cities. Following early arrivals from the same towns in Latin America— just as the European immigrants had done—they moved to immigrant enclaves outside the central cities. In the nation's three suburban metropolises flanking New York City, foreigners accounted for more than 14 percent of the population in Nassau-Suffolk Counties on Long Island and, in New Jersey, 25 percent in Bergen-Passaic and over 20 percent in Middlesex-Somerset-Hunterdon. Dawson County, Nebraska, which recorded 138 foreign-born residents in 1990, counted 3,866 in 2000. Dalton, Georgia, attracted so many foreign workers to its carpet mills that its public schools had to recruit teachers from Mexico. More than 2 in 3 of the foreigners living in Nashville in 2000 arrived there in the 1990s.

Some cities, like New York, which gained a million immigrants in the 1990s, and Miami, which drew more than 300,000, were always natural magnets for newcomers, rich and poor alike. Foreign-born people now account for fully 29.6 percent of the people in metropolitan Los Angeles and nearly 23 percent in metropolitan New York. "We never dreamed that New York would again become a major city of immigrants," said Nathan Glazer, coauthor of *Beyond the Melting Pot*, "but then the immigration laws changed in 1965." No county in the country is more diverse than Queens in New York City, where 167 nationalities speak 116 languages—personifying the welcoming "Gateway to America" sign at the borough's Kennedy International Airport. In the 1990s, the number of Mexicans in New York City nearly quadrupled to more than 133,000; the number of South Asians from India, Pakistan, and Bangladesh more than doubled to over 150,000. Those new immigrants have transformed entire neighborhoods— neighborhoods that had been built for, and by, earlier generations of immigrants. New York's Little Italy is largely Chinese. In Astoria, the capital of New York's Greek community, businesses owned by Middle Eastern newcomers are thriving. (New York also has more American Indians—87,000 at last count—than any city in the country.)

Other cities, fearing embarrassing or debilitating population losses and labor shortages and seeking to replenish abandoned neighborhoods, actually recruited foreigners, in sharp contrast to earlier concerns that all immigrants would burden local schools and social services. As the 1990s progressed, the Internet boom sparked a demand for labor. Immigrants helped meet that demand. In California alone, the labor force swelled by 1.4 million— more than one million of whom were legal immigrants.

"We've got a people problem," said Grant Oliphant, planning director for Heinz Endowments, a Pittsburgh foundation that awarded $800,000 to four local groups in 2001 to lure immigrants with jobs and to persuade students from abroad to remain after graduation. "Regional economies today are heavily dependent on people and people skills, and it's difficult to attract new businesses in a region that's losing people." In the 1990s, Pittsburgh's population fell 9.5 percent to 334,000 and would have dipped even more except for an influx of 9,000 immigrants. Louisville, Kentucky, established an office of international and cultural affairs after a population decline of 5 percent that would have been worse except for the 20,000 newcomers from overseas, including immigrants and refugees from Cuba, Somalia, and Vietnam, who tripled the city's immigrant population. Albuquerque, where an influx of immigrants from Latin America helped boost the population by 16 percent in the 1990s, formally declared itself "immigrant-friendly." North Carolina, which earlier in the century had the smallest proportion of foreigners, was so eager for immigrant workers that it has administered its driver's license test in Chinese, Japanese, Korean, and Spanish. Its Hispanic population nearly quadrupled in the 1990s.

"The most important factor for public officials to be aware of in the next ten to twenty years is that the vitality of cities will depend on their ability to attract and be a hospitable environment for minorities," says John R. Logan, director of the Lewis Mumford Center for Comparative Urban and Regional Research at the State University of New York at Albany.

✦   ✦   ✦

On average, 95,000 foreigners enter the United States every day. But most don't stay.

Demographers from the Population Reference Bureau figure that more than 90,000 of them are tourists, students, workers, diplomats, and executives who arrive legally, primarily at the nation's airports. About 3,000—still a considerable number—are immigrants also welcomed at the nation's ports of entry as permanent residents. The rest, 1,000 or so a day, manage to evade border controls and sneak into the country undetected, generally to seek low-paying jobs as day laborers in construction and other manual labor fields, as migrant farmworkers, and as back-of-the-house help in hotels and restaurants. Most immigrants stay, although air transportation makes going home much easier than it was for earlier generations of Italians and others who made their fortune, returned to Europe, and then emigrated again when they needed to make another fortune.

In 2001, more than one million legal immigrants entered the United States. The vast majority, 675,000, were sponsored by relatives already here. Another 179,000 were admitted because they possessed special job skills. The biggest group of other immigrants was the 108,000 people granted asylum or designated as refugees. During the same year, about 220,000 foreigners left the country. Among non-immigrants, the government counted nearly 30 million visitors for business or pleasure, 688,000 foreign students (most of the record of nearly 583,000 foreign students enrolled in American colleges and universities in 2001 were from India, about 67,000, followed by China, about 63,000), and 990,000 temporary foreign workers. (Officials apprehended nearly 1.4 million illegal immigrants, but estimate that up to 500,000 more slipped into the country.)

About half the nation's foreign-born have become citizens. By the beginning of the twenty-first century, about 45 percent of the immigrants who had entered the United States legally in the 1980s had been naturalized. Naturalization rates varied widely, though, with about 2 in 3 of the eligible Asians, 1 in 2 Europeans, and 1 in 3 Latin Americans becoming citizens. The rate surged in the 1990s, after the Clinton administration expedited the process and after non-citizens were denied certain welfare benefits, but then leveled off again. About 4 in 10 of the foreign-born arrived in the United States in the 1990s and, not surprisingly, they have the lowest rate of citizenship—about 1 in 10, compared to almost 30 percent among those who arrived in the 1980s and 1970s and about 33 percent among those who arrived before 1970. In only seven states (Alaska, Hawaii, Maine, Montana, Pennsylvania, Vermont, and West Virginia), did the foreign-born who were naturalized

United States citizens in 2000 outnumber foreign-born residents who were non-citizens.

Do immigrants cost Americans money or contribute to the nation's economy? Economists disagree. One comprehensive study by the National Research Council in 1997 can be encapsulated in two words: *it depends*. What it depends on most, according to the council, is age and education. Those are the variables that appear most likely to determine the difference between how much an immigrant costs society in services provided over his lifetime and what the government gains in taxes. An adult arriving with less than a high school education costs about $89,000 (in 1996 dollars) over his lifetime. An adult who graduated from high school would cost $31,000. An adult with more than a high school degree would eventually contribute $105,000. Those numbers do not reflect the intangible costs and benefits generated by the influx of foreigners. Nor do they measure the fiscal impact of their descendants, which, generally, is projected to be more of a financial gain to society than a cost.

◆   ◆   ◆

The census doesn't distinguish between immigrants who arrive legally and those who do not. But it does provide a tool for estimating the number of illegal immigrants living in the United States. The Immigration and Naturalization Service (now split into the Directorate of Border and Transportation Security and the Bureau of Citizenship and Immigration Services in the new Department of Homeland Security) had estimated that the number grew by several hundred thousand a year in the 1990s to about 7 million in 2000 (nearly half from Mexico, and most of the rest from Latin America, but with as many—about 30,000—from Ireland as from South Korea or Peru).

Barricades and border crackdowns in California and Texas, especially after the terror attacks of September 11, 2001, transformed the 261-mile border between Mexico and Arizona into the nation's busiest illegal crossing. *Polleros*—chicken ranchers, in Spanish—smuggle Mexicans across the border for $1,500 or so apiece and Central and South Americans for even more—payable in cash on delivery. Typically, a would-be migrant is driven from a Mexican border town into the desert where, led by a *pollero,* he risks poisonous snakes and insects and dehydration on a three-day trek to an isolated spot somewhere in Arizona. There, he is picked up by a van or truck, transported to a house in some city where he is locked up until a friend arrives to buy his freedom.

The INS estimated that there were about 2.2 million illegal immigrants in California, more than 1 million in Texas, nearly 500,000 in New York, about 432,000 in Illinois, 337,000 in Florida, and more than 200,000 each in Arizona, Georgia, North Carolina, and New Jersey. By subtracting the number of legal residents from the total number of foreign-born counted by the 2000 census, Jeff Passel of the Urban Institute calculated the pool of undocumented aliens at closer to 8.5 million—more than half of them from Mexico. Other organizations have even higher estimates.

✦   ✦   ✦

No immigrant group promises to have a greater impact in the beginning of the twenty-first century than Hispanics from Mexico and the rest of Latin America.

By the mid-1900s, pockets of Mexicans (in California and Texas) and of Puerto Ricans (in New York and New Jersey) punctuated the nation's ethnic landscape. Then, waves of Cubans escaping the communist revolution of 1959 settled in Florida. With each decade, those immigrants assimilated, some more quickly than others. Mexicans, in particular, were less likely to become citizens, with many—like Italians earlier in the century or like Canadians more recently—expecting to return to their native country or unwilling to relinquish property or inheritance rights at home. Puerto Ricans, already Americans by birth, found them-selves elbowed aside by more recent newcomers with whom they had less common ground—other than language—than many non-Hispanic whites had imagined. In 1990, Puerto Ricans were a majority among Hispanics in New York City, but by 2000 their share had declined to about one-third as the number of Mexicans more than tripled to 187,000 and other nationalities grew in number as well.

A trickle of Mexicans, mostly from the southern state of Puebla, that began in the 1980s gushed in the 1990s as the num-ber of Mexicans tripled to become the third-largest Latino group behind Puerto Ricans, who began arriving en masse in the 1940s, and Dominicans, who came in the 1960s. Even a trickle begins with a single drop. One 2,800-mile-long stream of Mexican mi-gration from the mountain villages of Cotija, Quitupan, and Jiquilpan to New York's Westchester County was credited largely to Antonio Valencia, a young deliveryman who overheard an Amer-ican couple tell a priest that they were looking for a "houseman." He spoke no English, but was hired by George Vergara, a former mayor of New Rochelle, and arrived in New York in 1954. Hun-dreds followed, as others had followed earlier pioneers, to work as laborers, gardeners, and kitchen help in Westchester's country clubs. Valencia became known as *el padrino,* the godfather, for helping them find jobs and housing. "The reason they come is be-cause Antonio came," Juan Sandoval, who owned a food market and liquor store in New Rochelle, told Lynda Richardson of the *New York Times.* "All they need is somebody to know. You need somebody to support you. We are all following the leader." The story behind Brazilian immigration is similar. Legend has it that in the 1960s two brothers from Governador Valadares in Brazil's arid interior formed the vanguard of an army of shoeshine men that encamped in midtown Manhattan. "Word filtered back of the money to be made, and by the end of the decade a small contingent of Brazilians were shining shoes in the vicinity of Grand Central Station," wrote Maxine L. Margolis, an anthropology professor at the University of Florida. "Their numbers slowly increased as networks of friends and relatives found shoeshine jobs for new arrivals in the city, and by the early 1980s this job sector, once the domain of African-Americans, was monopolized by Brazilians."

Similar immigrant streams developed elsewhere. Tougher enforcement for transients at the Mexican border helped lure more Mexicans to jobs in hotels, restaurants, and the meatpacking plants of the Midwest. The Mexican population more than doubled during the 1990s in Minnesota, Iowa, Indiana, and Wisconsin. Chicago is now home to more Mexicans than San Antonio— 530,000, or 50 percent more than in 1990—and it ranks second in Mexican immigrants, behind only Los Angeles. It is now estimated that Mexican migrant workers living in the United States send more money home—over $6 billion—than foreigners invest in Mexico or than tourists spend there.

In the 1990s, the number of U.S. residents of Mexican ancestry soared by 53 percent. The influx was attributed, in part, to a "migration hump"—displacement of agricultural workers caused by provisions of the North American Free Trade Agreement. The nation's more than 20 million Mexicans account for almost 60 percent of all Latinos—far exceeding the 3.4 million Puerto Ricans, who grew by 25 percent, and 1.2 million Cubans, who increased by 19 percent. The number of Hispanics from Central and South America nearly doubled (with Salvadorans and Guatemalans representing the largest proportion among Central American immigrants). The census counted 35.3 million Latinos, about 3 million more than demographers had projected, which reflected, in part, a larger than expected influx of illegal immigrants.

Spurred by estimates that the Hispanic share of the population will soar to 18 percent by 2025 (compared to 9 percent as recently as 1990), major newspaper publishers are tailoring their publications to attract Hispanic readers. The Tribune Company announced that it would expand *Hoy,* its Spanish-language daily in New York, to Chicago. The *New York Post* began publishing a monthly supplement called *NYP Tempo,* this one in English, aimed at second- and third-generation Latino teenagers. On radio, Spanish-language programming is now the fifth most popular format after country, news and talk, oldies, and adult contemporary. According to M Street, a research company, 361 Spanish stations were broadcasting in 1993. Ten years later, 655 were on the air, accounting for 6 percent of all commercial stations.

Hispanics now constitute 42 percent of the population of New Mexico and 32 percent in California and more than 90 percent in East Los Angeles, as well as in Laredo and Brownsville, Texas, and in Hialeah, Florida. In 1996, Jose became the most popular baby name in Texas, although it remains to be seen how long the grip of non-Anglicized names endures. "The Latinization of the country is not just happening in New York, Miami, or L.A.," said Juan Figueroa, president of the Puerto Rican Legal Defense and Education Fund. "Its greatest impact is in the heartland in places like Reading, Pennsylvania; Lorain, Ohio; and Lowell, Massachusetts."

There is growing diversity even among immigrants. Many second- and third-generation Cuban-Americans developed political and cultural values reflecting the fact that the homeland their Cuban exile parents longed to reclaim was a mythical anachronism they had never even visited. In 2003, as thousands of people in Miami and New York mourned Celia Cruz, the queen of salsa, Maria Vazquez, a fifty-three-year-old Florida businesswoman who was eight when she left Cuba, proclaimed the end of an era. "I call her and people like her, the last of the true Cubans," she said. "She was part of the Cuba of our parents, a

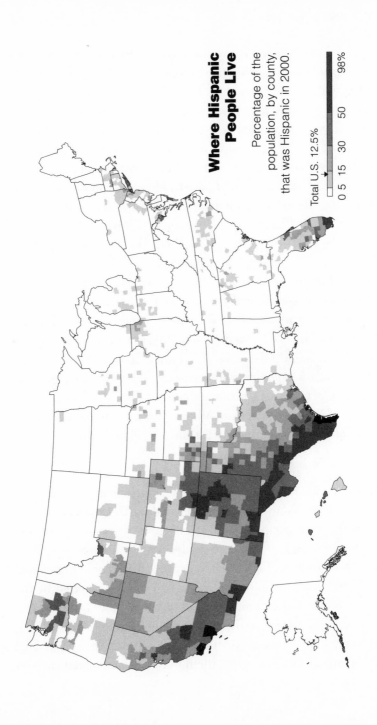

Where Hispanic People Live

Percentage of the population, by county, that was Hispanic in 2000.

Total U.S. 12.5%

0 5 15 30 50 98%

Cuba we didn't really know and that doesn't exist anymore. It's the Cuba of our imagination, a virtual Cuba, if you will."

Only about 12 percent of Hispanic immigrants marry non-Hispanics, but the proportion grows to more than 50 percent by the third generation. And despite the demands to declare English the nation's official language, newcomers seem to be accommodating to and adapting American culture, even as that culture embraces the Hispanic idiom. "I have third-generation Latino kids in my classes," Harry P. Pachon, president of the Tomas Rivera Policy Institute at Claremont Colleges in California, told Dean Murphy of the *New York Times*. "I ask them, do they speak Spanish? They say no. Do they eat Mexican food? They go to McDonald's. Do they like *rancheras* music? They listen to Power 106."

In Whittier, a historically white and middle-class suburb of Los Angeles, 1 in 5 residents are foreign-born and 1 in 3 speak Spanish at home. In 1947, when Martin Ortiz arrived, he was the only Hispanic student in his class at Whittier College. A half-century later, about 1 in 4 students are Hispanic. "Now the problem is different," says Ortiz, who recently retired as director of the college's Center of Mexican-American Affairs. "You speak to those students in Spanish and they wonder what you are talking about."

✦   ✦   ✦

Asian immigrants, too, have become much more diverse. The streams of Asian immigration developed much the same as they did with other groups: drawn at first from the same small geographic area and to the same profession. In metropolitan New York, for instance, Filipinos are defined by a single profession. Fully 30 percent of the 175,000 or so Filipinos counted by the census reported their professions as nurses or other health practitioners. Hospitals value them for their education, English skills, and work ethic and have recruited them for decades and lobbied immigration officials to grant them work visas and green cards as permanent residents. Filipino enclaves developed near major hospitals, along Manila Avenue in Jersey City, where the census counted nearly 16,000 Filipinos, and in Bergenfield, New Jersey, which elected a Filipino mayor in 1999. Their demographic profile is distinct: in New York City, 57 percent are women, 49.7 percent have college degrees, and their median income is $41,000, compared to the citywide average of $34,000. Many return to their families in the Philippines for vacations and some even leave or send their children with relatives there and send money to pay for better schooling. "We come from a Third World country, and I think this is our passport to earn a good living," said Maria Dolores Egasan, who came to the United States in 1989 and is an intensive care nurse at Montefiore Medical Center in the Bronx. She met her husband through his sister, also a nurse. Three of her husband's brothers are married to nurses; one is a nurse himself.

Within ten years, the Asian population of Fremont, California, in the Bay Area of San Francisco, just about doubled, from 19 percent to 37 percent, transforming a largely white bedroom community into a magnet for immigrants and creating previously unimaginable cultural conflicts. Police struck a compromise with the local Sikh community, allowing public school students to wear their sacred ceremonial swords that signify baptism, but only if the swords are concealed, wired into a scabbard, and the blade blunted. When Hillside Drive was named Gurdwara Road in honor of a temple that Sikh residents built there, Mayor Gus Morrison recalled, "at a public meeting, someone got up and said, 'I can't pronounce Gurwarda.' Then a Sikh stands up and says, 'I can't pronounce Paseo Padre.'"

In Washington State, a Chinese-American, Gary Locke, was elected governor in 1996. In Louisiana, Bobby Jindal, a thirty-two-year-old Rhodes scholar and son of immigrants from New Delhi, finished first in the initial round of voting for governor in 2003, though he was defeated in the general election. Jindal, a

Republican who changed his name to Bobby from Piyush when he was only four, has gotten further than any other Indian-American in state politics anywhere, much less in Louisiana, where foreign-born people constitute less than 3 percent of the population.

In Cupertino, California, the headquarters of Apple Computer, nearly half the population of 50,000 is Asian, compared to less than 10 percent in 1980. What distinguishes Cupertino even in the Bay Area is that the staggering demographic shift from just a few decades ago has transformed the political landscape. A third of the elected officials are Asian-American; a Chinese-American who teaches Asian-American studies at De Anza Community College has already served as mayor. But the pace of change has come with controversy, such as whether a Chinese dragon and lion dance are appropriate additions to the annual Fourth of July parade. Richard Lowenthal, a Cupertino city councilman who is co-chairman of the city's Lunar New Year Unity parade, told the *New York Times*'s Patricia Leigh Brown: "In San Francisco, change happened over a century, but here it's happened very fast. There's a certain sense people have that there's not enough room for two cultures. There are people making change and resisting change."

In 2000, for the first time, less than half the Asian population lived in the West. And though more than 1 in 3 Asians live in California, the census found concentrations of Asians in disparate states including Georgia, Pennsylvania, and Minnesota. With three hundred houses of worship, Fort Wayne, Indiana, proclaims itself the City of Churches, and so many of them sponsored refugees fleeing Myanmar that by 2000 the city had accommodated more Burmese than any place else in the United States. The 1,000 or so of them were the city's biggest immigrant group. In New York, Chinese-Americans now account for less than half the city's Asian population as new immigrants arrive from Bangladesh, Pakistan, Japan, and other nations. Asian-

Indians, who in 1990 were the fifth-largest group among Asian-Americans, after Chinese and Filipinos, catapulted to third largest.

✦   ✦   ✦

The influx of foreigners in the last decade of the twentieth century—especially of Hispanic people—profoundly altered the ethnic and racial complexion of a country where color has always counted. The proportion of Americans who described themselves as non-Hispanic whites, as the census calls them, slid from 76 percent to 69 percent. Non-Hispanic whites now constitute a minority of the population in the nation's hundred largest urban centers; nearly half the hundred largest cities have more blacks, Hispanics, and people of other races than non-Hispanic whites. So many foreigners flooded California and neighboring states that by 1990, for the first time in the century, the West overtook the South as the region with the highest proportion of nonwhites. More than 4 in 10 New Mexicans are of Hispanic heritage. While plenty of pockets of racial separation remain—in some places, the degree of residential segregation actually increased—diversity has become more widespread. By 2000, only ten states still had populations that were more than 90 percent white.

Except for Alabama, Arkansas, Mississippi, South Carolina, and West Virginia, in every state the percentage of nonwhites was higher in 2000 than it was in 1950. By then, California had the highest proportion of Asians—1.5 percent. Today, it has well over 11 percent, and the Asian share of the population in Washington, New Jersey, and New York exceeds 5 percent. As recently as 1980, Colorado was the only state that didn't border Mexico where Hispanics accounted for at least 10 percent of the population. By 2000, Florida, New York, Nevada, Illinois, and New Jersey each had a population that was more than 10 percent Hispanic. Hispanics, who constituted less than 8 percent of the population in New York's inner suburbs in 1990, grew to more than 12 percent in Nassau, Rockland, and Westchester Counties by 2000. In Farmingville, Long Island, population 15,000, America's appetite for cheap labor drew about 1,500 illegal immigrants in the 1990s, most of them manual laborers from Mexico. Nationally, influxes of Hispanics and Asians helped increase the minority population of America's larger suburbs from 19 percent in 1990 to 27 percent in 2000.

By 2000, non-Hispanic whites had dwindled to a minority in 48 of the nation's 100 largest cities, compared to 30 in 1990. (Among those that shifted were Boston, Philadelphia, Albuquerque, Sacramento, Anaheim, and San Diego.) Analyses by the Brookings Institution and the Center on Urban and Metropolitan Policy found that Hispanics grew in number by 43 percent and Asians by 38 percent in the hundred largest cities and by even more—67 percent and 58 percent, respectively—in the next tier of cities, ranked 101 to 200 in total population. Among that group, 33 cities had majority minority populations in 2000, compared to 20 in 1990. Another analysis, this one by the National League of Cities, found that the minority population of the 100 largest cities jumped from 48 percent in 1990 to 56 percent in 2000. In St. Paul, Minnesota, 1 in 8 residents are Asian. The city in which Hispanics are growing fastest isn't in California or Texas but in North Carolina. Between 1990 and 2000, the Hispanic population of the Raleigh-Durham metropolitan area exploded by 631 percent, from fewer than 10,000 to nearly 73,000. Two trends contribute to those changes. Whites are moving out or dying—71 of the 100 largest cities lost white residents in the 1990s—and Hispanics are moving in and having more children. The National League of Cities analysis contrasted Santa Ana, California, where 3 of 4 residents are Hispanic, with Yonkers, New York, which lost 20 percent of its whites in the 1990s. In Santa Ana, the median age was twenty-six. In Yonkers, it was over thirty-five.

In his new book, *Who Are We*, published in 2004, the political scientist Samuel P. Huntington invokes his global clash of civilizations to warn against the dangers at home of immigration, particularly of Hispanics and especially of Mexicans who, he warns, represent "the single most immediate and most serious challenge to America's traditional identity." He argues that Mexican-Americans are increasingly comfortable with their own culture and are contemptuous of the basic American creed. "There is no Americano dream," Huntington argues. "There is only the American dream created by an Anglo-Protestant society. Mexican-Americans will share in that dream and in that society only if they dream in English." To which the columnist David Brooks responded in the *New York Times* that if Mexican-Americans often lag in school it is largely because "our integration machinery is broken. But if we close our borders to new immigration, you can kiss good-bye the new energy, new tastes, and new strivers who want to lunge into the future." Assimilation, Tamar Jacoby reminds us in *Reinventing the Melting Pot,* can take a lifetime, even two, and "a Mexican farmhand with a sixth-grade education takes a different path into the mainstream than an Indian engineer working on an M.B.A." And in California, where about 25 percent of the population, including the governor, is foreign-born, a recent study of immigration since the 1970s by the University of Southern California concludes that "earnings, home ownership, and voting participation all rise markedly with growing length of settlement."

In New York City, where the proportion of foreign-born residents skyrocketed from 28 percent in 1990 to 40 percent in 2000, the late Senator Daniel Patrick Moynihan, coauthor with Nathan Glazer of *Beyond the Melting Pot,* the seminal work on race and ethnicity, expressed astonishment at the dimension of the increase. "It's an enriching experience for us," he said in 2000. "It's wonderful—I mean, we have to think of it that way. If we think of it any other way, it won't be."

8

How We Live
in Black and White

Since the very first federal census in 1790, only three questions have survived the inevitable political and bureaucratic second-guessing to return on every survey: age, gender, and race. The government has redefined race periodically, primarily to accommodate the prevailing political mood. But the focus on race, whether as a vehicle to divide and to sustain those divisions or to rectify centuries of discrimination, has persisted. The one indelible distinction that has endured since 1790 is between black and white.

"Why has the way we count and sort by race always been such a volatile issue?" asked Kenneth Prewitt, the former Census Bureau director. "Because throughout American history, starting with the 1790 census, a classification of racial groups has been used to regulate relations among the races and to support discriminatory policies designed to protect the numerical and political supremacy of white Americans of European ancestry."

Since 1790, said Claudette Bennett, chief of racial statistics for the Census Bureau, "politics have continued to play a vital role in influencing the number of racial categories and the definitions that might influence how people identify themselves." A separate column for "color" was introduced to the census in 1850, which merely codified the presumption of whiteness. In the era before self-identification, marshals were instructed to leave the column blank if a person was white by (1870, however, the first census after the Civil War, they were instructed to write W, B for black, and an M for mulatto, although it was largely left to the enumerators how to differentiate one from the other or, for that matter, how to describe Indians and Asians). By 1890, the politics of race had intruded further. Enumeraters were advised: "Be particularly careful to distinguish between blacks, mulattoes, quadroons, and octoroons. The word 'black' should be used to describe those persons who have three-fourths or more black blood; 'mulatto,' those persons who have from three-eighths to five-eighths black blood; 'quadroon,' those persons who have one-fourth black blood; and 'octoroon,' those persons who have one-eighth or any trace of black blood."

In the twentieth century, America gradually evolved from a largely black or white racial perspective to a more multicultural one, but the obsession with race died hard. In 1900, the census introduced the term *Negro* and dropped its attempt to fractionalize the black population by blood, though ten years later it returned, with the census defining mulattoes as persons with "some proportion or perceptible trace of Negro blood." The census soon stopped differentiating between Negroes and mulattoes, a simplification that, intentionally or not, removed any ambiguity about whether they were black or white. (Until then, a Virginian could be up to 24 percent black, but still be considered white under the law.) By 1930, enumerators were advised that "a person of mixed White and Negro blood was to be returned as Negro, no matter how small the percentage of Negro blood." In 1960, census forms were mailed to most Americans for the first time, which meant they could identify themselves however they pleased, as long as they confined their choices to the official categories, subject to the eyeballing of the enumerator who came to collect the questionnaire.

If divining traces of Negro blood was challenging, what constitutes "white" has always been problematic, too. Mexicans were listed as a separate race in the 1930 census only, but were magically, and statistically, assimilated with whites when the category was eliminated ten years later, when new racial groups, including Hindu, were added. Puerto Ricans and Latin Americans were white (as were Europeans, of course, and Near Easterners) unless they were demonstrably Negro or American Indian. Asian Indians were considered white as recently as 1970. No wonder that as far back as 1962, Crayola changed the name of its pale "flesh" colored crayons to "peach." In 1992, Crayola introduced a carton of "multicultural crayons" with sixteen colors, including eight skin tones.

◆   ◆   ◆

"Nothing is more clearly written in the book of destiny than the emancipation of the blacks," Thomas Jefferson predicted in his memoirs, "and it is equally certain that the two races will never live in a state of equal freedom under the same government, so insurmountable are the barriers which nature, habit and opinion have established between them." More than 150 years ago, Tocqueville wrote: "Although the law may abolish slavery, God alone can obliterate the traces of its existence. You may set the Negro free, but you cannot make him otherwise than an alien to those of European origin." A century later, Gunnar Myrdal dubbed that legacy "the American dilemma."

Beginning with the first census in 1790, blacks have constituted the largest minority group in the United States, and they continue to suffer from a wrenching upheaval that has distinguished them from every other immigrant group for hundreds of years: they, too, were huddled masses yearning to breathe free, but they were kidnapped, chained together in the holds of fetid ships, and auctioned off as slave labor to maintain the cotton economy of the South. While the importation of slaves was legally banned nearly two centuries ago and the Civil War officially won those who were already here their freedom, they were not liberated from the hardscrabble plantation fields until the invention of the mechanical cotton picker after World War II. And, rather than liberate blacks, that machine merely transformed them into economic refugees, fleeing the rural South for factory jobs and the slum housing to which they were relegated or which was all they could afford in the big industrial cities of the North. Arguably, the legal revolution, the one that was accompanied by force of law and, if necessary, by force of federal troops, did not begin until only a half-century ago, when the United States Supreme Court ruled in 1954 that even if localities provided black students with an equal education those governments were violating the Constitution by segregating blacks in separate schools. Ten years later, President Lyndon Johnson prodded Congress into codifying and enforcing the principals of civil rights and voting rights.

By many social, economic, and political yardsticks, blacks have progressed enormously since then. But staggering disparities between native-born blacks and other Americans only begin to suggest the separate and unequal divisions that corrosive racism and its lingering consequences have etched in our society. Black infants are still twice as likely to die as white ones. Black children are three times more likely to live in poverty. Black children can expect to live about six years less than white children born at the same time. The death rate for black men from murder is seven times higher than for whites. As many black households are now headed by single women as by married couples. With the number of people incarcerated in American jails and prisons surpassing 2 million for the first time, a record proportion of black men in their twenties—12 percent—are among the inmates.

Blacks are apart from the larger whole—in W. E. B. Du Bois's words—in less tangible ways, too. A *New York Times* survey of 471 covers from an array of thirty-one magazines published in 2002 found that about 1 in 5 featured an ethnic or racial minority—an increase, actually, from the 1 in 8 or so five years earlier. In December 2002, Halle Berry became only the fifth black woman to appear on the cover of *Cosmopolitan* since the magazine began using cover photographs in 1964. Daniel Peres, the editor of *Details,* the men's magazine, explained, "While most people in the business would prefer it to go unspoken because they are horrified at being perceived as racist, it is a well-known legend that blacks, especially black males, do not help generate newsstand sales." Even in so-called alternative papers like New York City's *Village Voice,* people answering the classified ads for jobs and apartments are protected against discrimination, but the racy personals invite responses not merely on the basis of a bizarre range of sexual preferences but by race—perhaps the one place left where even ladies and gentlemen can proclaim, Blacks (or Whites or Asians, for that matter) Need Not Apply. Professor Randall Kennedy recalls the awkward silence in his Harvard Law School class when he asked a student unequivocally opposed to all varieties of racial discrimination whether he would condemn a friend who placed a personal ad specifying a preference by race. "Perhaps most revealing of all is the small number of black dental hygienists," Andrew Hacker of Queens College has written. "While white patients seem willing to be cared for by black nurses. They apparently draw the line at having black fingers in their mouths."

Nathan Glazer, who wrote *Beyond the Melting Pot* with Daniel Patrick Moynihan in 1964, later acknowledged that he was laboring under a "New York illusion" when he predicted that American-born blacks, like other newcomers to the city, would overcome the ghetto. However much ethnic ingredients can be merged in the city's simmering brew, he realized, blacks and whites will always be distinguishable. Ethnic identity, Glazer said, "is pretty thin gruel compared to race."

◆ ◆ ◆

Blacks accounted for 19.6 percent of the people recorded in the 1790 census, although for purposes of political representation, it took 1.67 blacks to equal 1 white—and even then blacks couldn't vote. Their proportion of the total population was at its peak in 1790, and their share would decline in every decade from 1810, two years after the importation of slaves was prohibited, until 1930, when they represented 9.7 percent of the population. Then the percentage began inching up again, until blacks accounted for 12.3 percent of the nation's population in 2000— about the same as their proportion in 1900. The proportion of blacks in the Northeast, Midwest, and West are at record highs, in the South at a record low.

When the century began, 90 percent of American blacks lived in the South, and they constituted 32 percent of the South's total population. The migration to the Northeast and Midwest that began in the 1930s and 1940s ended and went into reverse after 1970, a reversal that accelerated as the century ended. In the 1990s, the South gained double the number of blacks that it had in the 1980s. By 2000, nearly 55 percent of blacks lived in the South, where they represented 19 percent of the population. In the 1990s, the proportion of blacks surged in booming cities like Orlando and Atlanta, both by about 62 percent, and in Miami by 43 percent. Despite the influx of Hispanics, the South largely remains a study in black and white, although the South that blacks returned to is a very different place from the one their parents, grandparents, and great-grandparents left.

Regionally, blacks and whites are much more evenly distributed than when the century began. In 1900, nonwhites constituted nearly 33 percent of the population of the south, but less

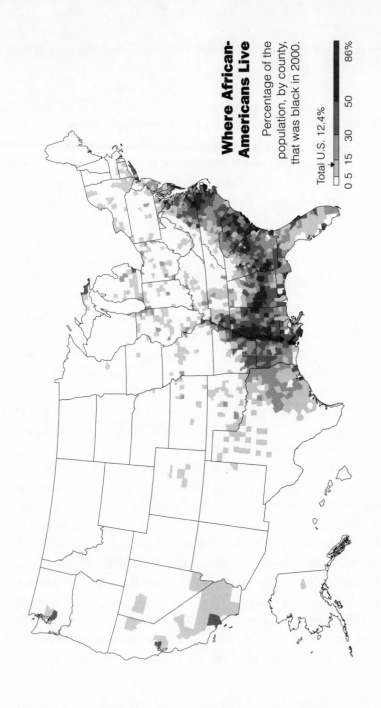

Where African-Americans Live

Percentage of the population, by county, that was black in 2000.

Total U.S. 12.4%

0 5 15   30   50   86%

than 2 percent in the Northeast. During the entire twentieth century, no state had a higher proportion of blacks than Mississippi, which with South Carolina were the only states in which blacks were a majority. Today, they are a minority in every state, but with wide disparities. Blacks constitute more than 36 percent of the population in Mississippi, but only 0.3 percent in Montana and less than 3 percent of the population in twelve other states. Among the ten largest cities in the United States, the proportion of blacks ranges from nearly 83 percent in Detroit to less than 6 percent in Phoenix. New York and Chicago alone account for 9 percent of the nation's black population. (New York, by virtue of its size, has the largest black population of any city—and also the largest white population.)

Blacks account for 22 percent of the big-city populations but only 8 percent of the suburbs. That's changing. In suburban Clayton County, Georgia, outside Atlanta, the influx of middle-class black families drove the proportion of blacks in the county from 24 percent in 1990 to 51 percent in 2000.

Even among blacks, whom whites have generally considered to be monolithic, cleavages have emerged and, in some cases, are widening: between the growing number who have succeeded and the seemingly intractable group mired in the socioeconomic cellar; and between the sexes, since black women now outnumber black men in the workforce; and between the American-born and immigrants. As recently as 1970, foreign-born blacks accounted for 1.3 percent of the black population. By 2000, they constituted 7.8 percent nationwide. Most came from the Caribbean—primarily Haiti, the Dominican Republic, and Jamaica—but an increasing number came from Africa. In New York, more than 1 in 4 blacks are foreign-born. In Florida and New Jersey, more than 1 in 5 are.

Between 1990 and 2000, the black population increased slightly faster than the total population, by 15.6 percent. But in the 1990s, the Hispanic population grew by more than 60 percent. By 2000, blacks were poised to be surpassed by Hispanics as the nation's largest ethnic or racial minority—a shift with potentially enormous implications. (In calculating who's ahead, one complication is that a person can be both black and Hispanic; also, the option of being able to choose more than one race complicates the count further.) In 2003, the Census Bureau announced that indeed the benchmark had been reached: in 2002, blacks constituted 13.1 percent of the population and Hispanics 13.4 percent.

✦   ✦   ✦

People can profess to get along, they can work next to one another and ride the same buses, subways, and commuter trains. But two discretionary choices reveal a lot more about the state of race relations and the extent to which a society is color blind: how willing people are to live next door to neighbors of a different race or ethnicity and how prone they are to socialize or even intermarry.

Residential integration may be proceeding more rapidly than compared to the experience of immigrant groups a century ago. "Italians and Jews were more segregated in the first thirty years after their arrival than Asian groups are today," said John R. Logan, the director of the Lewis Mumford Center for Comparative Urban and Regional Research at the State University of New York at Albany. While Hispanics and Asians are living in more heavily Hispanic and Asian neighborhoods than they were a decade ago, many began arriving a lot more recently than thirty years ago. It is also true that blacks and whites are only barely more integrated than they were in 1990 and—more disturbingly—that even middle-class and wealthier blacks are as segregated from whites in the suburbs and in better urban neighborhoods as the blacks whose poverty has relegated them to ghetto slums. Moreover, blacks tend to be more concentrated—in neighborhoods that are

80 percent or even 90 percent nonwhite—while other racial and ethnic groups, especially among the second generation of immigrants, tend to live in more mixed neighborhoods. The dominant ethnic group in enclaves like New York's Little Italy rarely accounted for about half the population, said Philip Kasinitz, a professor of sociology at Hunter College in New York.

According to John Logan's analysis of census data, the average white American living in a metropolitan area resides in a neighborhood that is 80 percent white and 7 percent black. That neighborhood was about 5 percentage points less white and 1 percent more black than it was in 1990. The average black metropolitan area resident lives in a neighborhood that is 33 percent white and 51 percent black, or about 5 percentage points fewer blacks than lived there in 1990.

The most integrated metropolitan areas were in the South or in largely military towns. The most segregated were in New York, Newark, Long Island, Detroit, Milwaukee, Chicago, Cleveland, Cincinnati, St. Louis, and Miami.

"The average white person continues to live in a neighborhood that looks very different from those neighborhoods where the average black, Hispanic, and Asian live," Professor Logan concluded. What Logan also found was that America's children (particularly in Northeast and Midwest metropolitan areas) have become more segregated—in part, because the whites who remained or moved into integrated urban neighborhoods were disproportionately childless. "It's a very big problem for white children who may think they're experiencing diversity in the country, but are only getting a taste of it," Logan said. "The problem for minority children is that, on average, they're growing up in neighborhoods where they are the majority, and that's not the world they will live in."

Still, among blacks who live in metropolitan areas, 4 in 10 now live in the suburbs, rather than the central cities. The average white suburbanite now lives in a neighborhood that is 84 percent white, compared to 89 percent white in 1990. In the cities, though, whites typically live in neighborhoods that are 72 percent white. Blacks live in neighborhoods that are 75 percent black. Generally, blacks are more likely to have Asian and Hispanic neighbors than they were in 1990, but not much more likely to have white neighbors.

The Census Bureau's own analysis of racial and ethnic residential segregation found that while blacks were still more segregated than other groups, they were more integrated in 2000 than in 1990 or 1980. "The reduction of African-American residential segregation remained slow, but steady," the bureau concluded. The most common index of segregation is the dissimilarity index, which measures what percentage of a group's population would have to move to evenly distribute its members within a metropolitan area. With 0 signifying complete integration, the dissimilarity index of blacks and non-Hispanic whites in American metropolitan areas declined from 73 in 1980 to 68 in 1990 to 64 in 2000. Examining 220 metropolitan areas where blacks constituted at least 3 percent of the population or 20,000 people in 1980, the bureau determined that residential segregation had declined by all five of its measures. Greater declines were recorded outside the Northeast and in metropolitan areas with fewer than 1 million people. The five most segregated metropolitan areas for blacks in 2000 were Milwaukee-Waukesha, Detroit, Cleveland-Lorian-Elyria, St. Louis, and Newark. Cincinnati, Buffalo-Niagara Falls, and New York were tied for sixth. By the same measurement, the least segregated metropolitan areas for blacks were Orange County, San Jose, Norfolk-Virginia Beach-Newport News, Tampa-St. Petersburg-Clearwater, and San Diego (the latter two pretty much tied with Providence-Fall River-Warwick). The broad pattern seemed to be more segregation in areas in the Northeast and Midwest, which have lost population, and less in the West and South, which have gained population. All five areas with the greatest decrease in residential segregation were in Florida, where population has boomed.

The picture for Hispanics was much more mixed, and, like Asians, probably was driven by two factors: the concentration of new immigrants and the diffusion of older, predominantly white residents. That helps explain why, while they are less segregated than blacks, the degree of Hispanic and Asian segregation remained about the same or increased between 1980 and 2000.

Using demographers' five measures of segregation, the most segregated areas for Hispanics were New York, Providence-Fall River-Warwick, Phoenix-Mesa, Los Angeles-Long Beach, Chicago, and Newark. The least segregated areas were Baltimore, St. Louis, Fort Lauderdale, Nassau-Suffolk, and Detroit. Between 1980 and 2000, Miami became less segregated for Hispanics.

The bureau found that in metropolitan areas, Asian-Americans were most segregated in San Francisco and least segregated on Long Island. The government's analysis concluded: "The more Asians and Pacific Islanders in an area as a percentage of the population, the more they are isolated, and the more they tend to live with one another."

Segregation is a consequence of several factors, including outright racial and ethnic discrimination, economic and social class, and the preferences of living with members of your own ethnic or racial group or, less benignly, the aversion to living with other groups. Discrimination still may be a dominant factor in determining where black, Hispanic, and Asian people live or, more to the point, where they don't live. But income plays a large part as does class, fluency in English, and other less tangible personal preferences that lead to the clustering among recent arrivals. "There's probably some discrimination against Latinos and Asians in the housing markets, but most immigrant groups have, to some degree, clustered when they arrived," said Reynolds Farley, the University of Michigan sociologist. "As they move up the economic

ladder, their clustering goes down." To which John Logan added:
"There are many places now where Mexicans or Guatemalans or
Dominicans or Puerto Ricans have greater disadvantage and perhaps not better prospects in the next twenty years than African-
Americans. There's a social process in place that makes
assimilation possible for them in a way that African-Americans do
not experience. But, particularly among Hispanics, only a relatively small share get the benefit of that."

As in so many other categories of human behavior, residential
segregation is no longer solely a black-white equation. "The conventional notions of integration and segregation need rethinking,"
George Galster, a professor of urban affairs at Wayne State University in Detroit, told Janny Scott of the *New York Times*. "We are
starting to see many more multiracial and ethnic neighborhoods.
And the dynamics of how and why those neighborhoods change
are relatively unknown to social scientists, compared to the dynamics of the traditional white-black transitions." For one thing,
Galster said, integration has progressed more between blacks and
non-blacks than between blacks and whites.

Drawing on earlier research as well as his own analyses, the
Census Bureau's John Iceland concluded that segregation has
been reduced by the influx of immigrants. More and more neighborhoods are multiracial or ethnic, rather than the exclusive domain of one group or another. Between 1970 and 1980 alone, the
number of census tracts that were at least 30 percent each of
blacks, Hispanics, and Asians rose from just under 20 percent to
more than 42 percent. Iceland found that while blacks and
whites have been the most segregated groups—by circumstance
or choice—"both white and African-American segregation decreased over the period, and quite considerably among the latter
group. Both these groups were moderately more evenly distributed across neighborhoods in metropolitan areas in 2000 than in
1980." He found that Hispanic segregation remained about the

same and that levels of Asian segregation increased slightly. Iceland also found that though the larger metropolitan areas are the most segregated, they underwent the greatest decline in segregation. "Greater diversity is associated with lower black segregation," Iceland concluded, which "is also consistent with the hypothesis that Hispanics and Asians and Pacific Islanders may serve as 'buffer' groups between initially white and black neighborhoods, resulting in less segregation between blacks and others." Moreover, he wrote, "It could be that continued high levels of immigration from Asia and Latin America may be increasing segregation even as the native-born of those groups are spreading outward into more integrated communities."

✦   ✦   ✦

In 1913, Wyoming became the 42nd and last state to prohibit interracial marriage—it had already been banned in every state where blacks had surpassed 5 percent of the population. Interracial marriage was still illegal in sixteen states in 1967 when the United States Supreme Court declared those bans unconstitutional. In 1960, when black-white marriages were still illegal in about one in three states, there were 51,000 of them. Since as recently as 1980, the number of black-white couples has more than doubled, from 167,000 to 395,000 in 2002. Of those, 279,000 were a black husband and a white wife; 116,000 were a white husband and a black wife. Although the number has multiplied, interracial marriage is still very much the exception, notwithstanding the rosy pronouncement in 2003 by Professor Randall Kennedy of Harvard Law School that "against the tragic backdrop of American history, the flowering of multiracial intimacy is a profoundly moving and encouraging development."

Overall, the number of interracial marriages and domestic partnerships quadrupled since 1970, from 500,000 to 2 million.

"If you come to a Filipino gathering, they are so diverse,"

Leonora A. G. Dubouzet, a nursing administrator in the Bronx, told Joseph Berger of the *New York Times*. She is married to a Puerto Rican man. A friend, a pediatric instructor at the same hospital, is married to a Chinese man. Sometimes, she said, "we don't know who we are." That's even more challenging for the next generation. They mix easily in multiethnic neighborhoods and, if they ever learned Tagalog, chances are they're in the process of forgetting it. "We're very vulnerable," said Pio Paunon, a Filipino father of two teenagers, who is the nurse manager at Montefiore Hospital in the Bronx and head of the Philippine Nurses Association of New York. "Our kids have nothing to hold on to. We blend in so well with other groups, we forget we're Filipino."

Blending is what Richard Rodriguez writes about in his book *Brown: The Last Discovery of America*: "I write about race in America in hopes of undermining the notion of race in America." Rodriguez celebrates what he calls "the browning of America" and suggests: "Because of Hispanics, Americans are coming to see the United States in terms of latitudinal vector, in terms of south-north, hot-cold; a new way of placing ourselves in the twenty-first century." But more fundamentally, he suggests, "what Latin America might give the United States is a playful notion of race." The bloodlines become diluted and even the markers of race blur. "Only further confusion can save us," Rodriguez concludes.

Further confusion seems inevitable. But will the passions that race and ethnicity engender dissipate as the bureaucratic boundaries, much less the biological ones, blur even further?

In Vallejo, California, one of the nation's most racially balanced cities, residents still typically congregate with members of their own racial or ethnic group. According to the 2000 census, the population of this working-class town of 116,000 was 24 percent black, 24 percent Asian, and 16 percent Hispanic. Its complexion was shaped, in part, by history—Filipinos who served as stewards on U.S. Navy ships settled in the area and blacks were drawn to construction jobs in the Mare Island Shipyard during World War II. Vallejo's ethnic and racial composition was also shaped by the navy's decision to close Mare Island in 1996. Whites, who constituted more than half the city's population in 1990, dropped to 36 percent by 2000. Despite the statistical diversity, each group pretty much goes its own way. Vallejo has a Black Chamber of Commerce, a Hispanic Chamber of Commerce, a Filipino Chamber of Commerce, and the Vallejo Chamber of Commerce, which is dominated by white business executives. The Vallejo chamber's president, Thomas Egidio, explained to Steven Holmes of the *New York Times:* "Every time we try to put ourselves together, we end up fighting with each other, so it was decided that each group would have its own organization." The city not only officially commemorates Juneteenth, celebrating the end of slavery, Cinco de Mayo, and Philippine Independence Day, but also inaugurated a Unity Day a few years ago so that at least one of the holidays would command some fully integrated display of public pageantry.

The new math of race in America has yet to be computed with certainty. When the website for Black Entertainment Television asked, "Does it bother you that Hispanics now outnumber African-Americans in the U.S.?" the response from its audience was torrential, but by no means unanimous. One person complained that "blacks are beginning to experience another wave of racial bias and favoritism not in our favor." Another warned: "Sounds like the same old trick to me. 'Divide and conquer.' Are we really going to let some numbers dictate how we treat one another?"

In 2003, the National Association of Hispanic Automobile Dealers merged with the black-led National Association of Minority Automobile Dealers. "There are some African-Americans that are going to see us as a threat, but a lot see the necessity of using each other," Lou Sobh, chairman of the Hispanic association, told the *New York Times*'s Mireya Navarro. Politically, the record of alliances has been mixed, which is why Hugh Price, the former president of the National Urban League, predicted that "floating coalitions around key issues" are more likely than enduring rainbow coalitions. In 2001, blacks and Hispanics generally supported the mayoral candidacy of Fernando Ferrer, a Democrat who lost his party's primary, but just barely. In Los Angeles, though, Latinos supported Antonio Villaraigosa, the former speaker of the Assembly for mayor, while blacks overwhelmingly voted for James K. Hahn, the white city attorney who won.

The challenge behind the numbers is whether the numerical ascendancy of one group means the decline of the other, whether there is as much natural competition as grounds for alliance—Hispanics generally favor fewer restrictions on immigration; blacks are concerned more immigrants will compete for lower-skilled jobs—and whether the old agenda of shared grievances remains valid given the diversity within each group.

Hispanics outnumber blacks, but fewer of them are citizens eligible to vote. Moreover, it's been hard enough to persuade Hispanics themselves to coalesce. Latinos have a common affinity for the Spanish language, but it's been difficult to identify, much less capitalize on, common ground among Mexicans, Cubans, Puerto Ricans, and newer arrivals from Latin America. "The national Latino organizations take the view that the legacy of the civil rights movement is to redress issues of discrimination, and if you are a person of color, you need to be protected from that as well, even if you just got here yesterday," said Angelo Falcon of the Puerto Rican Legal Defense and Education Fund in New York. "You have people who come here and say, 'I don't know what this Latino and minority stuff is all about. I'm Colombian.'" But if that Colombian winds up in the wrong neighborhood and becomes the target of an insult denigrating Latinos, Falcon said, "all of a sudden you're a minority."

Races Other Than White

Nonwhite percentage of the population in 1900, 1950, and 2000.

0%   10   20   30   76%

1900

1950

2000

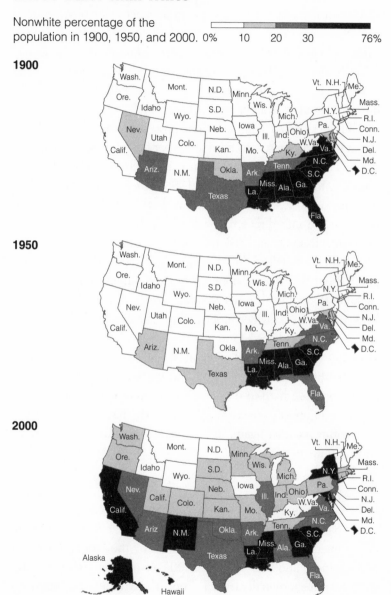

"Whether you're an African-American in the South or a Latino in California, you have the right to advance your own agenda," said Nicolas C. Vaca, a sociologist who has written *The Presumed Alliance: The Unspoken Conflict between Latinos and Blacks and What It Means for America*. "To the extent they can do it cooperatively, great. To the extent they can't they're going to have to work out some kind of strategy to avoid conflict."

Failure to avoid conflict might pose a more serious political threat to black Americans than to Hispanics, who are in the ascendancy. The Washington-based journalist Michael Lind predicted in *The New York Times Magazine* in 1998, "There is not going to be a nonwhite majority in the 21st century. Rather, there is going to be a mostly white mixed-race majority. The only way to stop this is to force all Hispanic and Asian-Americans from now on to marry within their officially defined groups. And that is not going to happen." What is going to happen, Lind concluded, is a variation of Richard Rodriguez's brown theme: "The U.S. population is not likely to be crisply divided among whites, blacks, Hispanics, Asians and American Indians," Lind wrote. "Nor is it likely to be split two ways, between whites and nonwhites. Rather we are more likely to see something more complicated: a white-Asian-Hispanic melting-pot majority—a hard-to-differentiate group of beige Americans— offset by a minority consisting of blacks who have been left out of the melting pot once again." If Lind is right, the American dilemma will continue to bedevil us.

◆   ◆   ◆

If the census is a portrait by numbers, the latest count provides a richer palate than ever before. Today, official racial categories are determined after a great deal of debate by the federal Office of Management and Budget. The 2000 census began with six categories: whites, originally from Europe, the Middle East, or North Africa, which would include those who identified themselves as, among other things, Italian or Arab; black, which describes people who originated in black racial groups of Africa, including African-American, Nigerian, or Haitian; American Indian and Alaska Native, those people who trace their heritage to the original peoples of North and South America, including Central America, and maintain a tribal or community attachment; Asian, or people originally from East Asia, Southeast Asia, or the Indian subcontinent, including Japanese, Vietnamese, and Pakistani; Native Hawaiian and other Pacific Islander, or people from Hawaii, Guam, Samoa, or other Pacific islands; and "some other race" for people who weren't comfortable with the other categories, and which could include those who described themselves as Moroccan or South African or anyone of Hispanic origin, from, among other places, Mexico, Cuba, or Puerto Rico. People who chose more than one of the six categories were automatically placed into a seventh, newly designated "two or more races" category, and 7 million Americans, or 2.4 percent of the population, chose this option. The rate for children was double what it was for adults, which suggests that the proportion will grow as the spectrum expands and our complexion changes and that race might someday diminish as the prism through which Americans define the politics of identity.

Of the 6.8 million Americans who identified themselves as of more than one race, 93 percent listed two and most of those reported "white and some other race" (followed by white and American Indian, white and Asian, and white and black). Between 1990 and 2000 the American Indian population increased by 26 percent to 2.4 million, but if Indians combined with other races are counted, the increase was 110 percent, to 4.1 million. Even the 2.4 million represent ten times the number recorded in 1900. Of that total, about 540,000 were living on reservations. More people identified themselves as American Indians and Alaska Natives—87,200—in New York than in any other city.

About 14 percent of Asians, 5 percent of blacks, 6 percent of Hispanics, and 2.5 percent of whites identified themselves as multiracial. (In all, 8,637 Americans claimed to belong to five races and 823 to all six.)

People who described themselves as white alone (211.5 million) or white combined with some other race (another 5.5 million) accounted for 77.1 percent of the population. Blacks, alone (34.7 million) or combined with one or more other races (an additional 1.8 million), made up 12.9 percent. But while only 3.3 percent of blacks age 18 and over described themselves as combined with one or more races, 8.1 percent under age 18 did, suggesting not only that younger people represent more of a racial and ethnic mosaic but also that they are more willing to acknowledge it.

The implications of so many options are enormous, some incalculable. (In Britain, for instance, 390,000 people, apparently *Star Wars* fans, wrote "Jedi" in response to an option question on religion in 2001—more than the number who identified themselves as Jewish, Buddhist, or Sikh.) "I think the multiple race issue is a tremor in 2000 for what is going to become a political earthquake that is coming down the road," said Kenneth Prewitt, the former census director. "In fifteen to twenty years, I would expect to see about a quarter of the population identifying themselves as multiracial."

The opportunity to combine the six racial categories (white, black, Asian, Native Indian/Native Alaskan, Native Hawaiian/Pacific Islander, and other race) creates sixty-three distinct racial groups. In addition, the census asked separately whether or not people consider themselves Spanish, Hispanic, or Latino—an ethnic category, not a racial one—which doubles the possibilities for self-identification to 126 categories of race and ethnicity. In 2000, nearly half—48 percent—of Hispanics identified themselves as white (down from 52 percent in 1990 and 58 percent in

1980). Most of the rest—42 percent—described themselves as some other race. Only 2 percent of Hispanics identified themselves as black. (Similarly, the vast majority of blacks described themselves as non-Hispanic.) Orlando Patterson, a professor of sociology at Harvard, invokes the 48 percent figure to dispute predictions—dire predictions, to some—that America will be mostly nonwhite by the middle of the twenty-first century. "Even if we view only the non-Hispanic white population, whites remain a robust 69.1 percent of the total population of the nation," Patterson wrote. "If we include Hispanic whites, as we should, whites constitute 75.14 percent of the total population, down by only 5 percent from the 1990 census."

Robert B. Hill, a statistician who has advised the Census Bureau, maintained that "many of those Hispanics who checked white feel they didn't have much of a choice. They didn't want to check black. They're not going to check Asian. But they sure don't see themselves as Anglos." And John Logan argued that self-identification by Hispanics as members of "some other race" was a healthy expression of ethnic pride. "There's a Latino identity that's neither white nor black, and it's a positive identity," Logan said.

"Being Latina implies mixed racial heritage," Patria Rodriguez, the advertising sales director for a women's magazine in New York, and a Hispanic who is often mistaken for Italian, told Mireya Navarro of the *New York Times*. "Why should I have to choose?" Moreover, identifying herself as either white or black suggests associations that she doesn't share. "White means mostly privilege and black means overcoming obstacles, a history of civil rights," she said. "As a Latina, I can't try to claim one of these."

"Ethnicity is a subjective feeling as well as an imposed category," said Harry Pachon of the Tomas Rivera Institute. "If it's imposed, because people make assumptions about you if you are dark-skinned and speak with an accent, then you have no option but to consider yourself Hispanic." Like other immigrant groups,

Hispanics are grappling with how to reconcile acculturation and assimilation. "If there is upward mobility," Pachon said, "that group identity loses its hold."

Which also means that self-identification can carry someone only so far.

Even if Hispanics tried, it's arguable whether white America is ready to identify them the way they identify themselves. "If you're Latino," said Letvia Arza-Goderich, a lawyer in Los Angeles whose family left Cuba in the late 1960s, "you're not white-white in the eyes of white-Americans."

"Is race really something we can choose," asks Russell Thornton, an anthropologist at the University of California at Los Angeles, "or is it chosen for us?" Self-identification has been a census staple for decades, but the 2000 count, which heralded a third century of census taking, carried the practice to a new dimension. "The 2000 census remains silent on whether the people around a given person consider him or her to be white, Asian-American, or something else altogether," Thornton said. "And that relative suspension of social judgment is the 2000 census's greatest innovation; it recognizes who you think you are as an important piece of information."

Fernando White, a twenty-eight-year-old community development worker who lives in Herndon, Virginia, is the son of a Salvadoran mother and a black father and marked Hispanic as his ethnicity but was stumped when it came to race. "I had to think twice about it and call a few friends to see what they put down," he told Eric Schmitt of the *New York Times*. Finally, he chose black and other. His wife, Vanessa, is Panamanian. One of her grandparents is from England, another from Italy, and still other ancestors are black. The Whites have two young daughters. "When you combine what their mother's side brings and what I bring," Fernando White said, "tell me what they get? It's all a personal perception."

"A man who looks African-American is typically going to be

treated as an African-American," said Russell Thornton of UCLA. "That the man may also be Native American, Asian-American, and/or white, and may have designated himself accordingly in the 2000 census may be of no importance to anyone other than himself. Americans are now relatively free to decide who they are, in racial terms, when filling out a census. But that is one of the few times when they are free to do so.

"Race," Thornton said, "is a social, not private, reality."

✦   ✦   ✦

For all the pretense of egalitarianism in the United States, gaps have always developed and, to one degree or another, persisted: between rich and poor, between North and South, between older groups of immigrants and greenhorns, between Americans of European stock and everybody else. None have been more enduring and insidious than the gap between blacks and whites. Today, a record 4 in 5 blacks have high school degrees, more than half of black married couples make more than $50,000, and half of black heads of households own their own homes. At the same time, blacks are disproportionately poor (about 1 in 5 black families, down from nearly 1 in 3 in 1993) and in prison (more than 1 in 10 black men in their late twenties are in state or federal correctional institutions, compared to about 2.4 percent of Hispanics and 1.2 percent of whites). Only 6 in 10 black men at most are in the labor force, fewer than half of black families consist of married couples (compared to more than 8 in 10 among whites), and a little more than 1 in 3 blacks (compared to nearly 6 in 10 whites) are now married.

Non-Hispanic whites who arrived in the New World were the first large minority group in America, but for the last two centuries, that distinction—more often than not, a dubious one—has belonged to the descendants of blacks originally kidnapped from Africa by slave traders. Now blacks have been consigned to an even more ambiguous status as members of the second-largest minority group. But America's changing complexion—the influx of Hispanics, as well as Asians—holds the potential to redefine the black-white paradigm of race in the twenty-first century in one of two ways: the so-called mongrelization that die-hard segregationists warned against will produce a browner multiracial nation where there is less cry over people's hue; or self-selected immigrants and their descendants will overtake American-born blacks economically, socially, and politically, leaving them again, as W. E. B. Du Bois said, "a part of the larger whole and yet apart from it."

Given the ethnic and racial transformation of America, who's a minority anymore? The word typically connoted a relatively small group oppressed to some degree by a white majority, but it's harder to be aggrieved when everyone is a minority. Maybe America will become like Queens County in New York City or the state of California. "California certainly represents what many states are moving toward," Dr. Paul Ong, the director of the Lewis Center for Regional Policy Studies at UCLA, told the *New York Times*'s Todd Purdum. "I don't think most states will end up at the same level of diversity. The truth of the matter is, the rest of the country is going in this direction, but it won't become this, in the same way that New York at the beginning of the last century represented an important trend, but the rest of the country didn't become New York."

When census figures confirmed that non-Hispanic whites had been relegated to a minority in California, a *New York Times* editorial observed: "The same is expected to happen nationwide within the next half-century because of the rapid Hispanic growth. Then everyone will be a minority. Some may differ, but that strikes us as a quintessentially American notion."

It's also a notion that's fraught with social and political implications as more and more cities and states adjust to the new math of what constitutes a minority. "Obviously," said Sonia M. Perez, a

deputy vice president of the National Council of La Raza, a Hispanic advocacy group, "we're moving beyond a black-white paradigm of race."

"In California, we are not using the word *minority* much anymore," said Juelle Taylor Gibbs, a retired professor at Berkeley.

The blurring that Richard Rodriguez writes of, the further
confusion that he craves, is already palpable.

"Asians and Koreans and Vietnamese and Indians and Russians
and Spanish people and everything up there," John Rocker of the
Atlanta Braves complained about New York. "How the hell did they
get into this country?" But, wherever they come from, most want
their children to grow up American. In New York City, the most
popular baby names for Hispanics are Ashley and Christopher; for
Asians, Michelle and Kevin. And in 2000, more than 20 million
Americans, or 7.3 percent—more than the proportion of Arabs,
Dutch, Greek, Polish, Ukrainians, and West Indians combined—
identified their ancestry as "American" or "United States."

9

What We're Worth

The census measures what we're worth mostly by asking how much money we make each year. Chances are, if you are a black, single woman under 24 or over 65, not a citizen, or living in the rural South, you make the least. If you're a married couple, Asian, 45 to 54, a naturalized citizen living in the suburbs of the Northeast, you make the most.

In the 1990s, economic conditions generally improved until the end of the decade when the latest recession struck. Overall, income rose and poverty declined. Adjusted for inflation, median family income rose 9.5 percent to $50,046—crossing the $50,000 threshold for the first time and further redefining what constitutes middle income. For decades, median household income has hewed to the same pattern: blacks make the least, Hispanics make a bit more, non-Hispanic whites make a lot more, and Asians make the most. In 2001, median household income was $29,470 for blacks, $33,565 for Hispanics, $46,305 for non-Hispanic whites, and $53,635 for Asians.

Median income for a foreign-born householder was $36,000,

but that ranged from a low of about $29,000 for newcomers from Latin America to more than $51,000 among immigrants from Asia.

The gap between rich and poor, which has been increasing since the late 1970s, widened, through more slowly, during the 1990s.

In 2000, poverty rates for blacks and women who headed households were the lowest on record and poverty rates dropped for the fourth consecutive year. The pattern varied, though, in part because of an uneven recovery from the recession in the early 1990s and the impact of immigration. "You see how the arithmetic works?" said Gary Burtless, a Brookings Institution economist. "When you have a lot of people entering from the rest of the world, and many of them enter at the lower rungs of the wage distribution, then you can have a situation where everyone is prospering and the median income is declining."

Net worth, which was falling after 1984, began climbing again in 1993, but didn't top the 1984 figure until 2000. Still, during the 1990s ordinary people achieved another economic benchmark with profound social and political implications: for the first time, one way or another—through pension plans or mutual funds or individual stock brokerage accounts—the majority of Americans owned a stake in Wall Street.

✦   ✦   ✦

Of the 281 million Americans counted by the census in 2000, about 140 million were employed civilians over age sixteen. More people were working in service occupations than in production. Nearly as many were employed in management and professional fields as in service, construction, and production. More people prepare and serve food than work in construction trades. More people now work in the information industry than in agriculture.

One measure of how specialized we've become—at least in

collecting statistics—is that the government's Standard Occupational Classification lists 31,000 job titles, a hundred times as many as when the compilation began with 322 titles in 1850 (as in jobs for men; women were included in the survey ten years later). By 1900, factory workers outnumbered farmers. The list was last revised in 1998 to include fifty titles that begin with the word *computer* as well as environmental engineers, preschool teachers, and personal service jobs like massage therapists and concierges.

In 1900, about 6 percent of American women worked outside the home. Most were single and had not yet married. By 1960, about 36 percent of women were in the workforce. The proportion hit 50 percent in 1980. By 2002, the proportion of working women had climbed to 60 percent (the proportion of men working declined, meanwhile, from 80 percent to 74 percent). The census found that, for the first time, families in which both parents work had become a majority, even among married couples with children. Women are more likely to be working if they have a higher education and older children and if they are raising a family by themselves. Half the separated, divorced, and widowed women with infants work full-time, compared to 39 percent of married women and 24 percent of women who had never married.

Women earned less than men in all occupations, but came closest in construction and maintenance. More men drive for a living than perform any other job. More women are secretaries and teachers. Women outnumbered men in professional and related occupations, but only because so many were employed in education and health care.

Since World War II, when women poured into the workforce, they made only about 60 percent of what men earned—mirroring the biblical equation in the book of Leviticus that a woman's life was valued at 30 shekels compared to a man's, which was worth 50. By 1960, more women were graduating from college; nearly half became teachers. By 1990, though, fewer than 1 in 10 chose that career path.

Overall, women working full-time made nearly $77.50 for every $100 that men made in 2002, breaking the previous high of $74 set in 1996. (In Australia, Denmark, and Spain, women make about 90 percent of what men make.) Among full-time workers, 6 percent of women and 16 percent of men earned $75,000 or more. That more women were working (and their median income rose while men's declined) also helped drive up median family income. Among couples who worked full-time, the proportion of wives who made more than their husbands rose, from 26 percent in 1990 to 32 percent in 2002.

In the 1990s, men's median income fell 2.3 percent. Women's rose 7 percent. Manufacturing and technology, industries in which men predominate, have been decimated by layoffs and pay cuts while service jobs in health care and government, which disproportionately employ women, have expanded.

Pay disparities are still pronounced between blacks and whites, but the gap is narrowing, particularly among full-time workers younger than 45. White lawyers earn a median income of $70,000 compared to $59,000 for black lawyers (but black and white paralegals make the same, $32,000). Black architects make a median $45,000, white ones $45,800. Black doctors and surgeons make $77,000 to whites' $106,000. Black teachers make $30,000 to white teachers' $31,300. But black and white painters, pilots, taxi drivers, and restaurant hostesses make the same, and blacks make more than whites as bookkeepers, editors, hotel clerks, machine operators, mail sorters, switchboard operators, tellers, psychologists, bus drivers, jewelers, dental lab technicians, tailors, travel agents, barbers, nurses aides, police officers, and waiters.

Blacks were disproportionately represented in production and transportation, Hispanics in farming, and Asians and non-Hispanic whites in management and professional occupations. About 12.4

Distribution of Wealth

Mean income received by each fifth of households in 2001.

	All Races	White	Black	Hispanic
Highest fifth in income	$145,970	$150,576	$96,569	$107,158
Second highest	$66,839	$69,254	$47,424	$51,459
Middle	$42,629	$44,628	$29,477	$33,624
Second lowest	$25,468	$26,985	$16,820	$20,854
Lowest fifth in income	$10,136	$11,118	$5,951	$8,822

percent of the workforce is foreign-born, and is disproportionately represented in service jobs, as laborers, in precision production and repair occupations, and in farming.

Lower Wages

Percentage of the population earning less than $15,000 a year, adjusted for inflation in 2001 dollars ($7.50 an hour, 2,000 hours a year).

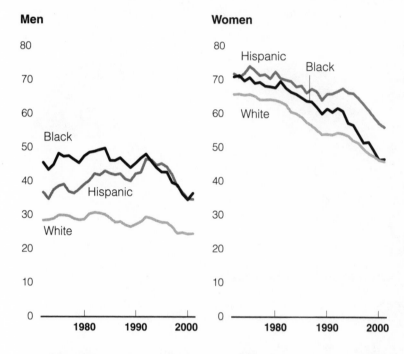

In Nevada, nearly 1 in 4 workers are employed in service jobs, reflecting the dominance of gambling and tourism. Idaho has the highest percentage in farming, but they represent only 2.7 percent of all workers there. In Indiana, more than 1 in 5 people is employed in production, more than any other state.

In Corvallis, Oregon, home to Hewlett Packard and Oregon State University, nearly half the workers are employed in management and professional occupations. In Las Vegas, nearly 27 percent hold service jobs. In Hickory, North Carolina, a hub of furniture manufacturing, more than 1 in 3 workers is employed in production and transportation.

The Growing Black Middle Class

Percentage of black families in each income group, in 2001 dollars.

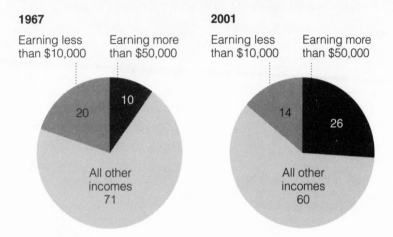

1967

Earning less than $10,000

Earning more than $50,000

20

10

All other incomes
71

2001

Earning less than $10,000

Earning more than $50,000

14

26

All other incomes
60

Black-White Income Gaps

Median income for black households as a percentage of median incomes for white households each year.

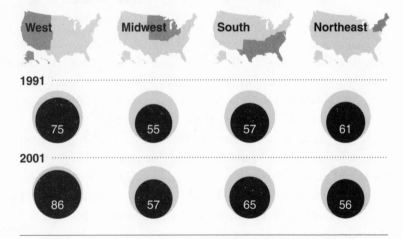

West   Midwest   South   Northeast

1991

75   55   57   61

2001

86   57   65   56

Labor participation rates range from more than 70 percent in Alaska and Minnesota to about 58 percent in Florida and 54 percent in West Virginia. Westminster, Colorado, between Denver and Boulder, claims the highest proportion of people in the labor force—77.7 percent—while Miami has the least—50.3 percent.

◆   ◆   ◆

One downside of having a job as the twenty-first century began: it took longer to get to work.

By 2000, mean travel time to work had stretched to 25.5 minutes, compared to 21.7 in 1980 and 22.4 in 1990. About 1 in 4 workers left home before 7 A.M. Most of the 128 million workers drove—87.9 percent—and the vast majority, fully 3 in 4 commuters, drove alone. Only 12.2 percent carpooled—a smaller proportion than in 1980, when 64.4 percent drove alone and 19.7 percent carpooled, or in 1990, when 73.2 percent drove to work alone and 13.4 percent carpooled. (Not surprisingly, the rate of driving alone was highest in three Detroit suburbs.) Fewer than 1 in 20 commuters took public transportation (2.5 percent bus, 1.5 percent by subway or elevated railroad). Nearly 3 in 10 of all the Americans who use mass transit live in New York City. Nearly 3.8 million Americans said they walked to work, compared to 488,000 who biked, 200,000 who took taxis, 142,000 who commuted by motorcycle, and 44,000 who rode a ferry. Another 3.3 percent, or nearly 4.2 million people, worked at home, more than in decades. In some rural counties, more than 1 in 5 working people work at home.

North Dakotans get to work in a record 16 minutes, on average. New Yorkers take twice that time, longer than residents of any other state. Residents of Elliott County, Kentucky, took longer to get to work than people in any other county—49 minutes. While most of the people who took 40 minutes or more to commute live on the edges of metropolitan areas, New York City residents who live outside Manhattan also spend that much time

Who Has Wheels

Percentage of households with
access to a motor vehicle in 2000.

BY HOME OWNERSHIP

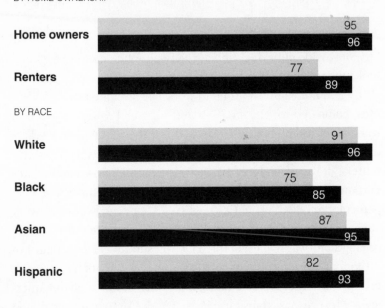

commuting (43.9 minutes from Staten Island), which is consistent with another law of transportation that applies in many places: the higher the rate of public transit ridership, the longer the typical travel time to work. New York City has the highest rate of mass transit ridership in the nation—55 percent, the only city where a majority of workers take public transportation to and from work. In New York, only 31 percent of workers go to work in a car, truck, or van. (In New York, a disproportionate share of the region's workers—about 40 percent—are employed in the central business district.) Among cities, residents of Palmdale, California, north of Los Angeles, had the longest commute, 43 minutes (compared to 40 minutes in New York City). Of the ten cities with the longest travel time to work, seven were in California.

Here's something to ponder the next time you're stuck in traffic on the way to work: congestion is good for you. Anthony Downs, a senior fellow at the Brookings Institution in Washington, argues that traffic is the way society rations finite space. "It is actually performing an important social function," he said. "Nobody believes this but me, but it's true."

◆   ◆   ◆

"Despite all our concerns with self-fulfillment," said Jerome M. Segal, a senior research scholar at the University of Maryland, "most Americans work to earn money, just as their forebears did one hundred years ago." In 1900, people in the nation's cities spent more on food than on anything else. It accounted for about half the budget of low-income families and about a third for wealthier Americans. Today, on average, we spend 15 percent of our household budgets on food (18 percent among the poorest households) and only 9 percent for food prepared at home (which they can earn in a little more than a month of work). In 1900 we spent about 10 to 15 percent on clothing, now only 5 percent. Transportation consumed about 1 or 2 percent of the budget a century ago. Now our cars and trucks and other means of commuting cost 20 percent. "Just to cover that, the average American family works from New Year's Day to March 14," Segal said. "No society in history has worked so much just to be able to get around." But today, the biggest expense is housing. At the beginning of the twentieth century, Americans spent about 25 percent on shelter. Today, renters and home owners spend about 27 percent.

Historically, lenders suggested that 25 percent or even 28 percent was the most home owners should be prudently spending on mortgage payments, taxes, and fuel, but that ceiling has inched upward. The Department of Housing and Urban Development defines homes and apartments as affordable if mortgage payments, rent, taxes, insurance, and utilities account for less than 30 percent of combined household income. In 2000, the census found that 21 percent lacked affordable housing, the same proportion as in 1990. But 11 percent were in even worse shape; their housing costs accounted for 50 percent of income. Among home owners, 15 percent lacked housing that met the official definition of affordability. Among renters, though, who generally have lower incomes, 31 percent lacked housing that was affordable and 18 percent were paying more than half their income for housing costs. Both renters and owners faced the biggest burden in California.

During the late 1990s, a half-dozen California coastal counties had the highest proportion of single-family home owners who spent more than 35 percent of their income on housing, but by the end of the decade Bronx, Brooklyn, and Queens in New York City; Hudson County, New Jersey; and Miami-Dade County topped the list. In the Bronx, more than 30 percent of single-family home owners spent at least 35 percent on mortgage payments, taxes, and fuel.

◆   ◆   ◆

Median household net worth hit $55,000 in 2000 and a home or apartment was the most valuable asset most people owned. More than 67 percent of households owned their home, nearly 86 percent owned a vehicle, and 27 percent had shares in stocks or mutual funds—not counting IRAs or 401(k) accounts.

Among blacks, Asians, and Hispanics who were foreign-born and became naturalized citizens, home ownership rates were higher than for their American-born racial and ethnic counterparts. By 2002, home ownership rates had reached record levels of 70 percent for American-born households, 68 percent for naturalized citizens, and 35 percent for non-citizens.

Black Americans achieved record levels of home ownership,

but when *The New York Times Magazine* drew on marketing surveys to furnish and stock typical kitchens and living rooms to reflect the average American home, those rooms looked very different depending on whether the home was inhabited by a black or a white household. Some of those differences were perfectly logical, attributable to the fact that whites are more likely to live in the suburbs, to earn more, and to own their homes, and that blacks are more likely to live in the South. Some differences seemed inexplicable. Among whites, 63 percent have a garage, 82 percent have a checking account, 72 percent own a cordless phone. The comparable figures for blacks were 34 percent, 58 percent, and 55 percent. Among whites, 40 percent have children and among those 76 percent live with both parents. Among blacks, 51 percent have children and in those households 42 percent live with both parents. Thirty-seven percent of whites but 65 percent of blacks buy refrigerated fruit drinks; 52 percent of whites but 25 percent of blacks buy dessert toppings. Ninety-five percent of both black and white typical households have toilet paper. (What, one wonders, do the other 5 percent use?)

Home ownership accounted for 32.3 percent of Americans' net worth. Stocks and mutual funds made up 15.6 percent, reflecting the market boom in the 1990s. Median home equity hit $59,000 in 2000, but mortgage payments generally increased faster than income.

Median net worth ranged widely, though. It was $7,396 for the lowest fifth of earners and $185,000 for the highest fifth. It was $7,240 for householders younger than 35 and $108,885 for householders 65 and older. It was $7,500 for households headed by a black person and $79,400 for households headed by a non-Hispanic white person. And it ranged from $23,028 for a household headed by a woman to $91,218 for a married-couple household.

Even the highest earners among blacks and Hispanics had accumulated a fraction of the net worth held by their non-Hispanic white counterparts. Among the top one-fifth of earners, net worth was $208,023 for non-Hispanic whites, $65,141 for blacks, and $73,032 for Hispanics.

◆   ◆   ◆

Statistical Policy Directive 14 from the Office of Management and Budget officially defines who's poor and who's not, but just try surviving on the official reassurance that you may be struggling, but you're not living in poverty. The definition counts only money income before taxes and does not include benefits such as public housing, Medicaid, or food stamps. It is updated for inflation but does not take into account geographic differentials. The threshold ranged in 2001 from $8,494 for a single elderly person to $18,022 for a mother with three children to $39,223 for a family of nine. The government also measures depth of poverty. In 2001, more than 13 million people were defined as severely poor, that is, with family incomes less than half the poverty threshold. Another 12 million were labeled near-poor, with incomes between 100 and 125 percent of their threshold. The income deficit—the difference between a family's income and its poverty threshold—averaged $7,231.

According to the official definition, in 2001 the overall poverty rate was 11.7 percent, about half of what it was in 1959. Social Security and Medicare drove the rate down among the elderly, from 35.2 percent in 1959 to 10.1 percent. Among blacks, it was 22.7 percent, less than half the peak of 55.1 in 1959. The rate among Hispanics, 21.4 percent, is about where it was when the government began measuring them in 1972, although the rate dropped considerably from the early 1990s. While about 1 in 5 Hispanics overall live below the poverty level, the rate varies even among Hispanics. In 2001, it ranged from 26.1 percent for Puerto Ricans to 22.8 percent for Mexicans and 16.5 percent for Cubans. Among the foreign-born, the rate was 16.8 percent in 1999; it was highest among foreigners who had lived in the United States less

Barometers of Change

Gain or loss between the 1990 census and the 2000 census.

MEDIAN HOUSEHOLD INCOME Adjusted for inflation

Greatest increase		Greatest decrease	
S.D.	+16.7%	Alaska	−7.3%
Colo.	+16.6	Hawaii	−4.5
Miss.	+15.8	Conn.	−2.8
Utah	+15.5	D.C.	−2.8
Minn.	+13.4	R.I.	−2.7

POVERTY RATE Percentage point change in rate

Greatest increase		Greatest decrease	
Calif.	+2.4%	S.D.	−5.3%
D.C.	+2.3	Miss.	−3.2
Hawaii	+1.7	La.	−2.7
N.Y.	+0.5	Ky.	−2.7
R.I.	+0.4	Ark.	−2.3

PERCENT FOREIGN-BORN Percentage point change in rate

Greatest change		Least change	
Nev.	+7.1%	Me.	−0.1%
Ariz.	+5.2	Mont.	+0.1
N.J.	+5.0	W.Va.	+0.2
Tex.	+4.9	N.D.	+0.4
N.Y.	+4.5	La.	+0.5

than ten years, children, non-citizens, and Mexicans. About 1 in 5 households headed by a foreigner were receiving food stamps, housing assistance, or Medicaid. Fewer than 1 in 10 were receiving cash benefits like welfare or Supplemental Security Insurance, compared to about 1 in 20 native-born households.

By 2002, while welfare overhaul pushed more single mothers into the workforce, nearly 35 million Americans, or 12.4 percent, were living below the poverty level, more than one-third of them children (a disproportionately large share, since children account for about one-fourth of the total population; in 2001 children in poverty included fully 30.2 percent of black children and 28 percent of Hispanic children).

In 2001, the proportion of poor people rose for the first time in eight years and the income of middle-class households dropped for the first time since 1991, when the previous recession ended. The poverty rate rose to 11.7 percent in 2001 from 11.3 percent a year earlier, compared to more than 12 percent every year from 1980 to 1998. The poverty rate is highest—more than 16 percent (down from a recent peak of 22.7 percent in 1993)—among children, especially blacks and Hispanics. Still, that 16 percent was the lowest rate in two decades. "Children are less likely to live in poverty, more likely to have a parent working full-time and more likely to have health insurance," said Duane Alexander, the director of the National Institute of Child Health and Human Development.

The largest numbers of poor people are non-Hispanic whites (about twice as many as blacks or Hispanics), aged 18 to 64, and native-born. The poverty rate for foreign-born naturalized citizens is lower than for native-born Americans. Almost 4 in 10 poor people 16 and older work, but only about 1 in 10 work full-time. Even so, a full-time job paying the minimum wage—which actually declined, when adjusted for inflation, from more than $6 an hour in the 1960s to about $5.25 in 2001—is not sufficient to lift a family out of poverty.

Nearly as many poor people live in the suburbs as in central cities. In fact, the Brookings Institution found that poor people dispersed in the 1990s, with the proportion of poor people who lived in high-poverty neighborhoods—those in which at least 40 percent of the residents were poor—declined from 15 percent to 10 percent. The trend was most pronounced among blacks and in the South and Midwest.

Among places of 100,000 people or more, Naperville, Illinois, just west of Chicago, had the lowest poverty rate, 2.2 percent. Brownsville, Texas, had the highest, 36 percent.

Families in Poverty

Percentage of families with children living below the poverty level.

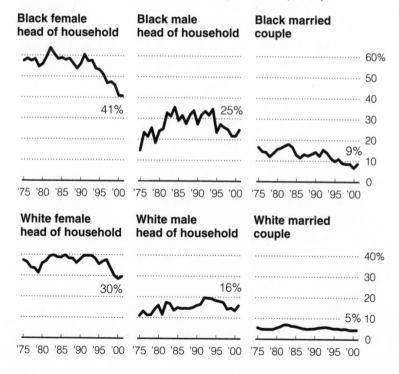

Black female head of household — 41%

Black male head of household — 25%

Black married couple — 9% (60% / 50 / 40 / 30 / 20 / 10 / 0)

White female head of household — 30%

White male head of household — 16%

White married couple — 5% (40% / 30 / 20 / 10 / 0)

'75 '80 '85 '90 '95 '00

A separate study by the Children's Defense Fund, though, found nearly 700,000 black children living in extreme poverty, the highest figure in the two decades since the government began counting that category. "Recent studies show overall poverty has declined among black children, but fail to show the record-breaking increase in extreme poverty among those children," the child welfare advocacy group concluded. Fewer Americans were collecting welfare by the end of the decade, the result of an economic boom that coincided with stricter federal requirements for receiving public assistance.

The government is experimenting with other definitions of poverty, some of them proposed by the National Academy of Sciences, to afford a more realistic measurement of how the other half really lives. Under each of those experimental standards, the poverty rate rose by roughly 1 percentage point and generally painted an even bleaker picture for older Americans (who have higher medical costs), Hispanics (who tend to live in places with higher housing costs), and poor people living in the Northeast.

"The ability to purchase basic goods and services is fundamental," said Sondra Beverly, an assistant professor at the University of Kansas School of Social Welfare, "but a comprehensive definition of economic well-being would also include the ability to fulfill personal and family responsibilities (like caregiving), the ability to reduce risk (through asset accumulation and insurance), and educational and training opportunities to improve long-term economic prospects."

Despite efforts to redefine poverty, it's still subjective. Research for the Heritage Foundation points out that the average American defined as poor by the government has a car, air conditioning, a refrigerator, a stove, a washing machine and dryer, two color televisions, cable or satellite TV service, and more living space than the average person living in Paris or London. But the

Heritage Foundation, which concludes that the two main reasons American children are poor are that "their parents don't work much, and fathers are absent from the home," also observes: "While the majority of poor households do not experience significant material problems, roughly a third do experience at least one problem, such as overcrowding, temporary hunger, or difficulty getting medical care." It is true that few Americans are starving, but many are hungry and certainly malnourished. And does owning a cellular phone or even a color television set automatically make a person non-poor, or has the price of appliances plunged to within nearly everyone's reach? Officially, poor meant earning less than $18,392 in 2003 for a family with one adult and three children. At forty hours a week, fifty-two weeks a year, that means a wage of $8.89 an hour—or $3.74 above the federal minimum wage. As David K. Shipler writes in his 2004 book, *The Working Poor: Invisible in America,* "At the bottom of the working world, millions live in the shadow of prosperity, in the twilight between poverty and well-being."

Virtually no one needs to be sleeping on the sidewalk or the steps of a church, but is the alternative—a public shelter—necessarily safe and sanitary, or even more devastating to self-esteem? Hardly anyone wears rags, or has to, but what's it like not to be able to afford the clothes your friends or classmates or colleagues covet? "A linen shirt, for example, is, strictly speaking, not a necessity of life," Adam Smith wrote in 1776. "The Greeks and Romans lived, I suppose, very comfortably though they had no linen. But in the present times, through the greater part of Europe, a creditable day laborer would be ashamed to appear in public without a linen shirt, the want of which would be supposed to denote that disgraceful degree of poverty which, it is presumed, nobody can well fall into without extreme bad conduct."

◆   ◆   ◆

"Some people thought you lost if you didn't do as well as the next guy," said Martha Farnsworth Riche, a former Census Bureau director. That depended on whom you lived next door to.

Between 1981 and 2000, the wages of ordinary American workers roughly doubled, before inflation. But, as Kevin Phillips has written, over the same period the average compensation among the ten highest-paid chief executive officers of American corporations soared 4,300 percent, from $3.5 million to $154 million. Nine communities reported average per capita income of over $100,000: Rancho Santa Fe, California; Atherton, California; Palm Beach, Florida; Bloomfield Hills, Michigan; Belle Meade, Tennessee; Woodside, California; Indian River Shores, Florida; and North Hills, New York, an enclave of former estates on Long Island only a mile from the Queens border.

Figuring income inequality is subject to lots of economic variables, much less political ones. The official definition of income is limited to money before taxes. But the amount available, and required, also depends on capital gains, employee contributions to health insurance, the value of Medicare and Medicaid, Social Security, veterans' benefits, supplemental security income, unemployment compensation, educational assistance, public assistance, and other government transfers based on need or not. The size of the gap depends, of course, on how it's measured. A census analysis concluded that "government transfers have a greater impact on lowering income inequality than the tax system" and that a standard that includes the impact of non-cash benefits and taxes reduces income inequality by about 8 percent.

In the last two decades, a study by the Center on Budget and Policy Priorities and the Economic Policy Institute concluded that the gap between rich and poor narrowed in only one state—Alaska, where part of the proceeds from oil leases were distributed as dividends to state residents (payments averaged about $8,000 a year to every family). In five other states—Arizona, California, New York,

Ohio, and Wyoming—income among the bottom fifth of house-holds actually fell, after inflation, but soared by double digits among the top fifth. Wall Street and the technology boom inflated incomes in California and New York, in particular; immigrants, meanwhile, filled low-paying jobs. "The year 2000 marked the final year of the longest recovery on record," said Jared Bernstein, an economist at the Economic Policy Institute. "Toward the end of the great '90s boom, we had a very low unemployment and finally saw some long-awaited real gains for families at the bottom of in-come scale. But it failed to reverse the growth of income inequal-ity." The study was conducted by two liberal groups. While conservatives disagree about the significance of the gap or how to mitigate it, they generally concur that it has widened. "I think they probably have a point that there is a growing distance between the top and the bottom, and a lot of that is policy driven," said William Beach, director for data analysis at the Heritage Foundation. Tax policy, he said, encourages the creation of wealth among higher in-come people, but not among poorer people.

On the basis of total money income, 14.6 percent of house-holds made under $10,000 (in 2001 dollars) in 1967 compared to 9 percent of households in 2001. During the same period, the proportion of households making $100,000 or more soared from 2.9 percent to 13.8 percent. Among black households, the pro-portion making under $10,000 decreased from 26.7 percent in 1967 to 17.7 percent in 2001. During the same period, the pro-portion making $100,000 or more rose from 0.8 percent to 5.6 percent. Income disparities may be inflicting a special toll on blacks. For every $1,000 earned by whites, black families make about $606, black men collect $731 and black women make $836 (down from $907 in 1990), although the gap narrows sub-stantially among younger people and recent college graduates in particular.

Statistically, at least, more black women graduating from college and getting higher-paying jobs are having a harder time finding black men with similar socioeconomic credentials. Among blacks, women earn nearly 66 percent of bachelor's and 61 percent of doctoral degrees, compared to 58 percent and 48 percent, respectively, among whites. "Black couples are less likely to marry when women are earning more, creating a hurdle between the formation of cohabitating unions and marriage," Philip N. Cohen, a Census Bureau demographer, has concluded. One consequence may be fewer marriages. Another may be that black women look elsewhere for a mate. "Better educated black women face a real dilemma: do they remain single or do they marry down?" said William Julius Wilson of Harvard. "All the various surveys reveal that people tend to marry within their own social class circles. One outcome could be not intraracial marriages, but more interracial marriages."

In 2001 the lowest fifth of all households received the smallest share of aggregate income ever—3.5 percent—while the top fifth received the most ever—50.1 percent. The second and third quintiles also dropped to their lowest share ever; the fourth quintile hadn't budged. The top 5 percent was collecting 22.4 percent of the income—the most ever recorded.

Edward N. Wolff, an economics professor at New York University, concluded: "Most of the prosperity has gone into the hands of the rich. The top 20 percent did well in the '90s. And even among that group, it's the top 1 percent that made out like bandits."

◆   ◆   ◆

How do Americans define who's rich? They're still very different from the rest of us, but there are more of them today and they are also very different from one another. "Today, wealth is much greater in its diversity," said George Fertitta, an advertising agency executive who specializes in luxury goods. "Unlike twenty years ago, the wealthy person isn't the kind of person you could paint a picture of and say, 'That's exactly who they are.'" In the last twenty years of the twentieth century, the number of households worth at least $1 million almost doubled, to 4.8 million, even after inflation. Of the 130 million families filing tax returns in 2001, the number reporting incomes of at least $200,000 more than doubled, from 1.3 million in 1995 to nearly 3 million in 2001.

Another way of measuring wealth is how much of all income in the United States went to the 400 wealthiest taxpayers. In 1992 their average income was $46.8 million and they accounted for 0.5 percent of all income. In 2000, they earned $174 million on average and accounted for 1.1 percent of all income. Their tax bills also grew, though more slowly, from 1 percent of all taxes in 1992 to 1.6 percent in 2000. (The Internal Revenue Service also reported that in 2000, a record 2,022 Americans with incomes of more than $200,000 paid no income tax at all.)

Two economists, Thomas Piketty and Emmanuel Saez, studied income inequality during much of the twentieth century for the National Bureau of Economic Research. In 2000, average income for the bottom 90 percent was $25,035, or $25 less, adjusted for inflation, than it was in 1970. Not only did the top 10 percent do much better, but the higher the income group, the better they did. David Cay Johnston, a *New York Times* reporter, calculated in his 2003 book, *Perfectly Legal: The Covert Campaign to Rig Our Tax System to Benefit the Super Rich—and Cheat Everybody Else,* just how dramatically the income gap has widened. In 1970, the top one-tenth of a percent of earners made 100 times the average income of all American households. In 2000, the average income of all households was $42,700. The 13,400 households at the very top made an average of $24 million each—or 560 times the average. Put another way, Johnston wrote, "for each dollar of additional income going to each of those in the bottom 99 percent of Americans the richest each averaged an astonishing $7,500." He added: "Applying the National Bureau of

Economic Research report to the incomes reported on tax returns in 2000 produces an astonishing result. The 13,400 top households had slightly more income than the 96 million poorest Americans." Money wasn't trickling down. Defying gravity, Johnston concluded, it was flowing uphill.

In the 1980s, the gap widened, largely because people at the bottom were getting pummeled. In the 1990s boom, inequality grew because the rich got even richer. And many got rich from salaries and stock options. Still, asked to describe themselves, 11 percent of Americans say they are upper income, 2 percent say rich, 59 percent say middle income, and 27 percent say low income or poor.

◆   ◆   ◆

Karl Marx preached that society's have-nots would finally converge with most of the haves into a single class, but it took a Republican to proclaim it. In 1997, Governor George E. Pataki of New York declared, "My plan to save rent control will ensure that every middle-class tenant has the right to remain in their apartment for the rest of their lives if they choose." And how did he define middle class? As any household making up to $175,000 a year. That placed a mere 1 percent of tenants at the mercy of the marketplace, protecting the other 99 percent as full-fledged members of the middle class. If this sounds more like Groucho than Karl, it's because in America the class struggle has meant trying to fit everyone into the middle.

Statistically, the middle can be whatever society decides it is, as long as its borders are equidistant from both extremes. In the American mind or myth, the middle is enormous. It always has been. Typically, when people are asked to choose among lower, middle, and upper in most polls—including surveys taken during the Depression—more than 8 in 10 Americans describe themselves as middle class. That includes 2 in 10 of the people who make less than $15,000 (that's below the poverty line for a family of four) and more than 9 in 10 of those who make over $75,000.

"I'm not a wealthy man," said former House Speaker Newt Gingrich, explaining why, despite his $171,500 salary, he needed a loan from former Senator Bob Dole to pay an Ethics Committee fine, "I'm a middle-class guy." His former congressional colleague, Fred Heineman, Republican of North Carolina, said his combined congressional salary and police pension (as an officer in New York City and the chief in Raleigh) of $183,500 defined him as lower middle class. "When I see someone who is making anywhere from $300,000 to $750,000," Heineman was quoted as saying, "that's middle class."

Profiling seven families, each of whom earns almost the same median American family income of $54,000, *The New York Times Magazine* found stark disparities in standards of living. On the same income, the Duhes in Louisiana could afford two cars and a 19½-foot boat, and pay $425 a month for the mortgage on their three-bedroom ranch home. The Alvarezes live in a $900-a-month, three-bedroom Bronx apartment (with a $2,100 wide-screen TV and entertainment center) but dream of buying a one-family house. The Anhalts in Wisconsin pay $2,475 monthly for the mortgage on their house and farm, $790 in car payments, and are also paying off $420,000 in agricultural loans.

More Americans may be better off today than in the 1950s. Back then, though, most toiled with the expectation that they would wind up better off. If some identified their parents with the blue-collar Kramdens, their own models were the white-collar Cleavers.

"Americans, especially, have blurred strictly economic class boundaries by reason of their hopes, not necessarily their wealth," wrote the historian Loren Baritz. Maybe our expectations are skewed. After all, as Gregg Easterbrook writes in his 2003 book, *The Progress Paradox,* the typical American is much better off today than a half-century ago, but, to the extent that it can be measured, is typically discontented or downright unhappy. Today, almost everybody has a television set; more Americans have two or more cars than have one or none. But it often costs more to get well, go to college (a four-year degree has become a minimal middle-class standard), or buy a house. Definitions of middle-class income depend on variables like the number of wage earners and dependents, the cost of living, whether food stamps are counted and how much wealth has been socked away. It's determined not only by disposable or discretionary income but by how it's spent, which also suggests social class, or to invoke an even more un-American term, status.

"In order to be middle class as our culture is coming to understand the term," Barbara Ehrenreich has written, "one almost has to be rich." What Jefferson viewed as a stabilizing buffer and Tocqueville described as "eager and apprehensive men of small property" has evolved into a mythology of classlessness. "That which in England we call the middle class is in America virtually the nation," Matthew Arnold wrote a century ago. "I never define it by money," says the social historian Paul Fussell, whose 1983 book, *Class,* skewered all but the abject poor. "The middle class is distinguishable more by its earnestness and psychic insecurity than by its middle income." Fussell devised a somewhat facetious "living room scale" to assess social class using various middle-class totems. Begin with a score of 100 and then subtract for items like original paintings by family members (minus four points each) and plastic covers on furniture (minus 6) and add points for others (6 for overflow books stacked on the floor and 3 for each family photograph in a sterling silver frame). Which only goes to show that, as Loren Baritz said, class may be determined less by Marx than by Flaubert.

It's the difference between classlessness and no class at all.

Are We Smarter?

Since 1840, in one form or another, the census has measured Americans' educational attainment. The first questions were about literacy: simply put, Could people over the age of twenty read and write? The answers provided one gauge of the nation's potential labor pool. Intentionally or not, the answers would also be used to argue the impact of immigrants on American culture: the extent to which foreigners were literate, educated, or could even speak English. In 1990, the questionnaire was expanded and in 2000 respondents had sixteen categories to choose from, ranging from no school completed to a doctoral degree. By the beginning of the twenty-first century, Americans were better educated—or, at least, had spent more time in school—than ever before. In 2002, of the more than 180 million Americans over the age of 25, a record 84 percent have graduated from high school. For the first time, more than 1 in 4—fully 27 percent—have a bachelor's degree. Nearly as many had doctorates as the number who said they hadn't completed any formal schooling.

Those figures reflect remarkable progress in the twentieth century, particularly in the second half. In 1940, only 24 percent of Americans 25 and over were high school graduates and 4.6 percent—fewer than 1 in 20—had a college degree. Fewer jobs demanded college or even high school diplomas then, more young people had to help support their families rather than complete high school or go on to college, and fewer opportunities were available to earn a college degree. The GI Bill changed that, offering the opportunity to returning veterans after World War II.

From kindergarten through college and graduate school, about 6.5 million teachers are educating more than 73 million students.

Of the population over age 25, 29 percent have only a high school diploma. But more than half of Americans in that age group—52 percent—have at least attended, if not completed, college. At least 16 percent are college graduates, 14 percent reported going to college for at least a year but not graduating, nearly 6 percent had earned a master's, 2 percent received professional degrees, and 1 percent had a doctorate. While the actual number of high school and college graduates increased in the 1990s, the number who hadn't completed high school actually declined during the decade.

Not surprisingly, educational attainment diverges widely by age. Among Americans in their late forties, 86 percent had at least a high school education, compared with 61 percent of those 75 and older—the age group reporting the lowest level of formal educational achievement. Among people in their early fifties, 13 percent reported having advanced degrees.

Half of all the students attending college today are 25 and over. "The Joe College stereotype—the eighteen- to twenty-two-year-old full-time student in residence on a campus—accounts for only 20 percent of the fifteen million students," says Harold Hodgkinson, the director of the Center for Demographic Policy at the Institute for Educational Leadership in Washington.

Overall, a slightly higher percentage of women 18 and older

have completed high school than men—84 percent compared to 83 percent. But the proportion of men with college degrees is higher—28.5 percent, compared to 25.1 percent of women. However, since 1979 women have outnumbered men among college students (since 1982, more women than men have been awarded bachelor's degrees every year), and they now account for 56 percent of the nation's college students. Among Americans age 25 to 39, more women have completed college than men.

The census found much larger disparities by race and ethnicity. High school graduation rates ranged from 52 percent for Hispanics to 72 percent for blacks, 80 percent for Asians, and nearly 85 percent for non-Hispanic whites. Only 10 percent of Hispanics said they were college graduates compared to 14 percent of blacks, 27 percent of non-Hispanic whites, and 44 percent of Asians.

About 1 in 4 foreign-born adults have bachelor's degrees—the same proportion as the native population—but immigrants lag in other measures of educational achievement. The same proportion, about 1 in 4, had less than a ninth-grade education, compared to 1 in 20 among the American-born population. Among foreign-born people over age 25, high school graduation rates ranged from 34 percent for immigrants from Mexico to 95 percent for newcomers from Africa. Asian immigrants were better educated for the most part than native Americans, with 87 percent having at least a high school diploma, compared to 84 percent of newcomers from Europe, and 50 percent from Latin America. Nearly 49 percent of Asian immigrants had at least a bachelor's degree.

But differences in educational attainment narrowed in the 1990s among regions and the states. States with the lowest proportion of high school graduates in 1990, including Mississippi and Kentucky, generally made the most progress, although they remained at the bottom, with high school graduates accounting for 73 percent and 74 percent, respectively, of their residents

Education's Advances

Percentage of people age 25 and older who had completed each level of schooling.

1940   2000

High school graduate or more

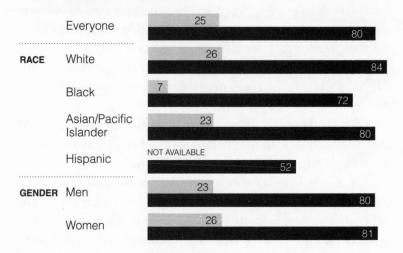

		1940	2000
	Everyone	25	80
RACE	White	26	84
	Black	7	72
	Asian/Pacific Islander	23	80
	Hispanic	NOT AVAILABLE	52
GENDER	Men	23	80
	Women	26	81

Bachelor's degree or higher

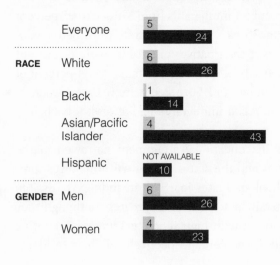

		1940	2000
	Everyone	5	24
RACE	White	6	26
	Black	1	14
	Asian/Pacific Islander	4	43
	Hispanic	NOT AVAILABLE	10
GENDER	Men	6	26
	Women	4	23

over 25. Places with a high percentage of people who hadn't completed high school tended to have a high proportion of Hispanics, poor people, and immigrants. In East Los Angeles, California, more than 66 percent of the people 25 and over don't have a high school diploma.

The proportion with college degrees ranged from less than 15 percent of West Virginia residents to more than 33 percent in Massachusetts, which also led in the share with advanced degrees, more than 13 percent. Not surprisingly, the highest proportion of people with advanced degrees are in university towns, like

America Is Becoming More Educated

Percentage of people in each age group who had obtained each level of education in 2000.

	High school graduate or some college	Bachelor's degree or higher
75 or older	47	13
70–74	51	16
65–69	54	18
60–64	56	20
55–59	57	25
50–54	56	29
45–49	58	29
40–44	60	26
35–39	59	26
30–34	56	28
25–29	56	27

Cambridge, Massachusetts—where 1 in 10 residents over age 25 has a doctorate—as well as in Ann Arbor, Michigan, and Berkeley, California.

◆   ◆   ◆

More than 50 million American children are enrolled in elementary and high schools. Enrollment surpasses the baby-boom peak of the early 1970s—in 1969, the last of the baby boomers swelled enrollment to nearly 52 million—but today's students are much more racially and ethnically diverse than their parents' generation. In 1972, 79 percent were non-Hispanic whites, 14 percent were black, 6 percent were Hispanic, and 1 percent were Asian. According to the latest count, about 64 percent are non-Hispanic whites, 16 percent are black, 15 percent are Hispanic, and 5 percent are Asian. Nearly 1 in 5 speak a foreign language at home—typically, Spanish—and have at least one foreign-born parent.

Among native-born Americans over age 25, a record 87 percent have a high school diploma. While the proportion among the foreign-born—67 percent—is much lower, it ranges among different immigrant groups: from 95 percent among Africans to 84 percent among Asians, 81 percent among Europeans, and 50 percent among Latin Americans.

In 2000, nearly 47 million Americans, or 18 percent, spoke a language other than English at home. That's 15 million more people than in 1990. Most speak Spanish—more than 28 million. The next biggest language category is Chinese, but with only 2 million. More than 1 million Americans each speak German, French, or Italian. In Los Angeles, 59 percent of the people age five and older speak a foreign language at home, mostly Spanish. In New York, 47 percent do. Historically, the language of immigrants has evolved from parents who speak broken English to bilingual children to English-only grandchildren. Notwithstanding the debates over bilingual education and the proliferation of

Spanish-language media, the assimilation to English speaking seems to be progressing more rapidly, in only two generations.

About 1 in 10 American schoolchildren are enrolled in private elementary and high schools. About 1 in 50—or 850,000 students—are schooled at home.

But the vast majority attend taxpayer-supported public school systems, constituted by more than 90,000 elementary and high schools. Many of those systems are increasingly strained by over-crowding and a growing number of students who aren't proficient in English and by higher standards being imposed by federal, state, and local governments.

In Fairfax County, Virginia, just west of Washington, more than 40 percent of the students are members of racial or ethnic minor-ity groups—double the proportion a decade earlier—and many of those are immigrants who, if they are taught English as a second language, cost $2,500 a year more to educate. In California, the backlash against immigrants resulted in a statewide referendum in 1998 in which a majority of voters repudiated bilingual education.

Schooling not only lasts longer, it now starts earlier, too. In 1970, 21 percent of three- and four-year-olds were enrolled in preschool or kindergarten programs. Today, more than 52 percent are. In 1970, 1 in 10 were enrolled in an all-day kindergarten. Now, 6 in 10 are—an increase driven both by the recognition that earlier school-ing can make a huge difference in academic achievement within a few years, and by the needs of working parents for child care.

✦   ✦   ✦

In the 1990s the cost of tuition, room, and board at four-year public colleges and universities soared by 75 percent and by 84 percent at private institutions. By most measures, though, it's still a good investment. Holders of a law, medical, dentistry, or veteri-nary degree will each earn an average of $4.4 million in their life-times, compared to $3.4 million for Ph.D.'s, $2.5 million for

Education's Link to Wages

Median income for full-time, year-round workers 25 and older, by gender and by level of education completed. Adjusted for inflation, in 2001 dollars.

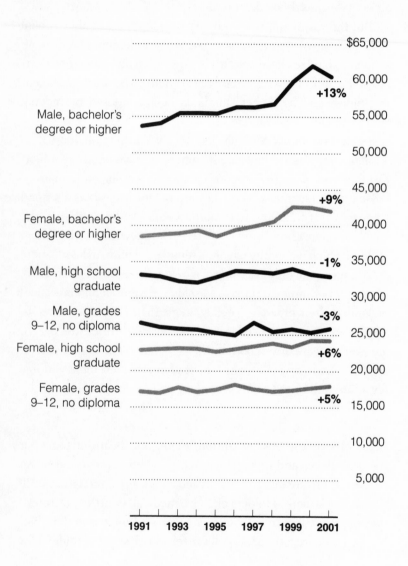

master's degree holders, $2.1 million for graduates with bache-lor's degrees, $1.2 million for those with only high school diplo-mas, and $1 million for high school dropouts. In 1999, average annual earnings ranged from $18,900 for high school dropouts to $25,900 for high school graduates, to $45,400 for college gradu-ates and $99,300 for people with professional degrees.

Even among those with just bachelor's degrees, starting salaries varied widely, from $30,653 for humanities majors to $54,761 for graduates who majored in petroleum engineering.

Earnings also diverge by race and gender. While it is better to be a non-Hispanic white male, the gap is narrowing. A non-Hispanic white college graduate, on average, will earn $1 million more over the course of his career than a non-Hispanic white armed with only a high school diploma. Comparable blacks, Asians, and Hispanics would earn about $700,000 more. Among people with professional degrees, men earn about $2 million more during their careers than women.

Even among recent graduates with bachelor's degrees, men in their late twenties make an average of $41,826 compared to $34,073 for women. And non-Hispanic whites make an average of $43,772 compared to $35,136 for blacks.

Still, says Harold Hodgkinson of the Institute for Educational Leadership, "No other country takes such a diverse group of people and turns them into the middle class. In the 1900s, it worked for Italians, Germans, French, and English-speaking im-migrants. Now it is working for Koreans and the Hmong. It is even working for the black population that is already here. Twenty percent of black households now have a higher income than the average for white households. That's never been true be-fore. The mobility machine is clicking along like it should."

11

Who in the World We Are

By one very rough estimate, about 1 in 20 of all the human beings ever born are alive today. But only 1 in 20 people on the planet are residents of the United States, which is another reminder that it's impossible to define who we are now as a nation or where we're going without hanging America's demographic portrait in a global gallery.

In so many ways that defied expectations, the dimensions and the composition of that gallery expanded dramatically during the twentieth century. Overall, life expectancy for all human beings more than doubled, from less than 30 years to about 67. In developed nations, life expectancy soared from 45 to 73 years. Even in the developing world, life expectancy more than doubled, from 25 years to 61. But in Sub-Saharan Africa, life expectancy is still only 49 years, or about what it was in the United States a century ago. In Mozambique, ravaged by AIDS, someone born today can expect to live only 34 years. (Within five years or so, AIDS may reduce life expectancies in some countries by more than thirty years from what they would have been otherwise.) The contrast in infant mortality is also pronounced. About six infants die for every 1,000 live births in North America and Western Europe, but the rate is five times higher in Latin America and the Caribbean, nearly ten times higher in the Near East and Asia, and fifteen times higher in Sub-Saharan Africa. Japan, the European Union, and Australia are among the nations with lower infant mortality rates than the United States, and the rate among blacks in the United States is only slightly better than among all people in Russia.

In 1900, more than 80 percent of the planet lived under the political hegemony of imperial Europe and North America. Only about three dozen countries could be described as politically independent. And just as the new century dawned, the reach of the United States' manifest destiny extended for the first time beyond the North American continent after the "splendid little war" with Spain. As Warren Zimmerman wrote in his 2002 book, *First Great Triumph,* "In 15 weeks the United States had gained island possessions on both the Atlantic and Pacific sides of its continental mass. It had put under its protection and control more than 10 million people: whites, blacks, Hispanics, Indians, Polynesians, Chinese, Japanese and the poly-ethnic peoples of the Philippine archipelago."

By 2000, the color-coded artificial boundaries that had neatly defined colonialism and marked the violent advance of fascism and communism had been blurred and redefined by the blood of nearly 90 million people who died as direct casualties of twentieth-century wars alone. (In his 1993 book, *Out of Control: Global Turmoil on the Eve of the Twenty-first Century,* Zbigniew Brzezinski estimated that, including those wars, up to 175 million lives were "deliberately extinguished by politically motivated carnage.") In 2000, the United Nations counted more than 190 independent members—more of them democratic, in theory, at least, than ever before, but many struggling with some of the same life-and-death conflicts that defined the last century compounded by the challenges of competition in an increasingly global marketplace.

At the beginning of the nineteenth century, the world's population stood at about one billion, then expanded to 1.6 billion by the start of the twentieth century. Since 1900, the world's population has nearly quadrupled. And in the minute or so it took you to read the first paragraphs of this chapter, global demographic changes have been geometric. If it was an average minute, 245 people were born. Another 107 died. The world's population increased by 138. In just one minute. At that rate, the population is exploding by nearly 8,300 people an hour, 200,000 a day, 6 million every month, and 73 million a year.

The United States is not only different from the world's less developed nations. It's also different from the other developed ones. And some of those differences are accentuating every day.

◆   ◆   ◆

Since well before the first humans migrated from Africa to the other continents, people have been moving from one place to another—some forced out by wars, famines, or oppression, others driven by wanderlust. By 2006, half the world's population is expected to be living in cities.

The United Nations estimates that 175 million people, or about 3 percent of the world's population, live outside the borders of the country in which they were born (of that total, about 9 percent, or 16 million, are considered refugees). That's about double the number thirty years earlier (although about 27 million of the 175 million are attributed to the collapse of the Soviet Union into separate countries). It's no surprise where they go. In the 1990s, the number of migrants in North America grew by 13 million, or 48 percent, and in Europe by 8 million, or 16 percent. Between 1995 and 2000, 12 million migrants, or about 2.3 million per year, left less developed regions for more developed ones. As a result, most migrants live in more developed countries, where they constitute about 1 in

The World Wide Population

Population in 2000.

Share of the world's population

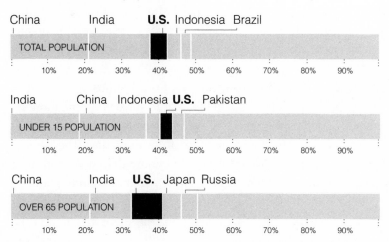

Contribution to world population increase, 1990 to 2000

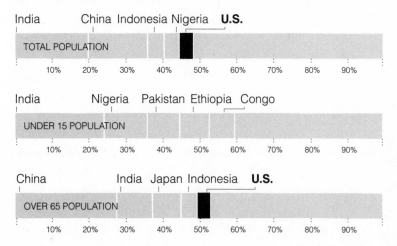

10 people. In developing countries, fewer than 1 in 70 people were born abroad.

In 2000, 60 percent of the population growth in the United States resulted from the greater number of births than deaths, with net immigration accounting for the rest. In contrast, immigration accounted for about two-thirds of the growth among members of the European Union, where demographers project about 650,000 immigrants arriving annually until about 2020. By 2025, the United Nations estimates, those countries would need more than a million immigrants a year to stave off population declines caused by the excess of deaths compared to births.

No country is home to more foreigners than the United States. (Americans, themselves, move more than people in most other countries, but almost exclusively within the United States.) United Nations demographers estimate the foreign-born population of the United States at 35 million—far more than that of the Russian Federation, in second place, with more than 13 million, followed by Germany, Ukraine, France, India, and Canada. None of those countries, though, are among the ten with the highest proportion of immigrants. That list is mostly dominated by Middle Eastern countries—whose petroleum industry attracts immigrants—followed by Switzerland and Australia, where about 1 in 4 people are foreign-born, and Canada, where nearly 1 in 5 are. To one degree or another, most nations—developed and less developed—seek to restrict newcomers. Some need workers, but have trouble accommodating or acculturating them, whether it's the homogeneous Japanese who complain about noisy Vietnamese or the secular French who have banned Muslim headscarves in the public schools. Some countries are also concerned about brain drains of their native-born workers, although a number of them—including Albania, El Salvador, Jamaica, Jordan, and Nicaragua—generate more than 10 percent of their gross domestic product from remittances by expatriates.

Adoptions constitute a tiny fraction of migrants, but they can have a disproportionate impact politically and culturally. More foreign babies are adopted in the United States than in any other country. The number of adoptions nearly doubled in the 1990s, to more than 20,000 by 2000 (or about 1 per every 200 births). China and Russia are each the source of about 25 percent of those adoptions, with most of the rest born in Guatemala, South Korea, and Ukraine (although international treaties to reduce trafficking in children and other abuses could alter that mix, reducing the number available for adoption from Guatemala, Vietnam, and Cambodia and increasing the number from Bolivia, Brazil, and Slovakia). "International adoptees add relatively little to national population growth, but they contribute to the United States' racial and ethnic diversity and links to foreign countries," said Allison Tarmann, an editor with the Population Reference Bureau. "And because many adopted children come from a different racial or ethnic background than their American parents, they contribute to the blurring of racial and ethnic boundaries."

✦   ✦   ✦

Much of the industrialized world is beginning to struggle with a challenge that the eighteenth-century economist Thomas Malthus never envisioned: too few people. In his *Essay on the Principle of Population*, Malthus made two postulations: "First, That food is necessary to the existence of man. Secondly, That the passion between the sexes is necessary and will remain nearly in its present state." More than two hundred years later, human beings still eat and they still engage in sexual intercourse. But the arithmetic increase in food supply and the geometric rise in population that Malthus postulated have not produced all the dire consequences that he preordained. People are still starving, but famines are largely a consequence of failures—deliberate or otherwise—in the means of distribution, not production. True, the competition for markets, for natural resources, for labor and, locally, for living room is as fierce as ever. Billions more people live on the planet today than when Malthus was alive, and passions between the sexes, presumably, haven't cooled. Still, by most estimates, global population growth appears to have slowed and may even peak within a century.

The AIDS pandemic and the decline in fertility rates reduced global population growth in the last few decades, but the number of human beings is still expanding exponentially. The world's population topped 6 billion in 1999. Within the next few decades, deaths will outnumber births in the world's most developed countries, which means that virtually all of the gain in global population will be generated by less developed countries.

According to the Population Reference Bureau, the total fertility rate in more developed countries has fallen to 1.5 children per woman between the ages of 15 and 45—compared to 3.1 in less developed countries, including China. (Without China, the rate in less developed countries rises to 3.5.) The United States became the last industrialized nation whose fertility rate fell below the replacement level of about 2.1 children per woman, dropping from 2.056 to 2.034 in 2001.

Predictions are notoriously suspect, because they are subject to so many variables, some not even imagined. But by one recent prediction in the journal *Nature,* the world's population will stop growing by the beginning of the twenty-second century and will level off at about 8.4 billion. And yet the Census Bureau projects that the world's population will reach nearly 8 billion by as soon as 2025 and grow to 9.3 billion by 2050. Even the United Nations population division, which a decade ago estimated that the world's population would peak at 12 billion, now suggests that because of surprisingly low fertility in some undeveloped nations—including India, Brazil, and Mexico (where the birthrate is about 2 per family compared to 7 as recently as the 1970s)—the world's population could level off at about 9 billion within fifty years.

The contrast in fertility also means that in developed nations, the elderly—those 65 and older—could outnumber youngsters under age 15 by 2025. By most measures, it means that people of working age in those nations will be increasingly hard-pressed to support their younger and elderly populations. Japan personifies this trend. In Japan, the size of the workforce peaked in 1998 and is expected to decline rapidly. Despite having the longest life span among industrialized nations, Japan has such low fertility that the population will start declining as soon as 2006. On the basis of current projections, by 2050 Japan's population will have declined by 30 percent, but will include a million centenarians. By then, about 800,000 more people will die each year than will be born. And by the end of the century, the United Nations estimates, Japan's population will have shrunk from 120 million today to half that.

Over the long term, the potential consequences of a baby bust—like the problems of overpopulation—could be catastrophic. Both are demographic time bombs. A declining population within a nation, and the resulting imbalance in workers and retired people, could bankrupt pension systems, create a shortage of skilled workers, and send health care costs skyrocketing. But, as Malthusians have learned, arithmetic and geometric projections are subject to lots of variables, some unimaginable. Birthrates have been reduced by contraception, by declines in infant and child mortality (making the number of children who live to maturity more predictable), and by gains in education and living standards (meaning a family needs to produce fewer workers to support itself). And just as some countries—Thailand, for one—have markedly reduced birthrates through government programs, others are beginning to grapple with the challenge of reversing population declines, or at least elevating the issue on the national agenda.

In Scotland, the government announced that in 2002, for the fifth consecutive year, more deaths than births were recorded. Not only had the birthrate dropped to the lowest since record keeping began 150 years ago, but Scots are living longer, too. Moreover, Scotland, unlike other countries with declining birthrates, such as Italy and Spain, has not gained population from immigration. Like some counties and states in America's midsection, the government of Scotland is seeking to lure expatriates and legal immigrants. In Glasgow, where the population dropped from one million to 600,000 in forty years, the city has offered thousands of asylum seekers vacant subsidized apartments. "Their children are educated in the local schools, and they are very keen to learn," Charles Gordon, the city council leader, told the *New York Times*'s Lizette Alvarez. "They have helped raise the educational standards. The asylum seekers also have skills the economy needs— medical skills, engineering skills."

Another solution is to encourage childbearing. Scotland is considering tax breaks or subsidies to encourage childbearing, as Sweden and Italy do. (Laviano, near Naples, was planning to pay couples nearly $12,000 for each child born; in 2002, only four babies were born in the town, whose population has shrunk from 3,000 in 1970 to 1,600.)

The government of Singapore, where the birthrate dipped to 1.4 in 2002, ingeniously applied its experience in social engineering to the latest challenge, which one sex consultant, Dr. Wei Siang Yu, blames on the population density and the highly competitive work ethic. "You're not supposed to be soft," he was quoted as saying. "Everything is supposed to be regimented. Family ties are very strong, and most young people move out only when they get married. So how am I going to have sex? How am I going to bring a girl home?" Singapore offers parents bonuses for having more than one child and also sponsors a state-run dating service, the Social Development Unit, which publishes an eight-page dating primer, "When Boy Meets Girl! The Chemistry Guide." It offers helpful hints, among them: "Smiling is a great way to break the ice, but don't grin

like a Cheshire cat the whole time." And: "A date is very similar to a
job interview. You have to sell yourself. People are drawn to good
listeners. But don't just sit there passively; engage whomever you
are with." After births fell to a fourteen-year low in 2002, the government also began a "Romancing Singapore" campaign of dances,
concerts, and drive-in movies to coincide with Valentine's Day and
to put young people "in the right mood for love." So far, there's little
proof that encouraging romance, Singapore-style, has contributed
to higher birthrates.

Still, there is evidence that government policy can affect fertility. In Sweden, the declining fertility rate reversed in the 1980s
after working women were granted paid maternity leave and leave
with full salary if they gave birth to a second child within two
years. (The United States is second only to the Scandinavian
countries in the proportion of women in the labor force.) In Europe, romance and even fertility seem to be less directly con-
nected to marriage. Unwed parents accounted for more than 6 in
10 births in Iceland, half the births in Norway, about 4 in 10 in
Britain and France, about 3 in 10 in Ireland (about the same proportion as in the United States), and even 1 in 10 in Italy. In
Britain, Alastair Campell, who was Prime Minister Tony Blair's
chief spokesman, has three children with his companion, who
also happens to be the top aide to Blair's wife. In Norway, Marit
Arnstad, an unmarried member of Parliament, became pregnant
while serving as oil minister, and is raising her son on her own.
Norway's crown prince, Haakon, lived with a single mother and
her toddler before marrying her. Marriage isn't dead by any means,
but government policies that provide equal benefits and rights to
all children, regardless of whether their parents are or ever were
married, and social mores seem to have replaced romance with
unadulterated pragmatism. Some people eventually marry, but
often for practical reasons, to ensure inheritance and other legal
rights or benefits for a surviving live-in partner or because one

partner is being transferred to work in another country and only a spouse gets to accompany the partner for free. Even when couples never marry, many explain that this decision is not a reflection on their commitment to parenting. In contrast to the United States, European governments apparently agree. "They've taken the marital status out of it and focused on the children," said Kathleen Kiernan, a professor of social policy and demography at the London School of Economics.

◆   ◆   ◆

In Japan, demographers warn that unless more women and immigrants are integrated into the labor force, the nation will be faced with a scarcity of workers and the potential collapse of its pension system. Already, immigrants—illegal and legal—are finding jobs, but the nation's rigid social and workplace structure and the lack of English speakers, particularly in the university system, has hampered Japan's ability to absorb enough newcomers to sustain the economy. The city of Himeji, about 250 miles west of Tokyo, embodies that insularity. Take Akio Nakashima and his wife, Yoshie, Vietnamese immigrants who arrived twenty-one years ago as boat people, but who today might be indistinguishable in a crowd of Japanese. They adopted Japanese names. Their two children speak perfect Japanese. But they worry about whether the children will be accepted. "As far as my life goes, it doesn't matter if I am Vietnamese or Japanese," Akio Nakashima, an engineer at a tire factory, told Howard French of the *New York Times*. "My biggest worry is prejudice and discrimination against my children. We pay the same taxes as anyone else, but will our children be able to work for a big company, or get jobs as civil servants?" Only about 1,000 Vietnamese live in Himeji, many of them workers in nearby leather factories, and even that relatively modest influx has created friction in some of the city's five-story apartment complexes over complaints that the foreigners park illegally, disobey strict regulations about garbage dumping, and disturb their neighbors with loud karaoke sing-alongs late at night. "Integration is easy to call for, but it is very difficult to achieve," said Masahiro Iba, an official in the public housing department. "You just can tell people that they must adjust to others." In Himeji's housing complexes, the solution was to impose an informal quota of 10 percent on the number of Vietnamese in any one building. "We are not refusing to take foreigners," explained Fusae Hirata, a widower who heads the complex's elderly residents' association. "We've all got the same red blood, and as long as we can communicate, things will be fine."

"We have already reached the point where the Japanese economy cannot function without foreign workers," said Mioko Honda of the Union of Migrant Workers. "The construction companies use Thais and Filipinos by day, because they are inconspicuous, and Africans and others are used at night or in factory work." Still, the United Nations estimates that to survive economically, Japan would need to admit 17 million foreign workers by 2050. Other projections place the demand for new immigrants at 400,000 a year. Admitting so many foreigners would amount to 18 percent of the population in a nation where immigrants now account for only 1 percent. "The kind of figures the demographers talk about are unimaginable for Japan," said Hiroshi Komai, a population expert at Tsukuba University. "In a quarter-century we have only absorbed one million immigrants."

◆   ◆   ◆

The world's elderly population is also growing by another 800,000 to 1 million people each month. Aging isn't a phenomenon limited to developed nations. Developing countries, which now produce about 99 percent of the world's population growth, also account for more than 75 percent of the net gain of older people.

"The changes that are going on are not paralleled in any century before the twentieth century," said Joseph Chamie, who directs the United Nations population division. "We will see this trend accelerating in the twenty-first century."

In 1950, only 8 percent of the world's population was older than sixty. By 2000, the number had inched up to about 10 percent. By 2050, it is projected to more than double, to 21 percent—including 1 in 5 people in poor countries and fully 1 in 3 in developed countries. By that year, according to United Nations estimates, the number of older people will exceed the number of younger ones for the first time. The pace of change is astounding. In France, the elderly rose from 7 to 14 percent of the population over the course of a century. China is expected to experience a comparable increase between 2000 and 2027.

The proportion of young and old people living in various countries diverges dramatically. In the Congo, more than 48 percent of the population is under 15. In Yemen, that figure is 47 percent. In Italy, Greece, and Japan, only 14 percent of the population is younger than 15. In Italy and Japan, more than 18 percent of the population is 65 and older. In Benin, Burundi, Niger, Saudi Arabia, and Sudan, less than 3 percent of the proportion is elderly.

The United States and other developed countries account for 1 in 5 people in the world, but 2 in 5 of the elderly. That means more than half the world's elderly live in developing countries. The proportion is expected to rise to more than 7 in 10 by 2030. In Sub-Saharan Africa, the elderly's share of the population is expected to rise only slightly by 2015, but the number of elderly is projected to soar by 50 percent, from 19 million to nearly 29 million.

But though America's population is older than the world average, immigration, which also helped produce a higher fertility rate, has also kept it younger than most other developed countries. It ranks 41st in the proportion of people over 65. Still, 19.1 percent of the world's children under five live in India; the United States ranks sixth, with 3.1 percent of the world's children.

Japan has the highest life expectancy at birth, 81 years (84 for females), followed by Singapore, Australia, Canada, Italy, Iceland, Sweden, and Switzerland. Life expectancy in most other developed countries, including the United States, ranges a little lower, from 76 to 78 years. The number of elderly in any country, though, is a consequence of two factors: longevity and the size of the total population. More than 1 in 3 people 80 and older live in just three countries: China, with 11.5 million; the United States, with 9.2 million; and India, with 6.2 million. People over 80 are the fastest-growing age group. By 2050, it's projected that their ranks worldwide will swell from about 70 million now to 350 million. In Japan, within twenty-five years nearly 40 percent of all the elderly are expected to be over 80.

In 2000, the median age in the world ranged from about 17 in Malawi to 41 in Japan. In Europe, the median age is expected to rise from about 37 to more than 52 by 2050 and 1 in 3 Germans and 1 in 4 Austrians are expected to be older than 60 as early as 2015. (More than six decades after World War II, the elderly populations of some countries are still affected by the toll; women are disproportionately represented among the oldest of the elderly in Russia and Germany, where they account for 80 and 74 percent of the population, respectively.)

In 2000, Italy succeeded Sweden as the world's oldest nation. Fully 18 percent of Italians—nearly 1 in 5—are 65 or older. In the 1990s, public pensions consumed 15 percent of Italy's gross domestic product, compared to about 7.2 percent in the United States. And in 2003, for the first time, the number of Britons 60 and older outnumbered those 16 and younger. In Austria, on the outskirts of Salzburg, Europe's first supermarket designed for shoppers over the age of 50 opened in 2003. It has bigger labels, wider aisles, nonskid floors, and plenty of seats. In America, the total number of children and retired people compared to the combined working-age population is called the dependency ratio. United Nations demographers call the difference between the pool of people between 15 and 64 and the retirees that, collectively, those people will have to sustain the "potential support ratio." In 1950, that ratio was estimated to have been 12 to 1. In 2000, it had diminished to 9 to 1. By 2050, the ratio of potential workers versus retirees is projected to plummet to only 4 to 1.

Marking his sixty-fourth birthday in 2002, UN Secretary-General Kofi Annan quoted the Beatles: "Will you still need me, will you still feed me, when I'm sixty-four?"

"I trust," he added, "the answer is yes."

◆ ◆ ◆

For most of the twentieth century, America was the fourth most populous nation on earth, and qualified for third place in 1991 only when the Soviet Union atomized. But if those numbers seem to minimize America's numerical might, consider this: since 1900, the United States swelled by more than 200 million people, which is more than the current population of every other country in the world, except for China, India, and Indonesia. That 200 million consists of two parts, both of which distinguish the United States from much of the rest of the developed world: the figure represents the difference between 330 million births and 165 million deaths; and it includes a net gain of 40 million people through immigration. Since 1950 alone, the population of the United States doubled. In the 1990s, the rate of population growth in the United States increased for the first time since the 1950s and the actual numerical increase was the greatest of any decade. The growth rate of 13 percent was five times the average increase in all the other developed countries—a dozen of which (in Eastern Europe and the former Soviet Union) actually lost population. In fact, during the last decade just five countries generated half the world's population growth: India, China, Indonesia, Nigeria, and the United States (at widely divergent rates, however, ranging from 33 percent in Nigeria, 19 percent in Indonesia, and 13 percent in the United States). The only developed nations that grew at even close to the same rate as the United States in the 1990s were two with much smaller populations, Australia and Canada.

But size is both a consequence and a symptom of other demographic forces. A country's growth rate and the ratio between its older and younger populations, among other measures, help to explain where it's going and the challenges it faces and poses to the rest of the world in getting there. India has four times the population of the United States, but fewer people 80 and older. Nigeria has half the population of the United States, but more children younger than five.

Considering all the growth in the United States, the nation is relatively uncrowded. America's population density more than tripled in the twentieth century, from 26 people per square mile in 1900 to 80 in 2000. That's well below the world's overall density of 120 people per square mile, though. Among the ten most populous nations, seven have much greater density than the United States (only Russia and Brazil also have a density of less than 100 per square mile). Density differs greatly all over the globe, which is one reason overpopulation is largely still a local problem. It ranges from about six people per square mile in Namibia and seven in Iceland up to 2,624 in Bangladesh and 70,868 in Macau.

◆   ◆   ◆

Since 1750, according to the best estimates, Asia peaked with its highest proportion of the world's population in 1800, Europe in 1900, and North America in 1950. The share living in Latin

America and the Caribbean have been rising steadily, and Africa's proportion has been climbing since about 1900.

During the entire twentieth century, China and India ranked first and second in population. Since 1950, Germany, Britain, and Italy were bumped from the top ten (by Pakistan, Bangladesh, and Nigeria) and Russia and Japan declined in rank (while Indonesia and Brazil advanced). France bounced from 12th to 20th, Poland from 19th to 31st, Spain from 17th to 29th.

America's share of the world's population declined from 6 percent in 1950 to about 4.5 percent in 2000, but the population of all developed countries shrank more sharply, from nearly 1 in 3 people in 1950 to fewer than 1 in 5. (Also, population aside, America predominates in supplying the rest of the world with, among other commodities, wheat, corn, and cigarettes; in turn, the United States is the most visited destination by foreign tourists, more than double the number of the runner-up, Spain.)

In 1900, six of the world's ten largest cities were in Europe, including the biggest, London, and also Paris, Berlin, Vienna, St. Petersburg, and Manchester. Europe accounted for 25 percent of the world's population, Africa 4.5 percent, and Latin America 3 percent. By 2000, Europe had declined to under 14 percent of the planet's population, Africa had more than doubled to 10 percent, and Latin America and the Caribbean nearly tripled to 8 percent. Asia decreased slightly, from 60 percent to 54 percent, and North America remained about the same, at 5 percent.

By 2000, Europe accounted for fewer than 1 in 8 of the more than 6 billion people on earth, and not one of the top ten cities (Mumbai, the former Bombay, is now the largest, followed by Buenos Aires, Karachi, Manila, and Delhi).

Growth of big cities has been one of the most dominant demographic trends of the twentieth century. In 1900, about 14 percent of the world's population lived in cities. Only twelve cities had a million or more people. Even by 1950, the proportion living in cities was below 20 percent. Today, for the first time, about half the people in the world live in cities, including 3 in 4 in more developed nations (85 percent of the people in Australia and New Zealand) and 4 in 10 in less developed nations (only 15 percent in Papua New Guinea). The Population Reference Bureau estimates that over 400 cities have more than a million inhabitants. By 2007, the United Nations says, a majority of the world's population will live in cities.

By 2050, the Population Reference Bureau estimates, the population of Middle Africa will soar by almost 200 percent, and West Africa by nearly 150 percent. In southern Africa, the population is projected to decline by about 22 percent—largely as the result of AIDS. In Asia, the western part of the continent is expected to grow by 105 percent, but the eastern part, including China, is projected to expand by only 5 percent. (Even in India's southern states, economic prosperity and the empowerment of women have reduced population growth to only the level required for the natural replacement of the population, or about 2.1 births per woman.) Growth rates are projected at 60 percent in Central America, 36 percent in the Caribbean, and 42 percent in South America. In 1950, Western Europe (which the Census Bureau defines as the non-communist nations during the Cold War) had twice as many people as the United States. And as recently as the late 1980s and early 1990s, more immigrants were settling in Europe than in the United States. But that pattern reversed, dramatically, by the mid-1990s. Also in the 1980s fertility rates began to diverge (possibly because European women, too, have been postponing childbirth). In the 1990s, while the population of the United States grew by 13 percent, the rest of the world's more developed countries grew by 2.5 percent combined.

By 2025, the population of the United States is projected to grow by about 23 percent. The rest of the more developed countries combined are expected to shrink by about 1 percent.

What that means is that by 2040 Americans may outnumber western Europeans. And by midcentury, according to the demographer William Frey, when the median age creeps up less than one year to 36.2 in the United States, it will rocket to 52.7 in Europe. "The contrast between youthful, exuberant, multicolored America and aging, decrepit, inward-looking Europe goes back almost to the foundation of the United States," *The Economist* noted, adding ruefully: "If Europeans are unwilling to spend what is needed to be full military partners of America now, when 65-year-olds amount to 30 percent of the working-age population, they will be even less likely to do more in 2050, when the proportion of old people will have doubled. In short, the long-term logic of demography seems likely to entrench America's power and to widen existing trans-Atlantic rifts."

12

Where We're Going

When the twentieth century began, H. G. Wells warned that humankind was racing between "education and catastrophe." What Wells meant, Paul Kennedy, the Yale history professor, recently recalled, was that "an explosion of knowledge, generated by the Enlightenment, and an explosion in new devices and machines, generated by the scientific and industrial revolutions, had combined to give Homo sapiens the capacity to transform his environment."

Wells was right. At the beginning of what Henry Luce would proclaim as the American Century, Senator Albert Beveridge outlined his vision of its mission: "God has not been preparing the English-speaking and Teutonic peoples for a thousand years for nothing but vain and idle self-contemplation and self-admiration. No! He has made us the master organizers of the world to establish system where chaos reigned." A chaotic world war followed, one that pitted the English-speaking and Teutonic peoples against each other, followed by a fragile peace that briefly codified another American vision, this one Woodrow Wilson's, of national self-determination. Even Wilson's secretary of state, Robert Lansing, cautioned: "The phrase is simply loaded with dynamite. It will raise hopes which can never be realized. It will, I fear, cost thousands of lives."

The twentieth century spanned the telegraph to the Internet, the cavalry to an entire catalogue of weapons of mass destruction, the single-engine biplane to the space shuttle, the more than doubling of average human life spans, the nearly quadrupling of the world's population, the decline of colonialism and the rise and fall of communism, and the ascendancy of isolationism, internationalism, and Islam. The race that Wells forecast cost more lives and saved more lives in the twentieth century than even Wells would have imagined.

What does the twenty-first century have in store?

Prophesizing the direction, much less the destination, for America and the rest of the world in the next hundred years is even more daunting. We know that in 2011 the first American baby boomers will turn 65, and that Halley's comet is due to intersect Earth's orbit in 2061. We've been offered a variety of prophetic visions, from the cinematic future in Hill Valley that Marty McFly and Doc Brown go back to in 2015, Isaac Newton's prediction that the apocalypse will occur in 2060, and Arthur C. Clarke's premillennial forecast that humans would be cloned in 2004 (pretty close), that the accidental detonation of a nuclear bomb would devastate a Third World city in 2009, that humans would land on Mars in 2021, and that nanotechnology would enable scientists to build a "Universal Replicator" in 2040 that could re-create any object—from diamonds to gourmet meals—from raw materials and the requisite information matrix.

We also know, or think we do, what to expect in the decades ahead by extrapolating from existing data, by placing a pencil or cursor on the point labeled with today's date and following current trend lines to their logical conclusion. Except that logic doesn't necessarily prevail or even apply all the time. Sometimes, a different, unpredictable logic imposes itself—the invention of a universal replicator that redefines the debate over sustainability and the adequacy of the food supply; or a vaccine that cures or prevents AIDS; or the outbreak of new diseases that afflict the elderly and reshape our assumptions about the world's aging population; or a medical breakthrough that promises to extend human survival indefinitely, or at least well beyond the seemingly arbitrary ceiling of 122 years; or the commercialization of space travel and the colonization of other worlds, which could upend our projections about population growth and migration on this planet—all these possibilities would send those comforting or alarming trend lines zigging and zagging into uncharted territory.

Sometimes simple extrapolation doesn't work because it fails to take into account obvious real world variables.

John McCarthy, professor emeritus of computer science at Stanford, facetiously suggests that current trends in fertility should challenge theologians to somehow reconcile the religious beliefs of Mormons and Hasidic Jews. "If we project these differential fertility trends over the next century," he wrote, "then we should imagine the Mormons expanding east from Utah to meet the Hasidic Jews expanding west from Brooklyn somewhere in Indiana at the end of the present century." Similarly, D. A. Coleman of Oxford concluded that maintaining the current ratio of working-age people to support the dependent population of children and elderly in Korea "would require the entire population of the world to live there by 2050." Moreover, Joseph A. McFalls Jr. of the Population Reference Bureau points out that if humans continue reproducing at current rates, "world population would rocket to 12 billion by 2050, 24 billion by 2100, and so on. Humanity would outweigh the Earth and then the solar system in a remarkably short period of time if the present growth continued indefinitely."

◆　　◆　　◆

The census and other surveys give us a pretty good idea of who we are now.

Americans today are better educated than ever—college graduates outnumber high school dropouts. We've got higher incomes. Almost all Americans have telephones and televisions and more own their own homes than ever before, but many still have trouble affording housing, health care, and higher education. Fewer of us work in factories—only about 1 in 5 men. Fewer still—about 1 in 50—have jobs related to farming. The nation's biggest industry, according to the census classification, is education, health, and social services. More of us were born abroad than at any time in our history, more are living in sprawling suburbs, and more are living longer and living alone.

On the basis of who we are now, we can make some educated guesses about where we're going.

We're getting bigger. Not just in girth, but in numbers. Nobody can be certain when, or if, the global population will ever stop growing, but while apocalyptic visions of mass starvation and competition for living space have largely been averted, virtually no projection suggests that a leveling off will occur before the middle of this century, at the very earliest. Given the commercial incentives for developing appetizing and healthful synthetic food, it's a good guess that waists might shrink before the overall population does.

We're getting older. Gains in life expectancy in developed nations in particular mean the overall population is aging. But in the less developed world, which will also have to come to grips with an older population, dependent children will continue to outnumber the dependent elderly. In the United States, the number of elderly will begin ballooning in less than a decade, when the first baby boomers turn 65. The fastest-growing group on the planet is people over 80.

We're getting darker. It's arguable whether widespread intermarriage between blacks and whites, as Professor Randall Kennedy of Harvard hopes, or the surge in immigrants and future generations of Hispanics, as Gregory Rodriguez of the New America Foundation envisions, will obliterate color lines in America and create a new multiracial minority. There's no question that the United States is growing more and more ethnically and racially diverse, attracting record numbers of foreigners from a record number of places. Someday, those flesh-colored crayons may be brown. Driven by a demand for workers, even more homogeneous countries in Europe and Asia are opening their doors a crack to immigrants, creating tensions that may lead to conflict in the future.

We're exporting jobs, but creating others. Not only factory jobs are moving overseas. So are white-collar jobs. In India, radiologists are reading X rays taken in America, and even journalists are covering business stories long distance. But there will still be plenty of jobs to fill at home, in addition to lower-paying service jobs in retail and food service industries. Projections through 2012 suggest a greater demand for, among other jobs, software engineers, network systems and data communications analysts, registered nurses, and college teachers.

We're still redefining the family. It's still not Ozzy Osbourne, but it's not Ozzie and Harriet either. Because Americans are marrying later and living longer, more young adults and older individuals are living alone. Fewer people are marrying, fewer marriages are permanent, fewer couples are producing children. The next edition of *The Oxford English Dictionary* will define marriage, ambiguously and nonjudgmentally, as "the legal or religious union of two people"—not specifying even that they be of different sexes. The definition of family in *The American Heritage Dictionary* has evolved in a decade from society's fundamental social group "typically consisting of a man and woman and their offspring" to one "typically consisting of one or two parents and their children."

+   +   +

Officially, the world's population topped six billion in 1999. Demographers project that it will grow a little more than 1 percent this year, which means that the population of the planet is swelling right now by about 200,000 a day, or between 70 million and 80 million a year. That's roughly the equivalent of adding the entire population of Egypt or Turkey, more than all the people in Britain, France, or Italy, and about three times the population of Iraq or Saudi Arabia. According to the latest projections, the world's population will hit 7 billion in around 2013, 8 billion in 2028, and 9 billion in 2048.

But the pace of growth regionally and in individual nations diverges greatly and those gaps appear likely to endure. Nearly all the population growth is projected to take place in less developed countries in Africa, Asia, and Latin America. (Less developed countries accounted for about 68 percent of the world's population in 1950, about 81 percent in 2003, and will constitute an estimated 86 percent by 2050.) Nearly all of the growth is expected to be in cities. Demographers at the United Nations estimate that Nigerians will outnumber Japanese in about a decade and Pakistanis will outnumber Brazilians. Over the next twenty years, Europe and Japan will actually lose population; the United States, Brazil, the Congo, and Bangladesh will each gain about 50 million people; China will swell by 200 million, India by more than 300 million, Pakistan by 100 million, Indonesia by 60 million, and Sub-Saharan Africa by 455 million. By the middle of the twenty-first century, India will surpass China as the most populous country.

The United States is expected to remain the world's third most populous nation.

As of January 1, 2004, the population was calculated at

292,287,454—up 2.8 million, or 1 percent, from one year earlier. At that rate, the United States began the new year with one birth every 8 seconds, one death every 13 seconds, and a net gain of one immigrant every 25 seconds. That produced an increase in the total population of about one person every 12 seconds. Beginning around 2011, the annual number of births in the United States is projected to be the highest ever.

Right now, the nation is adding double the number of people each decade as it did a century ago. According to the bureau's middle-level projections, the number of Americans will rise to 300 million by 2007, 338 million in 2025, 404 million in 2050, and 571 million by the end of the twenty-first century.

Nearly 800 people are moving into the Los Angeles-Long Beach metropolitan area every day—nearly one-third of them immigrants. That rate of growth swelled the area's population in 2001 alone by more than 285,000, or a larger population than all but sixty American cities. At the same time, on average about 640 people moved each day to metropolitan Chicago, 609 to New York, 557 to Riverside-San Bernardino, and 502 to Atlanta. Los Angeles registered the largest number of migrants from abroad (more than 91,000 for the year) and Miami the highest percentage of foreigners (59 percent) among all newcomers to metropolitan areas.

By 2020 Florida is expected to displace New York as the third most populous state.

✦   ✦   ✦

Forget about those red states and blue states and even the traditional divisions among urban, suburban, and rural America. William Frey, the University of Michigan demographer, foresees a new political map reconfigured to reflect three regional divides shaped by economics, culture, race, and ethnicity in the last decade. The Melting Pot States—California, Texas, Florida, New York, Hawaii, New Jersey, and New Mexico—added 10 million voting-age Hispanics and Asians in the 1990s alone. In those states, Hispanics and Asians now constitute more than 29 percent of the voting-age population and non-Hispanic whites make up just 61 percent (compared to 74 percent nationwide). Frey's second region is the New Sun Belt—not just Florida, California, and Texas, but Nevada, Georgia, and Colorado and other states where the influx of more cosmopolitan whites from New York and coastal California and of blacks returning to the South may alter the political bent. Frey's third region is the Heartland, including New England, Pennsylvania, Ohio, Indiana, and the upper Midwest with its disproportionately large share of aging, mostly white baby boomers.

It's uncertain how those regional divisions will play politically. For one thing, about 1 in 3 Latinos are younger than 18 and many aren't citizens. Even though Latinos outnumber blacks nationally, in Congress they hold about half the number of seats as blacks.

In the 2000 presidential election, George W. Bush captured about one-third of the Latino vote, the best showing for a Republican since Ronald Reagan in 1984. He still lost the popular vote overall. And because the number and proportion of black and Hispanic voters are growing, after the 2000 election Matthew Dowd, director of polling and media planning for the Bush campaign, warned that if Bush won only the same share of minority voters in 2004 as he did in 2000, he would lose reelection by three million votes. (Dowd estimated then that Bush would have to raise his share of the Hispanic vote to about 40 percent and his share of the black vote from 9 percent in 2000 to 15 percent.)

✦   ✦   ✦

In 1900, about 5 percent of the population of more developed countries was elderly. By 2000, the proportion had tripled to 15 percent. Depending on migration, their share could rise to as high as 35 percent.

Between 2000 and 2025 in the United States alone, the number of elderly will more than double to 70 million. And in a majority of the states, over 20 percent of the population will be elderly (none has that proportion of elderly right now, although Florida is close). While baby boomers will drive much of that increase, they will decline as a proportion of the total population, from about 25 percent in 2011, when the first turns 65, to 16 percent in 2029, when the last one turns 65.

By 2020, the elderly population of the United States is projected to top 54 million. By 2050, the number of Americans 65 and older is expected to be more than 80 million, or more than double what it is today. By 2060, regardless of whether the elderly keep expanding as a proportion of the total population, the number of people over 65 is expected to reach 90 million.

Today, about 13 percent of the American population is elderly. By as soon as 2030, their share may rise to 20 percent. By 2050, the proportion 85 and older is expected to more than triple, from 1.5 percent to 4.8 percent. Large increases are projected among some of the most vulnerable groups, according to the federal government, especially people living alone and elderly unmarried people with no children or siblings.

Still, the median age of Americans is expected to rise only slightly, to 38 by 2015 and, perhaps, peak at around 39 in 2035.

The overall dependency ratio—the number of children and elderly for every 100 people of working age—was 51:100 in 2000, compared to 48:100 in the world's other more developed nations and 61:100 in the less developed ones. It is projected to rise to 60.2 in 2010, 68.2 by 2020, 78.7 by 2030, and 79.9 by 2050—ratios that still fall below the 1960s levels before baby boomers turned 18 years old.

But while the ratio of children to working-age people is expected to remain roughly constant, the elderly dependency ratio is projected to continue climbing beyond current record highs. In

2000, for every 100 people of working age, there were 19 people 65 and over in the United States—double the ratio in less developed countries but lower than in most developed countries. It's estimated that the ratio will remain around 20 to 100 until 2010 and then surge to 35.7 to 100 in 2030 once all baby boomers reach the customary retirement age. By then, the elderly dependency ratio—now about half the youthful dependency ratio—would be about the same as the youthful ratio unless society responds by, among other alternatives, generating more jobs for working-age people and raising the retirement age.

Several trends are expected to profoundly skew the definition of dependency overall. In 1900, more than 1 in 4 American boys and 1 in 10 girls between the ages of 10 and 15 were "gainfully occupied," by which the government meant they were employed. Today, by law, younger people spend more years in school and more often go on to college and graduate school. They also tend to take longer to find work and to form their own families. That means they also are dependent on their parents longer. About 56 percent of 18- to 24-year-old men and 43 percent of women still live with parents or other relatives. Only about 10 percent of the men and 18 percent of the women are married and living with their spouses.

At the other end of the age spectrum, older, healthier people may take longer and longer to become dependent.

How much will healthier living and medical breakthroughs extend life spans? Nobody knows. But scientists suggest that longer life might not conform to earlier expectations of poor health and other disabilities that reduce our ability to cope. Each new generation of American octogenarians entered their eighties with fewer disabilities than the preceding generation. And technology is keeping pace. In Japan, one company has developed a washing machine for older people and others are marketing a battery-operated, motorized robot suit to help the frail elderly remain mobile. Still, without a dramatic expansion in elder hostels, of elderly people moving in with their children or grandchildren, as earlier generations did, or other alternative living arrangements, more and more vulnerable groups like the oldest old, older people who have been widowed or were never married, and the elderly without children or siblings will abound. In the 1990s, 4 percent of those aged 65 and older never married, a record low. This proportion is certain to grow in succeeding decades.

The Census Bureau estimates that by 2040 about 14 million Americans will be over age 85. But if death rates continue falling at recent rates, the number easily could be three times higher.

By 2050, according to the bureau, life expectancy at birth could be as high as 86 years for men and 92 for women. Men who survived until 65 could expect to live another 25 years, women another 30. Even the bureau's middle-level projections suggest that boys born in 2050 will live to be 80, girls to 84, and that life expectancy for those who turn 65 around midcentury will be another 20 years for men and 22 for women. Under the bureau's most optimistic forecast, women who reach the age of 85 in 2050 will have another 14.9 years of life expectancy. Racial disparities will remain, though. Girls born in 2050, according to the middle range of forecasts, can expect to live to 86 if they are white, 80 if they are black. The comparable estimates for boys are 82 and 71, respectively.

Today, Japanese women have the longest life expectancy, 84 years. Icelandic men, on average, live to 78. But while some cases of centenarians and supercentenarians have not been well documented, the assumption that 122 or so is the upper limit of human life seems to be less and less defensible.

◆   ◆   ◆

If mortality rates were the same in 2000 as they had been in 1900, only about half of today's population would be alive. In fact, demographers say that the decline in mortality played a greater role in America's population growth in the twentieth century than immigration did. At the beginning of the century, the leading causes of death in the United States were mostly infectious diseases: tuberculosis, pneumonia, diarrhea, and enteritis, along with heart disease, which is not infectious. By 2000, as people were living much longer, the leading causes of death were mostly chronic, degenerative diseases—heart disease, cancer, stroke, and lung disease—each, for the most part, a consequence of aging. (By 1990, among women, lung cancer was claiming more lives than breast cancer, a consequence of changes in smoking habits decades earlier.)

In the 1990s, fertility rates and immigration—to say nothing of previously unimagined plagues like AIDS—imposed profound demographic changes on individual countries and, sometimes, on whole continents. In the twenty-first century, genetic engineering holds the greatest promise of imposing, or perhaps inflicting, fundamental changes in medical care and ultimately on human life spans. Scientists have already expanded the life span of roundworms sixfold by manipulating two genes. They are challenging the so-called Hayflick limit, the natural barrier to how many times individual cells can divide. And they are hoping to harvest custom-made hearts and lungs from pigs specially bred to manufacture human organs. By the beginning of the next century, people in developed nations may not have achieved immortality, but may be able to live indefinitely.

"Our life expectancy will be in the region of five thousand years," says Aubrey de Grey of Cambridge University.

A world increasingly worried about daily survival might not pause long enough to reflect on that possibility. But the implications are boundless.

◆   ◆   ◆

America's complexion will change even more dramatically in the twenty-first century.

In 1900, whites accounted for about 90 percent of the nation's population. Blacks made up most of the rest, about half the share they constituted in the first census in 1790. By 1900, the population of American Indians had declined to a low of 237,000 and the census counted only 114,000 Asians. Hispanics weren't even counted separately.

In 2015, nearly 15 percent of Americans will be Hispanic, more than 13 percent black, and a little more than 5 percent Asian. Non-Hispanic whites will constitute about 67 percent. Hispanics will account for about half of all Californians.

By 2025, more than 18 percent of the population will be Hispanic, 14 percent black, and nearly 7 percent Asian, depressing the proportion of non-Hispanic whites to between 60 and 70 percent. Asians will account for about 1 in 4 Californians.

As soon as 2030, non-Hispanic whites will be a minority of Americans under 18 (but still 3 in 4 people 65 and older).

In 2050, more than 24 percent of the more than 400 million Americans will be Hispanic, nearly 15 percent black, more than 9 percent Asian, and just under 53 percent non-Hispanic white. By the midpoint of the century, 1 in 3 births will be to Hispanic parents, 2 in 5 to non-Hispanic whites, 1 in 5 to blacks, and 1 in 10 to Asians.

At those rates of growth, non-Hispanic whites will officially become a minority between 2055 and 2060.

By 2100, nonwhites and Hispanics are projected to make up 60 percent of the U.S. population, with Hispanics alone accounting for 33 percent. While immigrants lag politically, a study by the National Association of Latino Elected and Appointed Officials found that in 122 of the nation's 435 congressional districts, the proportion of Hispanics is higher than the national average. Still, their political impact is only beginning to be realized. In 2000, of the 35 million Hispanic-Americans, only 13 million were citizens of voting age, and of those only 6 million voted.

That represented 5 percent of the total turnout, compared to non-Hispanic whites, who accounted for 81 percent. These proportions will change, too, in the decades to come.

In 2000, about 6.8 million people identified themselves as multiracial—including 10,672 who, like Tiger Woods, identified themselves as white, black, Asian, and American-Indian, or, as he put it, Cablinasian.

Nathan Glazer, the Harvard sociology professor, proposes condensing the questionnaire on race and ethnicity to two questions: Do you consider yourself black (or African-American)? In which country were you born (and, perhaps, were your parents or grand-

The Immigration Factor

Census Bureau projections of the population for the United States, in millions. The total population is projected to be 420 million in 2050.

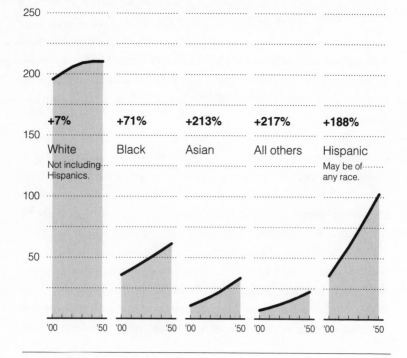

parents born)? Glazer argued for retaining the distinction for blacks: "This is the group that has suffered from prejudice, discrimination, and a lower caste status since the origins of the Republic. In law, all this is now thankfully overcome and does not exist. But African-Americans, despite their presence in large numbers from our country's earliest origins, are less integrated in American society than any other large group. They are more segregated residentially. Their rate of intermarriage, even if rapidly increasing, is the lowest for any minority. Moreover, they have a clear sense of their identity. When they answer the race question, one can depend on a high degree of reliability in the answer, as census research has shown." Glazer argued that his second set of questions would suffice because of the rapid rate of assimilation of other groups and because by the third or fourth generation "the mix of ethnicities is extensive."

Given the number of nonwhites already here, their higher fertility rates, and the government's present reluctance to reimpose stricter ceilings on immigration, the trend seems unmistakable. Martha Farnsworth Riche, a former census director, pointed out that "as many young Mexicans reached age 15 each year during the 1990s as young Americans, yet the Mexican economy was only one-tenth the size of the U.S. economy." Which country would you live in, if you had the choice?

Assessing the ethnic and racial makeup of Americans, one of her successors, Kenneth Prewitt, observed: "The young are more diverse than the old, giving weight to the assertion that there is no reversal in sight."

◆   ◆   ◆

The composition of households has changed as fundamentally as the nation's complexion, and it promises to keep changing.

The census defines a household as one or more persons sharing living quarters. A family is two or more persons living together and related by birth, marriage, or adoption. In 1950, 90 percent of all households were families. Now, fewer than 70 percent are.

Since 1960, the proportion of children living with both their natural parents plummeted from 88 percent to 68 percent. At least 40 percent of American children live with two working parents—about the same proportion as those who live with a single working parent and fully twice the proportion who live with the traditional working father and homemaker mother.

Families maintained by women grew rapidly, single-person households multiplied, and married couples slipped from 79 to 76 percent of all families (married couples with children made up only 39 percent of black family households with children). For the first time married couples with children accounted for fewer than 1 in 4 households. These figures reflect a number of factors: rearing children takes up a smaller proportion of adult life, so couples are together longer after the children are grown; elderly parents are less likely to move in with their adult children. More couples were cohabitating—living together without marrying. Births to unmarried women accounted for about a third of all births, and reached 28 percent among non-Hispanic whites. While rising divorce rates may have leveled off, more marriages now end in divorce than in death.

"The trends of increasing illegitimate births, increasing importance of female-headed households, and higher ratios of adults living alone, which had previously appeared as the deviant behavior of the black minority, now begin to appear with increasing frequency in the white majority," writes Herbert S. Klein of Columbia University in *A Population History of the United States*. "Whereas the black family structure may have emerged from dire poverty, the white family patterns had their origins in affluence." As critics of immigration are complaining that the influx of immigrants from Asia and Latin America are further detaching America from its European roots, Klein makes the point that, in some ways, the United States is becoming more like Europe: "In terms of family structures and changing household organization"—including the decline of the dual parent family, the increase in cohabitation and in births to unmarried mothers—"the trends evident in the United States tended to be common for all groups and in turn are paralleling the experience in the advanced European nations."

The Census Bureau projects even more changes by 2010: married-couple households will decline to barely half—51.7 percent—of all households and only 1 in 5 households will include a mother, father, and at least one child under 18. Slightly more than 70 percent of all families with children, a record low, will be headed by a married couple, and more than 20 percent of families with children will be headed by a single mother. Three of every five families will have no children living at home, and average family size is expected to decline further, to 3.05. Finally, the proportion of households consisting of people living alone will edge up to about 27 percent.

By 2010, nearly 1 in 3 Americans in their early thirties will have never been married. The proportion of all adults who have never married will inch up to 22.5 percent, those who have ever been married will dip to 77.5 percent and the proportion that are married and living with their spouse will decline further to 52.8 percent.

◆　◆　◆

In 1800, demographers estimated that the population of the United States would grow to 100 million within a century. The official count in 1900 was 76 million. In 1901, Robert P. Porter, a former census commissioner, estimated that by the end of the twentieth century the population of the United States would pass 300 million—which turned out to be a good guess. But the result of the 2000 census surprised more contemporary demographers, some of whom as recently as the 1990s had identified the trends but miscalculated the pace of change. America's population grew faster than expected in the last decade, largely because of immigration. That influx of foreigners, combined with their higher fertility rates, also accelerated the overtaking of blacks by Hispanics as the nation's largest minority. And while demographers remembered the birth dearth during the Great Depression, few experts predicted that the elderly, on the verge of transforming what's left of the population pyramid into a pillar, would decline as a proportion of the total population.

What about the next decade, much less the next quarter-century?

"The demographic book on 2025 is already written," Alison Stein Wellner argued in *American Demographics* in 2003, "as most of the people who will be alive in 22 years in the country are alive today."

Most—but by no means all—of the characters may, indeed, already be assembled. Many of the protagonists are well-known. Some of the broadest themes have already been brush-stroked onto paper or spreadsheets or computer screens. But not the precise plotlines, not the twists and turns that nobody can imagine, much less predict, not the immutable forces of personality, not the title of the Book on 2010, much less on 2025 or 2050.

Before it was even half over, the twentieth century was described as the American Century. How soon will the lessons of that century be forgotten? Already, the number of eyewitnesses is dwindling. "There are now very few people living who remember World War I," Paul Kennedy, the Yale historian, wrote recently. "Within a few decades, there will be nobody alive when the Holocaust occurred, when the first jet flew, when oral contraceptives became broadly available, or when women did not have the vote."

The twenty-first century began catastrophically with 9/11. Challenges to American hegemony continue to echo from Afghan caves and from satellite dishes on the Arabian peninsula. Changes within the United States are redefining who we are and how America's 300 million people—native-born and newcomers alike—relate to the other 6 billion or so people on the planet. How many more can the planet comfortably sustain simultaneously? Some experts say 10 billion at most—in between the 8.5 billion to 12 billion that many demographers predict is the peak that will be reached if and when the world, in one way or another, returns to the zero growth that characterized 99 percent of human history so far.

As those numbers grow larger, even small shifts can produce greater consequences. But Malthusian alarms about natural growth often fail to take into account the scope of human ingenuity and of human savagery committed in pursuit of our instincts to survive and to prevail.

Will America provide for the growing number of elderly? Will it continue to ration health care unequally? Will it devote the resources to reduce poverty among the young as it did in recent decades among the elderly? Will it acknowledge that plenty of people who work every day, own a television, a cell phone, and even an air conditioner can still be poor? Will it cleave politically and generationally into an older, whiter majority of voters worried about taxes and medical care and a younger, darker majority of the population that cares about health, but also about schools, day care, and mass transit?

The race between education and catastrophe, as H. G. Wells described it, is far from over. How this new century is defined will be determined not only by the numerological framework of demography but by the vagaries of human nature.

Count on it.

APPENDIX A

DEMOGRAPHIC CHARACTERISTICS OF THE UNITED STATES, 2000

Subject	Number	Percent
Total population	281,421,906	100.0
SEX AND AGE		
Male	138,053,563	49.1
Female	143,368,343	50.0
Under 5 years	19,175,798	6.8
5 to 9 years	20,549,505	7.3
10 to 14 years	20,528,072	7.3
15 to 19 years	20,219,890	7.2
20 to 24 years	18,964,001	6.7
25 to 34 years	39,891,724	14.2
35 to 44 years	45,148,527	16.0
45 to 54 years	37,677,952	13.4
55 to 59 years	13,469,237	4.8
60 to 64 years	10,805,447	3.8
65 to 74 years	18,390,986	6.5
75 to 84 years	12,361,180	4.4
85 years and over	4,239,587	1.5
Median age (years)	35.3	(X)
18 years and over	209,128,094	74.3
Male	100,994,367	35.9
Female	108,133,727	38.4
21 years and over	196,899,193	70.0
62 years and over	41,256,029	14.7
65 years and over	34,991,753	12.4
Male	14,409,625	5.1
Female	20,582,128	7.3

Subject	Number	Percent
RACE		
One race	274,595,678	97.6
White	211,460,626	75.1
Black or African-American	34,658,190	12.3
American Indian and Alaska Native	2,475,956	0.9
Asian	10,242,998	3.6
Asian Indian	1,678,765	0.6
Chinese	2,432,585	0.9
Filipino	1,850,314	0.7
Japanese	796,700	0.3
Korean	1,076,872	0.4
Vietnamese	1,122,528	0.4
Other Asian[1]	1,285,234	0.5
Native Hawaiian and Other Pacific Islander	398,835	0.1
Native Hawaiian	140,652	0.0
Guamanian or Chamorro	58,240	0.0
Samoan	91,029	0.0
Other Pacific Islander[2]	108,914	0.0
Some other race	15,359,073	5.5
Two or more races	6,826,228	2.4

Subject	Number	Percent
RACE ALONE OR IN COMBINATION WITH ONE OR MORE OTHER RACES[3]		
White	216,930,975	77.1
Black or African-American	36,419,434	12.9
American Indian and Alaska Native	4,119,301	1.5
Asian	11,898,828	4.2
Native Hawaiian and Other Pacific Islander	874,414	0.3
Some other race	18,521,486	6.6
HISPANIC OR LATINO AND RACE		
Total population	**281,421,906**	**100.0**
Hispanic or Latino (of any race)	35,305,818	12.5
Mexican	20,640,711	7.3
Puerto Rican	3,406,178	1.2
Cuban	1,241,685	0.4
Other Hispanic or Latino	10,017,244	3.6
Non-Hispanic or Latino	246,116,088	87.5
White alone	194,552,774	69.1
RELATIONSHIP		
Total population	**281,421,906**	**100.0**
In households	273,643,273	97.2
Householder	105,480,101	37.5
Spouse	54,493,232	19.4
Child	83,393,392	29.6
With own child under 18 years	64,494,637	22.9
Other relatives	15,684,318	5.6
Under 18 years	6,042,435	2.1

Subject	Number	Percent
Nonrelatives	14,592,230	5.2
Unmarried partner	5,475,768	1.9
In group quarters	7,778,633	2.8
Institutionalized population	4,059,039	1.4
Noninstitutionalized population	3,719,594	1.3
HOUSEHOLDS BY TYPE		
Total households	**105,480,101**	**100.0**
Family households (families)	71,787,347	68.1
With own children under 18 years	34,588,368	32.8
Married-couple family	54,493,232	51.7
With own children under 18 years	24,835,505	23.5
Female householder, no husband present	12,900,103	12.2
With own children under 18 years	7,561,874	7.2
Nonfamily households	33,692,754	31.9
Householder living alone	27,230,075	25.8
Householder 65 years and over	9,722,857	9.2
Households with individuals under 18 years	38,022,115	36.0
Households with individuals 65 years and over	24,672,708	23.4
Average household size	2.59	(X)
Average family size	3.14	(X)

Subject	Number	Percent
HOUSING OCCUPANCY		
Total housing units	**115,904,641**	**100.0**
Occupied housing units	105,480,101	91.0
Vacant housing units	10,424,540	9.0
For seasonal, recreational, or occasional use	3,578,718	3.1
Homeowner vacancy rate (percent)	1.7	(X)
Rental vacancy rate (percent)	6.8	(X)

Subject	Number	Percent
HOUSING TENURE		
Occupied housing units	**105,480,101**	**100.0**
Owner-occupied housing units	69,815,753	66.2
Renter-occupied housing units	35,664,348	33.8
Average household size of owner-occupied unit	2.69	(X)
Average household size of renter-occupied unit	2.4	(X)

(X) Not applicable

APPENDIX B

SELECTED SOCIAL CHARACTERISTICS IN 2000

Subject	Number	Percent
SCHOOL ENROLLMENT		
Population 3 years and over enrolled in school	**76,632,927**	**100.0**
Nursery school, preschool	4,957,582	6.5
Kindergarten	4,157,491	5.4
Elementary school (grades 1–8)	33,653,641	43.9
High school (grades 9–12)	16,380,951	21.4
College or graduate school	17,483,262	22.8
EDUCATIONAL ATTAINMENT		
Population 25 years and over	**182,211,639**	**100.0**
Less than 9th grade	13,755,477	7.5
9th to 12th grade, no diploma	21,960,148	12.1
High school graduate (includes equivalency)	52,168,981	28.6
Some college, no degree	38,351,595	21.0
Associate degree	11,512,833	6.3
Bachelor's degree	28,317,792	15.5
Graduate or professional degree	16,144,813	8.9
Percent high school graduate or higher	80.4	(X)

Subject	Number	Percent
Percent bachelor's degree or higher	24.4	(X)
MARITAL STATUS		
Population 15 years and over	**221,148,671**	**100.0**
Never married	59,913,370	27.1
Now married, except separated	120,231,273	54.4
Separated	4,769,220	2.2
Widowed	14,674,500	6.6
Female	11,975,325	5.4
Divorced	21,560,308	9.7
Female	12,305,294	5.6
GRANDPARENTS AS CAREGIVERS		
Grandparent living in household with one or more own grandchildren under 18 years	**5,771,671**	**100.0**
Grandparent responsible for grandchildren	2,426,730	42.0
VETERAN STATUS		
Civilian population 18 years and over	**208,130,352**	**100.0**
Civilian veterans	26,403,703	12.7

Subject	Number	Percent
DISABILITY STATUS OF THE CIVILIAN NON-INSTITUTIONALIZED POPULATION		
Population 5 to 20 years	**64,689,357**	**100.0**
With a disability	5,214,334	8.1
Population 21 to 64 years	**159,131,544**	**100.0**
With a disability	30,553,796	19.2
Percent employed	56.6	(X)
No disability	128,577,748	80.8
Percent employed	77.2	(X)
Population 65 years and over	**33,346,626**	**100.0**
With a disability	13,978,118	41.9
RESIDENCE IN 1995		
Population 5 years and over	**262,375,152**	**100.0**
Same house in 1995	142,027,478	54.1
Different house in the U.S. in 1995	112,851,828	43.0
Same county	65,435,013	24.9
Different county	47,416,815	18.1
Same state	25,327,355	9.7
Different state	22,089,460	8.4
Elsewhere in 1995	7,495,846	2.9
NATIVITY AND PLACE OF BIRTH		
Total population	**281,421,906**	**100.0**
Native	250,314,017	88.9
Born in United States	246,786,466	87.7
State of residence	168,729,388	60.0
Different state	78,057,078	27.7
Born outside United States	3,527,551	1.3

Subject	Number	Percent
Foreign born	31,107,889	11.1
Entered 1990 to March 2000	13,178,276	4.7
Naturalized citizen	12,542,626	4.5
Not a citizen	18,565,263	6.6
REGION OF BIRTH OF FOREIGN-BORN		
Total (excluding born at sea)	**31,107,573**	**100.0**
Europe	4,915,557	15.8
Asia	8,226,254	26.4
Africa	881,300	2.8
Oceania	168,046	0.5
Latin America	16,086,974	51.7
Northern America	829,442	2.7
LANGUAGE SPOKEN AT HOME		
Population 5 years and over	**262,375,152**	**100.0**
English only	215,423,557	82.1
Language other than English	46,951,595	17.9
Speak English less than "very well"	21,320,407	8.1
Spanish	28,101,052	10.7
Speak English less than "very well"	13,751,256	5.2
Other Indo-European languages	10,017,989	3.8
Speak English less than "very well"	3,390,301	1.3
Asian and Pacific Island languages	6,960,065	2.7
Speak English less than "very well"	3,590,024	1.4

Subject	Number	Percent
ANCESTRY (SINGLE OR MULTIPLE)		
Total population	**281,421,906**	**100.0**
Total ancestries reported	287,304,886	102.1
Arab	1,202,871	0.4
Czech	1,703,930	0.6
Danish	1,430,897	0.5
Dutch	4,542,494	1.6
English	24,515,138	8.7
French (except Basque)	8,325,509	3.0
French Canadian	2,435,098	0.9
German	42,885,162	15.2
Greek	1,153,307	0.4
Hungarian	1,398,724	0.5
Irish	30,594,130	10.9
Italian	15,723,555	5.6
Lithuanian	659,992	0.2

Subject	Number	Percent
Norwegian	4,477,725	1.6
Polish	8,977,444	3.2
Portuguese	1,177,112	0.4
Russian	2,652,214	0.9
Scotch-Irish	4,319,232	1.5
Scottish	4,890,581	1.7
Slovak	797,764	0.3
Sub-Saharan African	1,781,877	0.6
Swedish	3,998,310	1.4
Swiss	911,502	0.3
Ukrainian	892,922	0.3
United States or American	20,625,093	7.3
Welsh	1,753,794	0.6
West Indian (excluding Hispanic groups)	1,869,504	0.7
Other ancestries	91,609,005	32.6

RACE OF THE POPULATION

All United States	281,421,906
Hispanic or Latino	35,305,818
Non-Hispanic or Latino:	246,116,088
Population of one race:	241,513,942
White alone	194,552,774
Black or African-American alone	33,947,837
American Indian and Alaska Native alone	2,068,883
Asian alone	10,123,169
Native Hawaiian and Other Pacific Islander alone	353,509
Some other race alone	467,770
Population of two or more races:	4,602,146
Population of two races:	4,257,110
White; Black or African-American	697,077
White; American Indian and Alaska Native	969,238
White; Asian	811,240
White; Native Hawaiian and Other Pacific Islander	100,702
White; some other race	731,719
Black or African-American; American Indian and Alaska Native	168,022
Black or African-American; Asian	99,513
Black or African-American; Native Hawaiian and Other Pacific Islander	27,479
Black or African-American; some other race	255,966
American Indian and Alaska Native; Asian-American Indian and Alaska Native; Native Hawaiian and Other Pacific Islander	5,453
American Indian and Alaska Native; some other race	21,477
Asian; Native Hawaiian and Other Pacific Islander	129,130
Asian; some other race	185,754
Native Hawaiian and Other Pacific Islander; some other race	11,288
Population of three races:	311,029
White; Black or African-American; American Indian and Alaska Native	94,161

White; Black or African-American; Asian	18,229
White; Black or African-American; Native Hawaiian and Other Pacific Islander	2,527
White; Black or African-American; some other race	27,691
White; American Indian and Alaska Native; Asian	18,405
White; American Indian and Alaska Native; Native Hawaiian and Other Pacific Islander	3,884
White; American Indian and Alaska Native; some other race	13,796
White; Asian; Native Hawaiian and Other Pacific Islander	77,616
White; Asian; some other race	21,964
White; Native Hawaiian and Other Pacific Islander; some other race	4,741
Black or African-American; American Indian and Alaska Native; Asian	4,849
Black or African-American; American Indian and Alaska Native; Native Hawaiian and Other Pacific Islander	753
Black or African-American; American Indian and Alaska Native; some other race	4,648
Black or African-American; Asian; Native Hawaiian and Other Pacific Islander	4,501
Black or African-American; Asian; some other race	6,217
Black or African-American; Native Hawaiian and Other Pacific Islander; some other race	1,289
American Indian and Alaska Native; Asian; Native Hawaiian and Other Pacific Islander	2,131
American Indian and Alaska Native; Asian; some other race	955
American Indian and Alaska Native; Native Hawaiian and Other Pacific Islander; some other race	200
Asian; Native Hawaiian and Other Pacific Islander; some other race	2,472
Population of four races:	27,155
White; Black or African-American; American Indian and Alaska Native; Asian	8,912
White; Black or African-American; American Indian and Alaska Native; Native Hawaiian and Other Pacific Islander	740
White; Black or African-American; American Indian and Alaska Native; some other race	2,576
White; Black or African-American; Asian; Native Hawaiian and Other Pacific Islander	1,635
White; Black or African-American; Asian; some other race	848
White; Black or African-American; Native Hawaiian and Other Pacific Islander; some other race	157
White; American Indian and Alaska Native; Asian; Native Hawaiian and Other Pacific Islander	4,411

White; American Indian and Alaska Native; Asian; some other race	491
White; American Indian and Alaska Native; Native Hawaiian and Other Pacific Islander; some other race	160
White; Asian; Native Hawaiian and Other Pacific Islander; some other race	5,493
Black or African-American; American Indian and Alaska Native; Asian; Native Hawaiian and Other Pacific Islander	530
Black or African-American; American Indian and Alaska Native; Asian; some other race	223
Black or African-American; American Indian and Alaska Native; Native Hawaiian and Other Pacific Islander; some other race	45
Black or African-American; Asian; Native Hawaiian and Other Pacific Islander; some other race	854
American Indian and Alaska Native; Asian; Native Hawaiian and Other Pacific Islander; some other race	80
Population of five races:	6,342
White; Black or African-American; American Indian and Alaska Native; Asian; Native Hawaiian and Other Pacific Islander	5,081
White; Black or African-American; American Indian and Alaska Native; Asian; some other race	483
White; Black or African-American; American Indian and Alaska Native; Native Hawaiian and Other Pacific Islander; some other race	32
White; Black or African-American; Asian; Native Hawaiian and Other Pacific Islander; some other race	227
White; American Indian and Alaska Native; Asian; Native Hawaiian and Other Pacific Islander; some other race	380
Black or African-American; American Indian and Alaska Native; Asian; Native Hawaiian and Other Pacific Islander; some other race	139
Population of six races:	510
White; Black or African-American; American Indian and Alaska Native; Asian; Native Hawaiian and Other Pacific Islander; some other race	510

APPENDIX D

RACE AND ETHNICITY BY STATE

PERCENTAGE OF TOTAL POPULATION

Geographic area	Total population	Race — ONE RACE							TWO OR MORE RACES	Hispanic or Latino (of any race)	Non-Hispanic White
		White	Black or African-American	American Indian and Alaska Native	Asian	Native Hawaiian and Other Pacific Islander	Some other race				
Alaska	626,932	69.3	3.5	15.6	4.0	0.5	1.6	5.4	4.1	67.6
Arizona	5,130,632	75.5	3.1	5.0	1.8	0.1	11.6	2.9	25.3	63.8
Arkansas	2,673,400	80.0	15.7	0.7	0.8	0.1	1.5	1.3	3.2	78.6
California	33,871,648	59.5	6.7	1.0	10.9	0.3	16.8	4.7	32.4	46.7
Colorado	4,301,261	82.8	3.8	1.0	2.2	0.1	7.2	2.8	17.1	74.5
Connecticut	3,405,565	81.6	9.1	0.3	2.4	0.0	4.3	2.2	9.4	77.5
Delaware	783,600	74.6	19.2	0.3	2.1	0.0	2.0	1.7	4.8	72.5
District of Columbia	572,059	30.8	60.0	0.3	2.7	0.1	3.8	2.4	7.9	27.8
Florida	15,982,378	78.0	14.6	0.3	1.7	0.1	3.0	2.4	16.8	65.4
Georgia	8,186,453	65.1	28.7	0.3	2.1	0.1	2.4	1.4	5.3	62.6
Hawaii	1,211,537	24.3	1.8	0.3	41.6	9.4	1.3	21.4	7.2	22.9
Idaho	1,293,953	91.0	0.4	1.4	0.9	0.1	4.2	2.0	7.9	88.0

Illinois	12,419,293	73.5	15.1	0.2	3.4	0.0	5.8	1.9	12.3	67.8
Indiana	6,080,485	87.5	8.4	0.3	1.0	0.0	1.6	1.2	3.5	85.8
Iowa	2,926,324	93.9	2.1	0.3	1.3	0.0	1.3	1.1	2.8	92.6
Kansas	2,688,418	86.1	5.7	0.9	1.7	0.0	3.4	2.1	7.0	83.1
Kentucky	4,041,769	90.1	7.3	0.2	0.7	0.0	0.6	1.1	1.5	89.3
Louisiana	4,468,976	63.9	32.5	0.6	1.2	0.0	0.7	1.1	2.4	62.5
Maine	1,274,923	96.9	0.5	0.6	0.7	0.0	0.2	1.0	0.7	96.5
Maryland	5,296,486	64.0	27.9	0.3	4.0	0.0	1.8	2.0	4.3	62.1
Massachusetts	6,349,097	84.5	5.4	0.2	3.8	0.0	3.7	2.3	6.8	81.9
Michigan	9,938,444	80.2	14.2	0.6	1.8	0.0	1.3	1.9	3.3	78.6
Minnesota	4,919,479	89.4	3.5	1.1	2.9	0.0	1.3	1.7	2.9	88.2
Mississippi	2,844,658	61.4	36.3	0.4	0.7	0.0	0.5	0.7	1.4	60.7
Missouri	5,595,211	84.9	11.2	0.4	1.1	0.1	0.8	1.5	2.1	83.8
Montana	902,195	90.6	0.3	6.2	0.5	0.1	0.6	1.7	2.0	89.5
Nebraska	1,711,263	89.6	4.0	0.9	1.3	0.0	2.8	1.4	5.5	87.3
Nevada	1,998,257	75.2	6.8	1.3	4.5	0.4	8.0	3.8	19.7	65.2
New Hampshire	1,235,786	96.0	0.7	0.2	1.3	0.0	0.6	1.1	1.7	95.1
New Jersey	8,414,350	72.6	13.6	0.2	5.7	0.0	5.4	2.5	13.3	66.0
New Mexico	1,819,046	66.8	1.9	9.5	1.1	0.1	17.0	3.6	42.1	44.7
New York	18,976,457	67.9	15.9	0.4	5.5	0.0	7.1	3.1	15.1	62.0
North Carolina	8,049,313	72.1	21.6	1.2	1.4	0.0	2.3	1.3	4.7	70.2
North Dakota	642,200	92.4	0.6	4.9	0.6	0.0	0.4	1.2	1.2	91.7
Ohio	11,353,140	85.0	11.5	0.2	1.2	0.0	0.8	1.4	1.9	84.0
Oklahoma	3,450,654	76.2	7.6	7.9	1.4	0.1	2.4	4.5	5.2	74.1

Geographic area	Total population	White	Black or African American	American Indian and Alaska Native	Asian	Native Hawaiian and Other Pacific Islander	Some other race	TWO OR MORE RACES	Hispanic or Latino (of any race)	Non-Hispanic White
		ONE RACE								
Oregon	3,421,399	86.6	1.6	1.3	3.0	0.2	4.2	3.1	8.0	83.5
Pennsylvania	12,281,054	85.4	10.0	0.1	1.8	0.0	1.5	1.2	3.2	84.1
Rhode Island	1,048,319	85.0	4.5	0.5	2.3	0.1	5.0	2.7	8.7	81.9
South Carolina	4,012,012	67.2	29.5	0.3	0.9	0.0	1.0	1.0	2.4	66.1
South Dakota	754,844	88.7	0.6	8.3	0.6	0.0	0.5	1.3	1.4	88.0
Tennessee	5,689,283	80.2	16.4	0.3	1.0	0.0	1.0	1.1	2.2	79.2
Texas	20,851,820	71.0	11.5	0.6	2.7	0.1	11.7	2.5	32.0	52.4
Utah	2,233,169	89.2	0.8	1.3	1.7	0.7	4.2	2.1	9.0	85.3
Vermont	608,827	96.8	0.5	0.4	0.9	0.0	0.2	1.2	0.9	96.2
Virginia	7,078,515	72.3	19.6	0.3	3.7	0.1	2.0	2.0	4.7	70.2
Washington	5,894,121	81.8	3.2	1.6	5.5	0.4	3.9	3.6	7.5	78.9
West Virginia	1,808,344	95.0	3.2	0.2	0.5	0.0	0.2	0.9	0.7	94.6
Wisconsin	5,363,675	88.9	5.7	0.9	1.7	0.0	1.6	1.2	3.6	87.3
Wyoming	493,782	92.1	0.8	2.3	0.6	0.1	2.5	1.8	6.4	88.9
Puerto Rico	3,808,610	80.5	8.0	0.4	0.2	0.0	6.8	4.2	98.8	0.9

SOURCE: U.S. Census Bureau, Census 2000 Summary File 1, Matrix P8.

APPENDIX E

FOREIGN-BORN POPULATION IN U.S. BY PLACE OF BIRTH

Region and country or area	Number	Percent
Foreign-born population	31,107,889	100.0
Europe	4,915,557	15.8
Northern Europe	974,619	3.1
United Kingdom	677,751	2.2
Ireland	156,474	0.5
Sweden	49,724	0.2
Western Europe	1,095,847	3.5
Austria	63,648	0.2
France	151,154	0.5
Germany	706,704	2.3
Netherlands	94,570	0.3
Southern Europe	934,665	3.0
Greece	165,750	0.5
Italy	473,338	1.5
Portugal	203,119	0.7
Spain	82,858	0.3
Eastern Europe	1,906,056	6.1
Czechoslovakia (includes Czech Republic and Slovakia)	83,081	0.3
Hungary	92,017	0.3
Poland	466,742	1.5
Romania	135,966	0.4
Belarus	38,503	0.1
Russia	340,177	1.1
Ukraine	275,153	0.9

Region and country or area	Number	Percent
Foreign-born population	31,107,889	100.0
Bosnia and Herzegovina	98,766	0.3
Yugoslavia	113,987	0.4
Europe, not elsewhere classified	4,370	0.0
Asia	8,226,254	26.4
Eastern Asia	2,739,510	8.8
China	1,518,652	4.9
Hong Kong	203,580	0.7
Taiwan	326,215	1.0
Japan	347,539	1.1
Korea	864,125	2.8
South Central Asia	1,745,201	5.6
Afghanistan	45,195	0.1
Bangladesh	95,294	0.3
India	1,022,552	3.3
Iran	283,226	0.9
Pakistan	223,477	0.7
South Eastern Asia	3,044,288	9.8
Cambodia	136,978	0.4
Indonesia	72,552	0.2
Laos	204,284	0.7
Malaysia	49,459	0.2
Philippines	1,369,070	4.4
Thailand	169,801	0.5
Vietnam	988,174	3.2

Region and country or area	Number	Percent
Foreign-born population	31,107,889	100.0
Western Asia	658,603	2.1
Iraq	89,892	0.3
Israel	109,719	0.4
Jordan	46,794	0.2
Lebanon	105,910	0.3
Syria	54,561	0.2
Turkey	78,378	0.3
Armenia	65,280	0.2
Asia, not elsewhere classified	38,652	0.1
Africa	881,300	2.8
East Africa	213,299	0.7
Ethiopia	69,531	0.2
Middle Africa	26,900	0.1
North Africa	190,491	0.6
Egypt	113,396	0.4
Southern Africa	66,496	0.2
South Africa	63,558	0.2
West Africa	326,507	1.0
Ghana	65,572	0.2
Nigeria	134,940	0.4
Sierra Leone	20,831	0.1
Africa, not elsewhere classified	57,607	0.2
Oceania	168,046	0.5
Australia and New Zealand Subregion	83,837	0.3
Australia	60,965	0.2
Melanesia	32,305	0.1
Micronesia	16,469	0.1
Polynesia	35,194	0.1
Oceania, not elsewhere classified	241	0.0

Region and country or area	Number	Percent
Foreign-born population	31,107,889	100.0
Latin America	16,086,974	51.7
Caribbean	2,953,066	9.5
Barbados	52,172	0.2
Cuba	872,716	2.8
Dominican Republic	687,677	2.2
Haiti	419,317	1.3
Jamaica	553,827	1.8
Trinidad and Tobago	197,398	0.6
Central America	11,203,637	36.0
Mexico	9,177,487	29.5
Other Central America	2,026,150	6.5
Costa Rica	71,870	0.2
El Salvador	817,336	2.6
Guatemala	480,665	1.5
Honduras	282,852	0.9
Nicaragua	220,335	0.7
Panama	105,177	0.3
South America	1,930,271	6.2
Argentina	125,218	0.4
Bolivia	53,278	0.2
Brazil	212,428	0.7
Chile	80,804	0.3
Colombia	509,872	1.6
Ecuador	298,626	1.0
Guyana	211,189	0.7
Peru	278,186	0.9
Venezuela	107,031	0.3
Northern America	829,442	2.7
Canada	820,771	2.6
Born at sea	316	0.0

APPENDIX F

PERCENT OF TOTAL POPULATION BY STATE THAT IS FOREIGN-BORN

Rank	State	Percent	Rank	State	Percent
	United States	**11.8**	26	Alaska	5.4
1	California	26.9	26	Idaho	5.4
2	New York	20.9	28	Pennsylvania	4.6
3	New Jersey	18.9	29	New Hampshire	4.5
4	Florida	17.9	30	Nebraska	4.4
4	Hawaii	17.9	31	Kansas	4.2
6	Nevada	17.0	31	Oklahoma	4.2
7	Texas	15.2	33	Wisconsin	4.0
8	District of Columbia	14.6	34	Vermont	3.8
9	Arizona	13.2	35	Iowa	3.5
10	Illinois	13.1	35	South Carolina	3.5
10	Massachusetts	13.1	37	Indiana	3.4
12	Connecticut	12.1	38	Ohio	3.3
13	Rhode Island	11.6	38	Tennessee	3.3
14	Maryland	10.8	40	Missouri	3.1
15	Washington	10.7	41	Maine	3.0
16	Colorado	9.8	42	Arkansas	2.9
17	Oregon	9.0	43	Alabama	2.6
18	New Mexico	8.9	43	Louisiana	2.6
19	Virginia	8.8	45	Wyoming	2.4
20	Georgia	7.7	46	Kentucky	2.1
21	Utah	7.1	46	North Dakota	2.1
22	Minnesota	6.4	48	South Dakota	1.9
23	Delaware	6.1	49	Montana	1.6
24	North Carolina	6.0	50	West Virginia	1.2
25	Michigan	5.5	51	Mississippi	1.1

TOP 50 PLACES RANKED BY PERCENT
OF POPULATION THAT IS FOREIGN-BORN

Rank	Place	Percent	Rank	Place	Percent
1	Miami, FL	60.6	27	Minneapolis, MN	17.6
2	Santa Ana, CA	48.4	28	Seattle, WA	17.2
3	Los Angeles, CA	41.3	29	Arlington, TX	16.6
3	Anaheim, CA	41.3	30	St. Paul, MN	16.3
5	San Francisco, CA	36.7	31	Fort Worth, TX	15.6
6	San Jose, CA	36.5	32	Washington, DC	14.6
7	New York, NY	36.0	33	Tampa, FL	14.0
8	Long Beach, CA	30.9	34	Tucson, AZ	13.8
9	Houston, TX	28.1	35	Bakersfield, CA	13.4
10	San Diego, CA	27.9	36	Portland, OR	12.9
11	Oakland, CA	27.1	37	Mesa, AZ	12.8
12	Boston, MA	27.0	38	Raleigh, NC	12.3
13	Dallas, TX	26.5	39	Charlotte, NC	12.0
14	Sacramento, CA	26.4	40	San Antonio, TX	11.2
15	Honolulu, HI	25.5	41	Oklahoma City, OK	10.5
16	El Paso, TX	24.9	42	Albuquerque, NM	10.0
17	Stockton, CA	24.2	43	Philadelphia, PA	10.0
18	Riverside, CA	23.9	44	Milwaukee, WI	9.5
19	Fresno, CA	22.7	45	Colorado Springs, CO	9.4
20	Chicago, IL	22.6	46	Nashville-Davidson, TN	9.0
21	Newark, NJ	22.4	47	Jacksonville, FL	8.5
22	Phoenix, AZ	21.1	48	Wichita, KS	8.2
23	Las Vegas, NV	21.1	49	Columbus, OH	8.1
24	Denver, CO	20.2	50	Anchorage, AK	8.0
25	Austin, TX	19.6			
26	Aurora, CO	17.7			

APPENDIX H

ANCESTRY OF THE U.S. POPULATION, 2000 CENSUS

Ancestry	Number	Percent of total population	Ancestry	Number	Percent of total population
Multiple ancestry	61,994,475	22	Brazilian	181,076	0.1
			British	1,085,720	0.4
Ancestry unclassified or not reported	56,111,495	19.9	Bulgarian	55,489	0.0
			Canadian	647,376	0.2
			Celtic	65,638	0.0
Total ancestries reported	**287,304,886**	**102.1**	Croatian	374,241	0.1
			Cypriot	7,663	0.0
Acadian/Cajun	85,414	0.0	Czech	1,262,527	0.4
Afghan	53,709	0.0	Czechoslovakian	441,403	0.2
Albanian	113,661	0.0	Danish	1,430,897	0.5
Alsatian	15,601	0.0	Dutch	4,542,494	1.6
Arab	1,202,871	0.4	English	24,515,138	8.7
Egyptian	142,832	0.1	Estonian	25,034	0.0
Iraqi	37,714	0.0	European	1,968,696	0.7
Jordanian	39,734	0.0	Finnish	623,573	0.2
Lebanese	440,279	0.2	French (except Basque)	8,309,908	3.0
Moroccan	38,923	0.0	French Canadian	2,349,684	0.8
Palestinian	72,112	0.0	German	42,885,162	15.2
Syrian	142,897	0.1	German Russian	10,535	0.0
Arab/Arabic	205,822	0.1	Greek	1,153,307	0.4
Other Arab	82,558	0.0	Guyanese	162,456	0.1
Armenian	385,488	0.1	Hungarian	1,398,724	0.5
Assyrian/Chaldean/ Syriac	82,355	0.0	Icelander	42,716	0.0
Australian	78,673	0.0	Iranian	338,266	0.1
Austrian	735,128	0.3	Irish	30,528,492	10.8
Basque	57,793	0.0	Israeli	106,839	0.0
Belgian	360,642	0.1	Italian	15,723,555	5.6

Ancestry	Number	Percent of total population
Latvian	87,564	0.0
Lithuanian	659,992	0.2
Luxemburger	45,139	0.0
Macedonian	38,051	0.0
Maltese	40,159	0.0
Norwegian	4,477,725	1.6
Pennsylvania German	255,807	0.1
Polish	8,977,444	3.2
Portuguese	1,177,112	0.4
Romanian	367,310	0.1
Russian	2,652,214	0.0
Scandinavian	425,099	0.2
Scots-Irish	4,319,232	1.5
Scottish	4,890,581	1.7
Serbian	140,337	0.0
Slavic	127,137	0.0
Slovak	797,764	0.3
Slovene	176,691	0.1
Sub-Saharan African	1,781,877	0.6
African	1,183,316	0.4
Cape Verdean	77,103	0.0
Ethiopian	86,918	0.0
Ghanian	49,944	0.0
Kenyan	17,336	0.0
Liberian	25,575	0.0
Nigerian	165,481	0.1
Sierra Leonean	12,410	0.0
Somalian	36,313	0.0

Ancestry	Number	Percent of total population
South African	45,569	0.0
Sudanese	14,936	0.0
Other Sub-Saharan African	66,976	0.0
Swedish	3,998,310	1.4
Swiss	911,502	0.3
Turkish	117,575	0.0
Ukrainian	892,922	0.3
United States or American	20,625,093	7.3
Welsh	1,753,794	0.6
West Indian (excluding Hispanic groups)	1,869,504	0.7
Bahamian	31,984	0.0
Barbadian	54,509	0.0
Belizean	37,688	0.0
British West Indian	84,671	0.0
Dutch West Indian	37,681	0.0
Haitian	548,199	0.2
Jamaican	736,513	0.3
Trinidadian or Tobagonian	164,778	0.1
U.S. Virgin Islander	15,014	0.0
West Indian	147,222	0.1
Other West Indian	11,245	0.0
Yugoslavian	328,547	0.1
Other ancestries	81,962,460	29.1

Note: Percent of total population is over 100 because some respondents identified more than one ancestry.

STATES RANKED BY NUMERIC POPULATION CHANGE: 1990–2000

| RANK | AREA | Census Population | | Change, 1990 to 2000 | |
		APRIL 1, 2000	APRIL 1, 1990	NUMBER	PERCENT
1	California	33,871,648	29,760,021	4,111,627	13.8
2	Texas	20,851,820	16,986,510	3,865,310	22.8
3	Florida	15,982,378	12,937,926	3,044,452	23.5
4	Georgia	8,186,453	6,478,216	1,708,237	26.4
5	Arizona	5,130,632	3,665,228	1,465,404	40.0
6	North Carolina	8,049,313	6,628,637	1,420,676	21.4
7	Washington	5,894,121	4,866,692	1,027,429	21.1
8	Colorado	4,301,261	3,294,394	1,006,867	30.6
9	Illinois	12,419,293	11,430,602	988,691	8.6
10	New York	18,976,457	17,990,455	986,002	5.5
11	Virginia	7,078,515	6,187,358	891,157	14.4
12	Tennessee	5,689,283	4,877,185	812,098	16.7
13	Nevada	1,998,257	1,201,833	796,424	66.3
14	New Jersey	8,414,350	7,730,188	684,162	8.9
15	Michigan	9,938,444	9,295,297	643,147	6.9
16	Oregon	3,421,399	2,842,321	579,078	20.4
17	Minnesota	4,919,479	4,375,099	544,380	12.4
18	Indiana	6,080,485	5,544,159	536,326	9.7
19	South Carolina	4,012,012	3,486,703	525,309	15.1
20	Maryland	5,296,486	4,781,468	515,018	10.8
21	Utah	2,233,169	1,722,850	510,319	29.6
22	Ohio	11,353,140	10,847,115	506,025	4.7
23	Missouri	5,595,211	5,117,073	478,138	9.3
24	Wisconsin	5,363,675	4,891,769	471,906	9.6
25	Alabama	4,447,100	4,040,587	406,513	10.1
26	Pennsylvania	12,281,054	11,881,643	399,411	3.4

RANK	AREA	Census Population		Change, 1990 to 2000	
		APRIL 1, 2000	APRIL 1, 1990	NUMBER	PERCENT
27	Kentucky	4,041,769	3,685,296	356,473	9.7
28	Massachusetts	6,349,097	6,016,425	332,672	5.5
29	Arkansas	2,673,400	2,350,725	322,675	13.7
30	Oklahoma	3,450,654	3,145,585	305,069	9.7
31	New Mexico	1,819,046	1,515,069	303,977	20.1
32	Idaho	1,293,953	1,006,749	287,204	28.5
33	Mississippi	2,844,658	2,573,216	271,442	10.5
34	Louisiana	4,468,976	4,219,973	249,003	5.9
35	Kansas	2,688,418	2,477,574	210,844	8.5
36	Iowa	2,926,324	2,776,755	149,569	5.4
37	Nebraska	1,711,263	1,578,385	132,878	8.4
38	New Hampshire	1,235,786	1,109,252	126,534	11.4
39	Connecticut	3,405,565	3,287,116	118,449	3.6
40	Delaware	783,600	666,168	117,432	17.6
41	Hawaii	1,211,537	1,108,229	103,308	9.3
42	Montana	902,195	799,065	103,130	12.9
43	Alaska	626,932	550,043	76,889	14.0
44	South Dakota	754,844	696,004	58,840	8.5
45	Maine	1,274,923	1,227,928	46,995	3.8
46	Vermont	608,827	562,758	46,069	8.2
47	Rhode Island	1,048,319	1,003,464	44,855	4.5
48	Wyoming	493,782	453,588	40,194	8.9
49	West Virginia	1,808,344	1,793,477	14,867	0.8
50	North Dakota	642,200	638,800	3,400	0.5
(NA)	District of Columbia	572,059	606,900	-34,841	-5.7
(N/A)	**United States**	281,421,906	248,709,873	32,712,033	13.2

MEDIAN HOUSEHOLD INCOME BY STATE

State	Median Income ($)	State	Median Income ($)
Maryland	55,912	New York	42,432
Alaska	55,412	Vermont	41,929
Minnesota	54,931	Iowa	41,827
New Hampshire	53,549	Indiana	41,581
Connecticut	53,325	Arizona	41,554
New Jersey	53,266	Texas	40,659
Delaware	50,878	Wyoming	40,499
Massachusetts	50,587	South Dakota	38,755
Virginia	49,974	Idaho	38,613
Hawaii	49,775	Florida	38,533
Colorado	49,617	South Carolina	38,460
Utah	48,537	North Carolina	38,432
California	48,113	Kentucky	37,893
Wisconsin	46,351	Maine	37,654
Nevada	46,289	Alabama	36,771
Illinois	45,906	North Dakota	36,717
Michigan	45,335	Tennessee	36,329
Rhode Island	44,311	Oklahoma	35,500
Washington	44,252	New Mexico	35,251
Missouri	43,955	Montana	33,900
Pennsylvania	43,577	Louisiana	33,312
Nebraska	43,566	Mississippi	32,447
Ohio	43,332	Arkansas	32,423
Georgia	43,316	West Virginia	30,072
Oregon	42,704		
Kansas	42,523		

(Three-year-average of inflation-adjusted single-year medians.)

APPENDIX K

METROPOLITAN AREAS RANKED BY POPULATION, 1990 AND 2000

RANK	AREA NAME	Census Population		Change, 1990 to 2000	
		APRIL 1, 2000	APRIL 1, 1990	NUMBER	PERCENT
1	New York–Northern New Jersey–Long Island, NY–NJ–CT–PA	21,199,865	19,549,649	1,650,216	8.4
2	Los Angeles–Riverside–Orange County, CA	16,373,645	14,531,529	1,842,116	12.7
3	Chicago–Gary–Kenosha, IL–IN–WI	9,157,540	8,239,820	917,720	11.1
4	Washington–Baltimore, D.C.–MD–VA–WV	7,608,070	6,727,050	881,020	13.1
5	San Francisco–Oakland–San Jose, CA	7,039,362	6,253,311	786,051	12.6
6	Philadelphia–Wilmington–Atlantic City, PA–NJ–DE–MD	6,188,463	5,892,937	295,526	5.0
7	Boston–Worcester–Lawrence, MA–NH–ME–CT	5,819,100	5,455,403	363,697	6.7
8	Detroit–Ann Arbor–Flint, MI	5,456,428	5,187,171	269,257	5.2
9	Dallas–Fort Worth, TX	5,221,801	4,037,282	1,184,519	29.3
10	Houston–Galveston–Brazoria, TX	4,669,571	3,731,131	938,440	25.2
11	Atlanta, GA	4,112,198	2,959,950	1,152,248	38.9
12	Miami–Fort Lauderdale, FL	3,876,380	3,192,582	683,798	21.4
13	Seattle–Tacoma–Bremerton, WA	3,554,760	2,970,328	584,432	19.7
14	Phoenix–Mesa, AZ	3,251,876	2,238,480	1,013,396	45.3
15	Minneapolis–St. Paul, MN–WI	2,968,806	2,538,834	429,972	16.9

16	Cleveland–Akron, OH	2,945,831	2,859,644	86,187	3.0
17	San Diego, CA	2,813,833	2,498,016	315,817	12.6
18	St. Louis, MO–IL	2,603,607	2,492,525	111,082	4.5
19	Denver–Boulder–Greeley, CO	2,581,506	1,980,140	601,366	30.4
20	San Juan–Caguas–Arecibo, PR	2,450,292	2,270,808	179,484	7.9
21	Tampa–St. Petersburg–Clearwater, FL	2,395,997	2,067,959	328,038	15.9
22	Pittsburgh, PA	2,358,695	2,394,811	-36,116	-1.5
23	Portland–Salem, OR–WA	2,265,223	1,793,476	471,747	26.3
24	Cincinnati–Hamilton, OH–KY–IN	1,979,202	1,817,571	161,631	8.9
25	Sacramento–Yolo, CA	1,796,857	1,481,102	315,755	21.3
26	Kansas City–MO–KS	1,776,062	1,582,875	193,187	12.2
27	Milwaukee–Racine, WI	1,689,572	1,607,183	82,389	5.1
28	Orlando, FL	1,644,561	1,224,852	419,709	34.3
29	Indianapolis, IN	1,607,486	1,380,491	226,995	16.4
30	San Antonio, TX	1,592,383	1,324,749	267,634	20.2
31	Norfolk–Virginia Beach–Newport News, VA–NC	1,569,541	1,443,244	126,297	8.8
32	Las Vegas, NV–AZ	1,563,282	852,737	710,545	83.3
33	Columbus, OH	1,540,157	1,345,450	194,707	14.5
34	Charlotte-Gastonia-Rock Hill, NC–SC	1,499,293	1,162,093	337,200	29.0
35	New Orleans, LA	1,337,726	1,285,270	52,456	4.1
36	Salt Lake City–Ogden, UT	1,333,914	1,072,227	261,687	24.4
37	Greensboro–Winston-Salem–High Point, NC	1,251,509	1,050,304	201,205	19.2
38	Austin–San Marcos, TX	1,249,763	846,227	403,536	47.7
39	Nashville, TN	1,231,311	985,026	246,285	25.0
40	Providence–Fall River-Warwick, RI–MA	1,188,613	1,134,350	54,263	4.8

RANK	AREA NAME	Census Population		Change, 1990 to 2000	
		APRIL 1, 2000	APRIL 1, 1990	NUMBER	PERCENT
41	Raleigh–Durham–Chapel Hill, NC	1,187,941	855,545	332,396	38.9
42	Hartford, CT	1,183,110	1,157,585	25,525	2.2
43	Buffalo–Niagara Falls, NY	1,170,111	1,189,288	-19,177	-1.6
44	Memphis, TN–AR–MS	1,135,614	1,007,306	128,308	12.7
45	West Palm Beach–Boca Raton, FL	1,131,184	863,518	267,666	31.0
46	Jacksonville, FL	1,100,491	906,727	193,764	21.4
47	Rochester, NY	1,098,201	1,062,470	35,731	3.4
48	Grand Rapids–Muskegon–Holland, MI	1,088,514	937,891	150,623	16.1
49	Oklahoma City, OK	1,083,346	958,839	124,507	13.0
50	Louisville, KY–IN	1,025,598	948,829	76,769	8.1
51	Richmond–Petersburg, VA	996,512	865,640	130,872	15.1
52	Greenville–Spartanburg–Anderson, SC	962,441	830,563	131,878	15.9
53	Dayton–Springfield, OH	950,558	951,270	-712	-0.1
54	Fresno, CA	922,516	755,580	166,936	22.1
55	Birmingham, AL	921,106	840,140	80,966	9.6
56	Honolulu, HI	876,156	836,231	39,925	4.8
57	Albany–Schenectady–Troy, NY	875,583	861,424	14,159	1.6
58	Tucson, AZ	843,746	666,880	176,866	26.5
59	Tulsa, OK	803,235	708,954	94,281	13.3
60	Syracuse, NY	732,117	742,177	-10,060	-1.4
61	Omaha, NE–IA	716,998	639,580	77,418	12.1

62	Albuquerque, NM	712,738	589,131	123,607	21.0
63	Knoxville, TN	687,249	585,960	101,289	17.3
64	El Paso, TX	679,622	591,610	88,012	14.9
65	Bakersfield, CA	661,645	543,477	118,168	21.7
66	Allentown–Bethlehem–Easton, PA	637,958	595,081	42,877	7.2
67	Harrisburg–Lebanon–Carlisle, PA	629,401	587,986	41,415	7.0
68	Scranton–Wilkes-Barre–Hazleton, PA	624,776	638,466	-13,690	-2.1
69	Toledo, OH	618,203	614,128	4,075	0.7
70	Baton Rouge, LA	602,894	528,264	74,630	14.1
71	Youngstown–Warren, OH	594,746	600,895	-6,149	-1.0
72	Springfield, MA	591,932	587,884	4,048	0.7
73	Sarasota–Bradenton, FL	589,959	489,483	100,476	20.5
74	Little Rock–North Little Rock, AR	583,845	513,117	70,728	13.8
75	McAllen–Edinburg–Mission, TX	569,463	383,545	185,918	48.5
76	Stockton–Lodi, CA	563,598	480,628	82,970	17.3
77	Charleston–North Charleston, SC	549,033	506,875	42,158	8.3
78	Wichita, KS	545,220	485,270	59,950	12.4
79	Mobile, AL	540,258	476,923	63,335	13.3
80	Columbia, SC	536,691	453,331	83,360	18.4
81	Colorado Springs, CO	516,929	397,014	119,915	30.2
82	Fort Wayne, IN	502,141	456,281	45,860	10.1
83	Daytona Beach, FL	493,175	399,413	93,762	23.5
84	Lakeland–Winter Haven, FL	483,924	405,382	78,542	19.4
85	Johnson City–Kingsport–Bristol, TN–VA	480,091	436,047	44,044	10.1
86	Lexington, KY	479,198	405,936	73,262	18.0

RANK	AREA NAME	Census Population		Change, 1990 to 2000	
		APRIL 1, 2000	APRIL 1, 1990	NUMBER	PERCENT
87	Augusta–Aiken, GA–SC	477,441	415,184	62,257	15.0
88	Melbourne–Titusville–Palm Bay, FL	476,230	398,978	77,252	19.4
89	Lancaster, PA	470,658	422,822	47,836	11.3
90	Chattanooga, TN–GA	465,161	424,347	40,814	9.6
91	Des Moines, IA	456,022	392,928	63,094	16.1
92	Kalamazoo–Battle Creek, MI	452,851	429,453	23,398	5.4
93	Lansing–East Lansing, MI	447,728	432,674	15,054	3.5
94	Modesto, CA	446,997	370,522	76,475	20.6
95	Fort Myers–Cape Coral, FL	440,888	335,113	105,775	31.6
96	Jackson, MS	440,801	395,396	45,405	11.5
97	Boise City, ID	432,345	295,851	136,494	46.1
98	Madison, WI	426,526	367,085	59,441	16.2
99	Spokane, WA	417,939	361,364	56,575	15.7
100	Pensacola, FL	412,153	344,406	67,747	19.7

APPENDIX L

INCORPORATED PLACES OF 100,000 OR MORE:
1990 AND 2000 POPULATION

CITY OR TOWN	Population		Change, 1990 to 2000	
	APRIL 1, 2000	APRIL 1, 1990	NUMBER	PERCENT
Abilene, TX	115,930	106,654	9,276	8.7
Akron, OH	217,074	223,019	-5,945	-2.7
Albuquerque, NM	448,607	384,736	63,871	16.6
Alexandria, VA	128,283	111,183	17,100	15.4
Allentown, PA	106,632	105,090	1,542	1.5
Amarillo, TX	173,627	157,615	16,012	10.2
Anaheim, CA	328,014	266,406	61,608	23.1
Anchorage, AK	260,283	226,338	33,945	15.0
Ann Arbor, MI	114,024	109,592	4,432	4.0
Arlington, TX	332,969	261,721	71,248	27.2
Arvada, CO	102,153	89,235	12,918	14.5
Athens-Clarke County, GA	101,489	45,734	55,755	121.9
Atlanta, GA	416,474	394,017	22,457	5.7
Augusta-Richmond County, GA	199,775	44,639	155,136	347.5
Aurora, CO	276,393	222,103	54,290	24.4
Aurora, IL	142,990	99,581	43,409	43.6
Austin, TX	656,562	465,622	190,940	41.0
Bakersfield, CA	247,057	174,820	72,237	41.3
Baltimore, MD	651,154	736,014	-84,860	-11.5
Baton Rouge, LA	227,818	219,531	8,287	3.8
Bayamon, PR	203,499	202,103	1,396	0.7
Beaumont, TX	113,866	114,323	-457	-0.4
Bellevue, WA	109,569	86,874	22,695	26.1
Berkeley, CA	102,743	102,724	19	0.0

CITY OR TOWN	Population		Change, 1990 to 2000	
	APRIL 1, 2000	APRIL 1, 1990	NUMBER	PERCENT
Birmingham, AL	242,820	265,968	-23,148	-8.7
Boise, ID	185,787	125,738	60,049	47.8
Boston, MA	589,141	574,283	14,858	2.6
Bridgeport, CT	139,529	141,686	-2,157	-1.5
Brownsville, TX	139,722	98,962	40,760	41.2
Buffalo, NY	292,648	328,123	-35,475	-10.8
Burbank, CA	100,316	93,643	6,673	7.1
Cambridge, MA	101,355	95,802	5,553	5.8
Cape Coral, FL	102,286	74,991	27,295	36.4
Carolina, PR	168,164	162,404	5,760	3.5
Carrollton, TX	109,576	82,169	27,407	33.4
Cedar Rapids, IA	120,758	108,751	12,007	11.0
Chandler, AZ	176,581	90,533	86,048	95.0
Charlotte, NC	540,828	395,934	144,894	36.6
Chattanooga, TN	155,554	152,466	3,088	2.0
Chesapeake, VA	199,184	151,976	47,208	31.1
Chicago, IL	2,896,016	2,783,726	112,290	4.0
Chula Vista, CA	173,556	135,163	38,393	28.4
Cincinnati, OH	331,285	364,040	-32,755	-9.0
Clarksville, TN	103,455	75,494	27,961	37.0
Clearwater, FL	108,787	98,784	10,003	10.1
Cleveland, OH	478,403	505,616	-27,213	-5.4
Colorado Springs, CO	360,890	281,140	79,750	28.4
Columbia, SC	116,278	98,052	18,226	18.6
Columbus, OH	711,470	632,910	78,560	12.4
Columbus, GA	186,291	179,278	7,013	3.9
Concord, CA	121,780	111,348	10,432	9.4
Coral Springs, FL	117,549	79,443	38,106	48.0
Corona, CA	124,966	76,095	48,871	64.2
Corpus Christi, TX	277,454	257,453	20,001	7.8
Costa Mesa, CA	108,724	96,357	12,367	12.8
Dallas, TX	1,188,580	1,006,877	181,703	18.0
Daly City, CA	103,621	92,311	11,310	12.3
Dayton, OH	166,179	182,044	-15,865	-8.7

	Population		Change, 1990 to 2000	
CITY OR TOWN	**APRIL 1, 2000**	**APRIL 1, 1990**	**NUMBER**	**PERCENT**
Denver, CO	554,636	467,610	87,026	18.6
Des Moines, IA	198,682	193,187	5,495	2.8
Detroit, MI	951,270	1,027,974	-76,704	-7.5
Downey, CA	107,323	91,444	15,879	17.4
Durham, NC	187,035	136,611	50,424	36.9
El Monte, CA	115,965	106,209	9,756	9.2
El Paso, TX	563,662	515,342	48,320	9.4
Elizabeth, NJ	120,568	110,002	10,566	9.6
Erie, PA	103,717	108,718	-5,001	-4.6
Escondido, CA	133,559	108,635	24,924	22.9
Eugene, OR	137,893	112,669	25,224	22.4
Evansville, IN	121,582	126,272	-4,690	-3.7
Fayetteville, NC	121,015	75,695	45,320	59.9
Flint, MI	124,943	140,761	-15,818	-11.2
Fontana, CA	128,929	87,535	41,394	47.3
Fort Collins, CO	118,652	87,758	30,894	35.2
Fort Lauderdale, FL	152,397	149,377	3,020	2.0
Fort Wayne, IN	205,727	173,072	32,655	18.9
Fort Worth, TX	534,694	447,619	87,075	19.5
Fremont, CA	203,413	173,339	30,074	17.3
Fresno, CA	427,652	354,202	73,450	20.7
Fullerton, CA	126,003	114,144	11,859	10.4
Garden Grove, CA	165,196	143,050	22,146	15.5
Garland, TX	215,768	180,650	35,118	19.4
Gary, IN	102,746	116,646	-13,900	-11.9
Gilbert, AZ	109,697	29,188	80,509	275.8
Glendale, AZ	218,812	148,134	70,678	47.7
Glendale, CA	194,973	180,038	14,935	8.3
Grand Prairie, TX	127,427	99,616	27,811	27.9
Grand Rapids, MI	197,800	189,126	8,674	4.6
Green Bay, WI	102,313	96,466	5,847	6.1
Greensboro, NC	223,891	183,521	40,370	22.0
Hampton, VA	146,437	133,793	12,644	9.5
Hartford, CT	121,578	139,739	-18,161	-13.0

CITY OR TOWN	Population		Change, 1990 to 2000	
	APRIL 1, 2000	APRIL 1, 1990	NUMBER	PERCENT
Hayward, CA	140,030	111,498	28,532	25.6
Henderson, NV	175,381	64,942	110,439	170.1
Hialeah, FL	226,419	188,004	38,415	20.4
Hollywood, FL	139,357	121,697	17,660	14.5
Honolulu, HI	371,657	365,272	6,385	1.7
Houston, TX	1,953,631	1,630,553	323,078	19.8
Huntington Beach, CA	189,594	181,519	8,075	4.4
Huntsville, AL	158,216	159,789	-1,573	-1.0
Independence, MO	113,288	112,301	987	0.9
Indianapolis, IN	791,926	741,952	49,974	6.7
Inglewood, CA	112,580	109,602	2,978	2.7
Irvine, CA	143,072	110,330	32,742	29.7
Irving, TX	191,615	155,037	36,578	23.6
Jackson, MS	184,256	196,637	-12,381	-6.3
Jacksonville, FL	735,617	635,230	100,387	15.8
Jersey City, NJ	240,055	228,537	11,518	5.0
Joliet, IL	106,221	76,836	29,385	38.2
Kansas City, MO	441,545	435,146	6,399	1.5
Kansas City, KS	146,866	149,767	-2,901	-1.9
Knoxville, TN	173,890	165,121	8,769	5.3
Lafayette, LA	110,257	94,440	15,817	16.7
Lakewood, CO	144,126	126,481	17,645	14.0
Lancaster, CA	118,718	97,291	21,427	22.0
Lansing, MI	119,128	127,321	-8,193	-6.4
Laredo, TX	176,576	122,899	53,677	43.7
Las Vegas, NV	478,434	258,295	220,139	85.2
Lexington-Fayette, KY	260,512	225,366	35,146	15.6
Lincoln, NE	225,581	191,972	33,609	17.5
Little Rock, AR	183,133	175,795	7,338	4.2
Livonia, MI	100,545	100,850	-305	-0.3
Long Beach, CA	461,522	429,433	32,089	7.5
Los Angeles, CA	3,694,820	3,485,398	209,422	6.0
Louisville, KY	256,231	269,063	-12,832	-4.8
Lowell, MA	105,167	103,439	1,728	1.7

CITY OR TOWN	Population		Change, 1990 to 2000	
	APRIL 1, 2000	APRIL 1, 1990	NUMBER	PERCENT
Lubbock, TX	199,564	186,206	13,358	7.2
Madison, WI	208,054	191,262	16,792	8.8
Manchester, NH	107,006	99,567	7,439	7.5
McAllen, TX	106,414	84,021	22,393	26.7
Memphis, TN	650,100	610,337	39,763	6.5
Mesa, AZ	396,375	288,091	108,284	37.6
Mesquite, TX	124,523	101,484	23,039	22.7
Miami, FL	362,470	358,548	3,922	1.1
Milwaukee, WI	596,974	628,088	-31,114	-5.0
Minneapolis, MN	382,618	368,383	14,235	3.9
Mobile, AL	198,915	196,278	2,637	1.3
Modesto, CA	188,856	164,730	24,126	14.6
Montgomery, AL	201,568	187,106	14,462	7.7
Moreno Valley, CA	142,381	118,779	23,602	19.9
Naperville, IL	128,358	85,351	43,007	50.4
Nashville-Davidson, TN	569,891	510,784	59,107	11.6
New Haven, CT	123,626	130,474	-6,848	-5.2
New Orleans, LA	484,674	496,938	-12,264	-2.5
New York, NY	8,008,278	7,322,564	685,714	9.4
Newark, NJ	273,546	275,221	-1,675	-0.6
Newport News, VA	180,150	170,045	10,105	5.9
Norfolk, VA	234,403	261,229	-26,826	-10.3
North Las Vegas, NV	115,488	47,707	67,781	142.1
Norwalk, CA	103,298	94,279	9,109	9.6
Oakland, CA	399,484	372,242	27,242	7.3
Oceanside, CA	161,029	128,398	32,631	25.4
Oklahoma City, OK	506,132	444,719	61,413	13.8
Omaha, NE	390,007	335,795	54,212	16.1
Ontario, CA	158,007	133,179	24,828	18.6
Orange, CA	128,821	110,658	18,163	16.4
Orlando, FL	185,951	164,693	21,258	12.9
Overland Park, KS	149,080	111,790	37,290	33.4
Oxnard, CA	170,358	142,216	28,142	19.8

CITY OR TOWN	Population		Change, 1990 to 2000	
	APRIL 1, 2000	APRIL 1, 1990	NUMBER	PERCENT
Palmdale, CA	116,670	68,842	47,828	69.5
Pasadena, TX	141,674	119,363	22,311	18.7
Pasadena, CA	133,936	131,591	2,345	1.8
Paterson, NJ	149,222	140,891	8,331	5.9
Pembroke Pines, FL	137,427	65,452	71,975	110.0
Peoria, AZ	108,364	50,618	57,746	114.1
Peoria, IL	112,936	113,504	-568	-0.5
Philadelphia, PA	1,517,550	1,585,577	-68,027	-4.3
Phoenix, AZ	1,321,045	983,403	337,642	34.3
Pittsburgh, PA	334,563	369,879	-35,316	-9.5
Plano, TX	222,030	128,713	93,317	72.5
Pomona, CA	149,473	131,723	17,750	13.5
Ponce, PR	155,038	159,151	-4,113	-2.6
Portland, OR	529,121	437,319	91,802	21.0
Portsmouth, VA	100,565	103,907	-3,342	-3.2
Providence, RI	173,618	160,728	12,890	8.0
Provo, UT	105,166	86,835	18,331	21.1
Pueblo, CO	102,121	98,640	3,481	3.5
Raleigh, NC	276,093	207,951	68,142	32.8
Rancho Cucamonga, CA	127,743	101,409	26,334	26.0
Reno, NV	180,480	133,850	46,630	34.8
Richmond, VA	197,790	203,056	-5,266	-2.6
Riverside, CA	255,166	226,505	28,661	12.7
Rochester, NY	219,773	231,636	-11,863	-5.1
Rockford, IL	150,115	139,426	10,689	7.7
Sacramento, CA	407,018	369,365	37,653	10.2
Salem, OR	136,924	107,786	29,138	27.0
Salinas, CA	151,060	108,777	42,283	38.9
Salt Lake City, UT	181,743	159,936	21,807	13.6
San Antonio, TX	1,144,646	935,933	208,713	22.3
San Bernardino, CA	185,401	164,164	21,237	12.9
San Buenaventura (Ventura), CA	100,916	92,575	8,341	9.0
San Diego, CA	1,223,400	1,110,549	112,851	10.2
San Francisco, CA	776,733	723, 959	52,774	7.3

	Population		Change, 1990 to 2000	
CITY OR TOWN	APRIL 1, 2000	APRIL 1, 1990	NUMBER	PERCENT
San Jose, CA	894,943	782,248	112,695	14.4
San Juan, PR	421,958	426,832	-4,874	-1.1
Santa Ana, CA	337,977	293,742	44,235	15.1
Santa Clara, CA	102,361	93,613	8,748	9.3
Santa Clarita, CA	151,088	110,642	40,446	36.6
Santa Rosa, CA	147,595	113,313	34,282	30.3
Savannah, GA	131,510	137,560	-6,050	-4.4
Scottsdale, AZ	202,705	130,069	72,636	55.8
Seattle, WA	563,374	516,259	47,115	9.1
Shreveport, LA	200,145	198,525	1,620	0.8
Simi Valley, CA	111,351	100,217	11,134	11.1
Sioux Falls, SD	123,975	100,814	23,161	23.0
South Bend, IN	107,789	105,511	2,278	2.2
Spokane, WA	195,629	177,196	18,433	10.4
Springfield, IL	111,454	105,227	6,227	5.9
Springfield, MA	152,082	156,983	-4,901	-3.1
Springfield, MO	151,580	140,494	11,086	7.9
St. Louis, MO	348,189	396,685	-48,496	-12.2
St. Paul, MN	287,151	272,235	14,916	5.5
St. Petersburg, FL	248,232	238,629	9,603	4.0
Stamford, CT	117,083	108,056	9,027	8.4
Sterling Heights, MI	124,471	117,810	6,661	5.7
Stockton, CA	243,771	210,943	32,828	15.6
Sunnyvale, CA	131,760	117,229	14,531	12.4
Syracuse, NY	147,306	163,860	-16,554	-10.1
Tacoma, WA	193,556	176,664	16,892	9.6
Tallahassee, FL	150,624	124,773	25,851	20.7
Tampa, FL	303,447	280,015	23,432	8.4
Tempe, AZ	158,625	141,865	16,760	11.8
Thousand Oaks, CA	117,005	104,352	12,653	12.1
Toledo, OH	313,619	332,943	-19,324	-5.8
Topeka, KS	122,377	119,883	2,494	2.1
Torrance, CA	137,946	133,107	4,839	3.6

CITY OR TOWN	Population		Change, 1990 to 2000	
	APRIL 1, 2000	APRIL 1, 1990	NUMBER	PERCENT
Tucson, AZ	486,699	405,390	81,309	20.1
Tulsa, OK	393,049	367,302	25,747	7.0
Vallejo, CA	116,760	109,199	7,561	6.9
Vancouver, WA	143,560	46,380	97,180	209.5
Virginia Beach, VA	425,257	393,069	32,188	8.2
Waco, TX	113,726	103,590	10,136	9.8
Warren, MI	138,247	144,864	-6,617	-4.6
Washington, DC	572,059	606,900	-34,841	-5.7
Waterbury, CT	107,271	108,961	-1,690	-1.6
West Covina, CA	105,080	96,086	8,994	9.4
West Valley City, UT	108,896	86,976	21,920	25.2
Westminster, CO	100,940	74,625	26,315	35.3
Wichita, KS	344,284	304,011	40,273	13.2
Wichita Falls, TX	104,197	96,259	7,938	8.2
Winston-Salem, NC	185,776	143,485	42,291	29.5
Worcester, MA	172,648	169,759	2,889	1.7
Yonkers, NY	196,086	188,082	8,004	4.3

APPENDIX M

PERCENT OF U.S. POPULATION 65 YEARS AND OVER

Rank	State	Percent	Rank	State	Percent
	United States	**9.6**	25	Nebraska	9.1
1	Mississippi	18.4	27	Massachusetts	9.0
2	District of Columbia	16.6	28	Oregon	8.9
3	Alabama	14.2	29	Kansas	8.8
3	Kentucky	14.2	30	Idaho	8.7
3	Louisiana	14.2	30	Illinois	8.7
3	North Dakota	14.2	30	New Hampshire	8.7
7	New Mexico	13.7	33	Iowa	8.5
8	Georgia	13.0	33	Ohio	8.5
9	South Carolina	12.6	35	Pennsylvania	8.3
9	Tennessee	12.6	36	Maryland	8.1
11	North Carolina	12.4	36	Wyoming	8.1
12	Texas	12.0	38	Arizona	8.0
13	New York	11.2	39	Indiana	7.9
14	Arkansas	10.9	40	Minnesota	7.8
15	Oklahoma	10.8	41	Delaware	7.7
16	West Virginia	10.5	41	Hawaii	7.7
17	Maine	10.4	43	Michigan	7.5
17	South Dakota	10.4	43	Vermont	7.5
19	Virginia	10.3	45	Wisconsin	7.4
20	Rhode Island	10.0	46	California	7.3
21	Florida	9.9	46	New Jersey	7.3
22	Nevada	9.7	48	Washington	7.0
23	Missouri	9.5	49	Connecticut	5.9
24	Colorado	9.3	50	Utah	5.1
25	Montana	9.1	51	Alaska	3.2

APPENDIX N

TOP 50 PLACES OF 100,000 OR MORE RANKED BY
PERCENT OF POPULATION 65 YEARS AND OVER

RANK	PLACE	TOTAL POPULATION	Population 65 Years and Over	
			NUMBER	PERCENT
1	Clearwater, FL	108,787	23,357	21.5
2	Cape Coral, FL	102,286	20,020	19.6
3	Honolulu, HI	371,657	66,257	17.8
4	St. Petersburg, FL	248,232	43,173	17.4
5	Hollywood, FL	139,357	24,159	17.3
5	Warren, MI	138,247	23,871	17.3
7	Miami, FL	362,470	61,768	17.0
8	Livonia, MI	100,545	16,988	16.9
9	Scottsdale, AZ	202,705	33,884	16.7
10	Hialeah, FL	226,419	37,679	16.6
10	Pueblo, CO	102,121	16,967	16.6
12	Pittsburgh, PA	334,563	55,034	16.4
12	Metairie, LA	146,136	24,033	16.4
14	Evansville, IN	121,582	19,746	16.2
15	Independence, MO	113,288	17,594	15.5
16	Erie, PA	103,717	15,931	15.4
17	Fort Lauderdale, FL	152,397	23,306	15.3
18	Chattanooga, TN	155,554	23,695	15.2
18	Pembroke Pines, FL	137,427	20,881	15.2
20	Allentown, PA	106,632	16,141	15.1
20	Topeka, KS	122,377	18,418	15.1
22	Yonkers, NY	196,086	29,377	15.0
22	Waterbury, CT	107,271	16,045	15.0
24	Springfield, MO	151,580	22,586	14.9
25	South Bend, IN	107,789	15,940	14.8

Population 65 Years and Over

RANK	PLACE	TOTAL POPULATION	NUMBER	PERCENT
26	Louisville, KY	256,231	37,457	14.6
27	Peoria, AZ	108,364	15,652	14.4
27	Springfield, IL	111,454	16,096	14.4
27	Knoxville, TN	173,890	24,994	14.4
30	Peoria, IL	112,936	16,033	14.2
31	Worcester, MA	172,648	24,389	14.1
31	Philadelphia, PA	1,517,550	213,722	14.1
31	Torrance, CA	137,946	19,427	14.1
31	Rockford, IL	150,115	21,109	14.1
35	Spokane, WA	195,629	27,301	14.0
36	Santa Rosa, CA	147,595	20,576	13.9
36	Glendale, CA	194,973	27,114	13.9
36	Shreveport, LA	200,145	27,770	13.9
39	Stamford, CT	117,083	16,175	13.8
39	Portsmouth, VA	100,565	13,854	13.8
41	St. Louis, MO	348,189	47,842	13.7
41	Mobile, AL	198,915	27,273	13.7
41	Winston-Salem, NC	185,776	25,404	13.7
41	San Francisco, CA	776,733	106,111	13.7
45	Oceanside, CA	161,029	21,859	13.6
46	Akron, OH	217,074	29,325	13.5
46	Birmingham, AL	242,820	32,682	13.5
48	Buffalo, NY	292,648	39,327	13.4
48	Waco, TX	113,726	15,249	13.4
48	Bellevue, WA	109,569	14,689	13.4

APPENDIX O

TOP 50 PLACES BY PERCENT OF POPULATION 25 YEARS AND OVER WITH A BACHELOR'S DEGREE OR MORE

Rank	Place	Percent	Rank	Place	Percent
1	Seattle, WA	48.8	29	New Orleans, LA	29.2
2	Raleigh, NC	48.0	30	Tulsa, OK	28.6
3	San Francisco, CA	47.8	31	Oklahoma City, OK	28.3
4	Washington, DC	42.5	32	Kansas City, MO	28.2
5	Atlanta, GA	41.2	32	Dallas, TX	28.2
6	Austin, TX	40.6	34	Houston, TX	28.1
7	Minneapolis, MN	40.5	35	Los Angeles, CA	28.0
7	Charlotte, NC	40.5	36	Indianapolis, IN	27.7
9	Lexington-Fayette, KY	39.7	37	Chicago, IL	26.9
10	Boston, MA	38.1	38	Tampa, FL	25.4
11	Colorado Springs, CO	36.9	39	Long Beach, CA	24.8
12	Portland, OR	36.8	40	Wichita, KS	24.7
13	Albuquerque, NM	36.5	41	Sacramento, CA	24.4
14	Oakland, CA	35.2	42	Aurora, CO	23.9
15	San Diego, CA	34.9	43	Tucson, AZ	23.7
16	St. Paul, MN	34.6	44	Phoenix, AZ	23.5
17	San Jose, CA	34.4	45	Miami, FL	22.2
18	Denver, CO	33.8	46	Corpus Christi, TX	21.6
19	Anchorage, AK	31.5	47	Jacksonville, FL	21.4
20	Honolulu, HI	31.4	47	Memphis, TN	21.4
21	Nashville-Davidson, TN	31.1	49	Anaheim, CA	21.3
22	Pittsburgh, PA	31.0	49	Fort Worth, TX	21.3
23	Arlington, TX	30.4			
24	Virginia Beach, VA	30.3			
25	Cincinnati, OH	29.6			
26	Omaha, NE	29.3			
26	New York, NY	29.3			
26	Columbus, OH	29.3			

BIBLIOGRAPHY

Allen, Frederick Lewis. *The Big Change: America Transforms Itself: 1900–1950*. New Brunswick: Transaction Publishers, 2002.

Brzezinski, Zbigniew. *Out of Control: Global Turmoil on the Eve of the Twenty-first Century*. New York: Maxwell Macmillan International, 1993.

Caplow, Theodore, et al. *The First Measured Century: An Illustrated Guide to Trends in America, 1900–2000*. Washington, D.C.: The AEI Press, 2001.

Farley, Reynolds. *The New American Reality: Who We Are, How We Got Here, Where We're Going*. New York: Russell Sage Foundation, 1966.

Fussell, Paul. *Class: A Guide through the American Status System*. New York: Summit Books, 1983.

Hacker, Andrew. *Mismatch: The Growing Gulf between Women and Men*. New York: Scribner, 2003.

———. *Money: Who Has How Much and Why*. New York: Scribner, 1997.

———. *Two Nations: Black and White, Separate, Hostile, Unequal*. New York: Scribner, 1992.

Haupt, Arthur, and Thomas T. Kane. *Population Handbook, 4th International Edition*. Washington, D.C.: Population Reference Bureau, 1998.

Hobbes, Frank, and Nicole Stoops, U.S. Census Bureau. *Demographic Trends in the 20th Century*. Washington, D.C.: U.S. Government Printing Office, 2002.

Huntington, Samuel P. *Who Are We: The Challenges to America's National Identity.* New York: Simon & Schuster, 2004.

Jacoby, Tamar, ed. *Reinventing the Melting Pot: The Immigrants and What It Means to Be American.* New York: Basic Books, 2004.

Johnston, David Cay. *Perfectly Legal: The Covert Campaign to Rig Our Tax System to Benefit the Super Rich—and Cheat Everybody Else.* New York: Portfolio, 2003.

Kinsella, Kevin, and Victoria A. Velkoff, U.S. Census Bureau. *An Aging World: 2001.* Washington, D.C.: U.S. Government Printing Office, 2001.

Klein, Herbert S. *A Population History of the United States.* Cambridge, Mass.: Cambridge University Press, 2004.

Lelyveld, Joseph. Introduction, *How Race Is Lived in America: Pulling Together, Pulling Apart.* New York: Times Books, 2001.

Martin, Philip, and Elizabeth Midgley. *Immigration: Shaping and Reshaping America.* Washington, D.C.: Population Reference Bureau, 2003.

McFalls, Joseph A. Jr. *Population: A Lively Introduction, 4th Edition.* Washington, D.C.: Population Reference Bureau, 2003.

Riche, Martha Farnsworth, and Deirdre A. Gaquin, ed. *The Who, What, and Where of America: Understanding the Census Results.* Lanham, Md.: Bernan Press, 2003.

Roberts, Sam. *Who We Are: A Portrait of America Based on the Latest U.S. Census.* New York: Times Books, 1994.

Rodriguez, Richard. *Brown: The Last Discovery of America.* New York: Viking, 2002.

Sevetson, Andrew, U.S. Census. *Census 2000 Basics.* Washington, D.C.: U.S. Government Printing Office, 2002.

Shipler, David K. *The Working Poor: Invisible in America.* New York: Alfred A. Knopf, 2004.

Spain, Daphne. *America's Diversity: On the Edge of Two Centuries.* Washington, D.C.: Population Reference Bureau, 1999.

Vaca, Nicholas. *The Presumed Alliance: The Unspoken Conflict between Latinos and Blacks and What It Means for America.* New York: Rayo, 2003.

ACKNOWLEDGMENTS

Thanks to the experts and entire staff, including all of the anonymous enumerators, of the Census Bureau whose original research and analysis, coupled with that of other demographers, especially from the Population Reference Bureau, provided much of the statistical backbone for this book, and to Professors Andrew Beveridge and Andrew Hacker of Queens College for their patience and expertise and to Susan Weber-Stoger for hers.

Thanks to my colleagues and friends at the *New York Times* whose published accounts, the product of the best reporting in America, are cited or excerpted in these pages: Lizette Alvarez, Joseph Berger, Patricia Leigh Brown, Timothy Egan, Alan Feuer, Blaine Harden, Steven Holmes, Peter Kilborn, Gina Kolata, Laura Mansnerus, Suketu Mehta, Dean Murphy, Mireya Navarro, Evelyn Nieves, Lydia Polgreen, Todd Purdum, Motoko Rich, Lynda Richardson, Kevin Sack, Eric Schmitt, and Janny Scott.

Much appreciation to my colleagues in the Week in Review for their support, guidance, and above all, their friendship: Marc Charney, Peter Edidin, Scott Garapolo, Kari Haskell, Katy Roberts,

Greg Ryan, Jeffrey Scales, Allison Silver, David Smith, Mary Suh, Michael Valenti, Scott Veale, Sarah Weissman, and Tom Zeller.

Thanks, too, to Matt Ericson of the *Times* for his skillful execution of the graphics in this book, to Linda Amster and her able and always willing research staff at the *Times,* to my editors at the *Times,* and to Marie Tirados for her research.

Gratitude to my dogged editor, Paul Golob, without whom this book would not have been possible, and to David Sobel and Brianna Smith of Times Books, and Mike Levitas, Susan Chira, and Alex Ward of the *Times.*

And, for so many kindnesses and for their indulgence, thanks to David and Jean Halberstam, Paul Neuthaler, Karen Salerno, Doris Bergman, and, above all, to my sons Michael and William Roberts and my wife, Marie.

INDEX

Land, Robert, 87, 103
Lang, Robert E., 13, 103
Lansing, Robert, 221–22
Las Vegas, Nevada, 89, 173
Latin America, 217–18, 219, 226
  immigration from, 121–22, 122, 130,
    131–36
Levy, Elisabeth, 36
Lewin, Tamar, 36
life expectancy, 8, 55–57, 202, 215, 224,
  230–31, 232
Lind, Michael, 160
living alone, population, 44–47, 225, 236
  home ownership among, 101
  in 1900, 1, 25, 44
  in 2000, 9, 13, 25, 26, 44–47
Livonia, Michigan, 59, 61
Locke, Gary, 137
Logan, John R., 128, 150, 151, 154, 163
Long Island, New York, 153
Lopatcong Township, New Jersey, 88
Lord, Walter, 2–3
Los Angeles, California, 89, 97, 105, 124,
  126, 133, 227
Louisiana:
  immigrants and, 137–38
  prison population, 109
Louisville, Kentucky, 128
Loving County, Texas, 97
Lowenthal, Richard, 138
Luce, Henry, 3, 6, 221

McCarthy, John, 223
McCracken, Reverend Dr. Robert J.,
  6–7
McFalls, Joseph A., Jr., 223
Madison, Wisconsin, 91
Malthus, Thomas, 207–8, 239
manifest destiny, 5, 203
Mansnerus, Laura, 89
manufactured housing, 106–8
Margolis, Maxine L., 132–33
marriage, 26–32, 165, 188
  age at, 24, 26–27, 37, 225
  annual number of, 31
  interracial, 155–56, 188, 225
  never married, 27–28, 31, 46, 237
  in 1900, 1, 26
  in 1950, 1, 8, 26–27
  in 2000, 24, 27–32

unmarried couple households, 37–38,
  211–12, 236, 237
  welfare reform and, 43–44
Martin, Philip, 114
Marx, Karl, 190
Massachusetts, home ownership in, 102,
  105
Mead, Margaret, 40
medical care, elderly and, 62–65
Medicare and Medicaid, 63–64, 66, 67,
  180, 182, 186
Mehta, Suketu, 112
melting pot, 23, 115
Melting Pot, The, 115
Melting Pot States, 227–28
Memphis, Tennessee, 91
Mesa, Arizona, 87
metropolitan areas, 85–93, 226
  blacks living in, 149, 151
  downtowns, 87
  fastest growing, 90
  fastest growing counties, 87–88
  growth of, 11–12, 68, 86
  home ownership in, 99–100
  immigrants settling in the, 88, 89, 126,
    227
  immigration and, 88
  in 1900, 4, 218
  in 1950, 1, 9, 218–19
  sex ratios, 94
  ten largest cities, 89–90
  in 2000, 9, 85–86
  world population living in, 204, 218–19
  world's ten largest cities, 218
Metuchen, New Jersey, 89
Mexico, 208
  immigration from, 122, 130, 131–32,
    133, 140, 141, 182, 235
Miami, Florida, 97, 124, 126, 227
Miami-Dade County, Florida, 124, 178
Michigan, 123
middle class, 182, 190–92
Midgley, Elizabeth, 114
Midwest, the, 228
  age statistics, 51, 57, 59, 60
  elderly population, 59, 60
  home ownership in, 99
  immigrants and, 76, 123, 133
  internal migration and, 72, 75, 76
  metropolitan areas, people living in, 86

About the Author

SAM ROBERTS has been a reporter, columnist, and editor at the *New York Times* since 1983 and is also the host of *New York Close-Up,* the *Times's* nightly television interview program on the cable news station New York 1. He is the author of *Who We Are* and *The Brother: The Untold Story of the Rosenberg Case.* He lives in New York City.